In search of Victorian values

Aspects of nineteenth-century thought and society

edited by

ERIC M. SIGSWORTH

MANCHESTER UNIVERSITY PRESS
Manchester and New York

Distributed exclusively in the USA and Canada by
St. Martin's Press, New York

Published by Manchester University Press
Oxford Road, Manchester M13 9PL, UK

Distributed exclusively in the USA and Canada
by St. Martin's Press, Inc.,
Room 400, 175 Fifth Avenue, New York, NY 10010, USA

British Library cataloguing in publication data
In search of Victorian values.
1. Social values 2. Great Britain—
Social conditions–19th century
I. Sigsworth, Eric M.
303.3'72 HN385

Library of Congress cataloging in publication data
In search of Victorian values / edited by Eric M. Sigsworth.
p. cm.
Includes index.
ISBN 0–7190–2569–9 : $35.00 (U.S. : est.)
1. England—Social conditions—19th century. 2. England—Moral conditions. 3. Social values—History—19th century.
I. Sigsworth, Eric M.
HN398.E515 1988
306'.0942—dc19 87–36709

ISBN 0–7190–2569 *hardback*

Photoset in Linotron Trump Mediaeval
by Northern Phototypesetting Co., Bolton

Printed and bound in Great Britain by
Anchor Brendon Ltd, Tiptree, Essex

Contents

Notes on contributors

Joan Bellamy is Dean of Arts and Director of Studies, Faculty of Arts, The Open University. She is the author of *Milton: A study guide* (for the Open University) and of units on Milton, and a contributor to the Open University Course 'The Nineteenth Century Novel and its Legacy' and to the OU's Arts Foundation Course. She is currently researching on feminist literary theory.

Ron Bellamy retired as Senior Lecturer in Economics, University of Leeds in 1982. He has also taught and researched in Oxford, Ghana and the USSR Academy of Sciences. Recent articles include 'Britain's crisis and alternative strategies of the Left' (*1986 Yearbook of the Institute for Marxist Studies and Research*, Frankfurt-am-Main), 'Maurice Dobb' (Marx Memorial Library), and 'The scientific–technical revolution and the structure of the working class' (*World Marxist Review*). He is currently researching on Marxist theory and its application.

Louis Billington is Head of the Department of American Studies, University of Hull. He is the author of many articles on eighteenth and nineteenth-century British and American history, and has a particular interest in the social history of religion. He is currently working on a study of popular evangelicalism in Britain and North America between 1750 and 1850 which will be published in 1988.

Rosamund Billington teaches sociology and socio-history, with particular emphasis on gender, culture and ideology, at Humberside College of Higher Education, where she is a Senior Lecturer in Sociology. She has published several articles on women and nineteenth-century feminism. At present she is collaborating on a book on the sociology of culture.

Lord Asa Briggs is Provost of Worcester College and was formerly Professor of History, Dean of the School of Social Studies and Vice-Chancellor of the University of Sussex. At present he is completing a trilogy which began with *Victorian People* and *Victorian Cities* with a volume called *Victorian Things*.

David Foster is Head of the Faculty of Arts, Humberside College of Higher Education. He has published on the regional history of Lancashire and East Yorkshire. He has worked for the last six years on police and crime with special reference to East Yorkshire; recent works include *The Rural Constabulary Act 1839* (1983) and articles in *Northern History* and the *Journal of Regional and Local Studies*.

Allen McLaurin has taught in universities in Britain and Japan and is currently Senior Lecturer at Humberside College of Higher Education. He has published various books and articles, mainly on early twentieth-century English literature and on the relationship between literature and the visual arts.

Michael E. Rose is Senior Lecturer in Economic History, University of Manchester. Published books include *The English Poor Law, 1780–1930, The Relief of Poverty 1834–1914* (ed.) and *The Poor and the City, 1834–1914*. His current research is on social settlements in Britain and the USA, 1880–1980.

John Saville is Emeritus Professor of Economic and Social History, University of Hull. He is co-editor of the *Dictionary of Labour Biography*, the author of *Ernest Jones: Chartist, Rural Depopulation in England and Wales, 1851–1951*, and *1848. The British State and the Chartist Movement*. He is currently Chairman of the Council for Academic Freedom and Democracy.

Eric M. Sigsworth is Reader in Humanities, Humberside College of Higher Education. He was formerly Professor of Economic and Social History, University of York and visiting Professor of Victorian Studies, University of Indiana. He has published widely, mainly on nineteenth-century topics, his books including *Black Dyke Mills*, and *Modern York* in the VCH. He is Editor of the *Journal of Regional and Local Studies*, and was until recently Chairman of the CNAA History Board. His forthcoming book is *Sir Montague Burton, 1885–1952*.

William Stafford is a Principal Lecturer in the Department of Humanities at Huddersfield Polytechnic. He has recently published *Socialism, Radicalism and Nostalgia: Social Criticism in Britain 1775–1830* and is presently working on the history of individualist and organic conceptions of society.

Sheelagh Strawbridge is a Senior Lecturer at Humberside College of Higher Education. her publications include articles on the work of Louis Althusser and contributions to texts on the sociology of knowledge. She is at present working with Rosamund Billington on a book on the sociology of culture.

'The Broad and Narrow Way' designed by
Mrs Charlotte Reihlen in 1862.

Eric M. Sigsworth

Introduction

The essays contained in this book were originally delivered as lectures in the Faculty of Arts at Humberside College of Higher Education in the Autumn Term of 1985 and the Spring Term of 1986. Given the way in which the phrase was being bandied about, it seemed timely to have 'Victorian values' examined critically.[1] Those who advocate a return to Victorian values usually choose examples suited to their prejudices, leaving aside other less attractive values which, however, are an inextricable part of the whole. Those values selected as worthy of emulation are not only wrenched out of context, but are usually presented in an over-simplified form – sometimes so as to distort misleadingly. Sir Keith Joseph, for example, introducing with evident approval that quintessentially Victorian text *Self Help* by Samuel Smiles as 'a book for our times', is commending a version which has been severely multilated. As Allen McLaurin points out, the cuts in the original text not only simplify but actually falsify Smiles. This comes close to breaching one of the Victorian values enshrined for posterity on the frieze of the concert hall in Leeds Town Hall, opened in the year before the publication of *Self Help* – 'Honesty is the Best Policy'.

It is, however, Mrs Thatcher's nostalgia for a Victorian past which has been most publicised. Sometimes it appears as a general yearning to return to those values which 'were the values when our country became great'.[2] More usually she focuses on specific examples, such as thrift, work, patriotism, family life. 'We were always taught to live within our income', was true no doubt of the Roberts family as it was for many

Victorians for whom financial prudence made sense. But there were also many for whom the exercise of thrift was a mockery. Towards the end of the century Charles Booth in London and Seebohm Rowntree in York made exhaustive studies of poverty and produced alarming figures of its extent. The richest, most powerful country in the world harboured a mass of people chronically living at or below a not very generously conceived poverty line. This, furthermore, was after a long period in which general living standards were apparently rising. Cutting across many popularly held notions of the causes of poverty as a fitting punishment for fecklessness and general moral unworthiness, was Rowntree's assertion that a powerful reason for being in a condition of poverty was low wages when in work. Yet it was work which was held to be one of the crucial Victorian virtues – 'we were taught to work jolly hard'. Indeed! There is no doubt about the amount of sheer drudgery which was required of the Victorian work force. The lapse into the vernacular of a small town grammar school, suggests the discussion of a hockey match. 'Jolly' is precisely what work in Victorian Britain was not.

To value hard work, nevertheless, made sense. It was a highly convenient doctrine for a ruling class which profited from the labour of the poor, brainwashed more often than not into acquiescence. At their annual dinner in 1867 the members of the Hull branch of the Boilermakers Society were treated to a poem, part of which exhorted

> Labour should co-operate
> And help with all their might
> Masters to compete.

To praise work as a Victorian value which we should emulate sounds a little strained when coming from someone presiding over an appalling unemployment record, but perhaps no more so than preaching thrift to a credit card society. Victorian values placed on work, ought also to recognise the gross forms of exploitation which were practised for so meagre a reward and frequently performed in atrocious conditions which broke the health and bodies of the workforce.

'You were taught that cleanliness is next to godliness.' This was, even in Mrs Thatcher's youth, so much pious nonsense for the denizens of the slums, which were to be found festering in every town and in the countryside as well. It was even more of a mockery in Victorian Britain – a dirty, smelly age in which a largely dirty, smelly population was sorely afflicted by all manner of diseases rooted in a chronic lack of hygiene at all levels. Crude mortality rates were steadily falling during the last quarter of a century, but the infant mortality remained obstinately high. Nor was dirt the exclusive characteristic of the poor. Imagine the layers of skirts and petticoats trailing in filth and the thick dark clothing worn by men of all ranks in which they sweated profusely. All this without much in the way of regular dry cleaning! Think of all that heavy furniture and the clutter of the prosperous Victorian household which defied cleaning, especially in the pre-vacuum cleaner age. A lot of Victorian cleaning rituals, however well intended, consisted of disturbing and re-distributing accumulations of dirt. Spring cleaning, more frequent sorties with duster and brush, the activities of the night soil man, all augmented the accumulations in the municipal dung hills and dust heaps, or fed rivers which were frequently a source of water for the poor. The practice of cleanliness is furthermore difficult without a bath and water closet. A cold water tap and a midden privy shared with other families often at some distance from the house was the lot of many Victorians.

One result of the absence of cleanliness, amongst other causes of ill health operating throughout Victorian times, was that an alarming proportion of would be recruits who flocked to join the army, in response to that other virtue 'tremendous pride in your country', failed to pass the not very stringent medical examination. This was sufficient to cause the convening of a Committee of enquiry in 1904. The stout resistance of Boer farmers, actuated no doubt by tremendous pride in *their* Country, and the protracted length of the war was a taste of what happens when that pride is not the monopoly of the British but is shared by other nations, as the world was to discover in 1914. The imperialist aspects of this patriotic fervour are dealt with by John Saville. It would be relevant to hear comments by inhabitants of countries, formerly parts of the Empire, on this aspect of the desirability of a return to Victorian values.

Over simplification of concepts which are intrinsically complicated and a failure to ask if the values held dear were shared by all Victorians during a long reign – which was nothing if not characterised by the most fundamental forces of change – is an essential mark of those seeking to erect monolithic structures, and attempting to popularise an edited version of the past which is to be a model for the future: all present the historian with a duty to qualify and correct. Not the least of these tasks is to point out that the practice of the values separately urged does not take place in a social vacuum, with results which are self contained. A single example should suffice. The sex of the audience which is being referred to is of crucial importance. The alleged value attached to family life, varied obviously with the social class concerned, but it also bore differentially on the sexes.

Long ago, G. M. Young alluded to the doctrine of the 'Two Spheres' when examining early Victorian society. He was particularly referring to the Victorian double standard of morality. The deep hypocrisy in which this standard was rooted was pertinently expressed in the Contagious Diseases Acts in which an all male Parliament attempted repeatedly to legislate to eradicate, or at least diminish, prostitution and its common result, the contraction of venereal disease. It is symptomatic of the values involved that the diseases in question had to be called the 'Contagious Diseases' and prostitution referred to as the 'The Social Evil'. The outrage of those who perceived not only the futility but the starkly sexist nature of these Laws provoked a campaign for their repeal, matched by a counter campaign for their retention. Trying to discern which values were held by whom in the resultant struggle, is complicated by class and gender. Men, especially working men, were active on the side of repeal, as well as women. Women as well as men supported retention and indeed the extension of the Acts to apply to the whole country, rather than just to military and naval depot towns. The fierce passions aroused by this issue which was of moral concern and an attempt to safeguard the family, as well as one of social injustice to women, well illustrates the complexity of the search for Victorian values.

More generally, the Victorians were being made increasingly aware of the disparities of treatment of men and women in a society in which men made the laws. In parenthesis it is worth noting that a return to Victorian values would disfranchise Mrs

Thatcher! Property, the custody of children, divorce, education, the franchise, were examples of areas seen increasingly as ones in which women were grossly discriminated against. The professions were reluctant to accept women. In fact the whole employment structure reflected their inferior status. The implications of the position of women for our understanding of values in Victorian society are considered by Rosamund Billington.

From a rather different point of view Joan Bellamy examines the position of women as expressed in some of the major novels written by women of the period. A notable supporter of the women's cause and critic of Victorian values was John Stuart Mill, aspects of whose thought are considered by William Stafford. It is worth recalling, if one is tempted by the idea that there were unanimously held values in Victorian society, that many of the leading thinkers of the day were highly critical of that society. Mill was one of these – sufficiently influential for his *Principles of Political Economy* to be required reading in Oxford during the whole of his lifetime. In it he advocated *laissez-faire* as a fundamental economic principle. His list of permissible, even desirable, departures from the principle, however, provides little comfort for those who see it as one of the values to which we should return. In fact 'although he thought he had steered between the opposing poles of centralisation and independent activity . . . [he] none the less opens the way . . . for a range of collectivist enterprises of an order calculated to make the strict libertarian blench'.[3] Many of these accepted interventions in the free working of a market economy were intended to protect the public, and particularly those most vulnerable to its unbridled excesses. The famous invisible hand to whose impersonal workings we are commended by latter day advocates of supposed Victorian values is and was, as Mill realised by implication 'if it is to be found anywhere . . . likely to be found in the pockets of the poor'.[4] It is worth recalling, in the context of the actuating forces of the Victorian economy, that Alfred Marshall, another celebrated Victorian economist, proclaimed

A new emphasis is given to the watchword *laissez-faire*: – Let everyone work with all his might: and most of all let the government arouse itself to do that work which is vital, and which none but government can do efficiently . . . So I cry *Laissez-faire*; let the State be up and doing.[5]

Another notion central to Victorian economic thinking, the economic theory of value itself, is rigorously explored by Ron Bellamy.

The problem posed by crime in Victorian society is the subject of David Foster's essay. Apparently opinion was that there was no link between poverty and crime. This is reminiscent of the contemporary view that there is no link between unemployment and crime. The attitude to poverty itself, which was widespread and into which those who thought themselves immune could so easily fall, as the blind forces of an imperfectly understood economy wreaked social havoc, is the subject of Michael Rose's contribution. Victorian Britain was not a very comfortable place to be for those who lacked defences against the ravages of ill health, old age or bereavement, or the involuntary unemployment created every few years as a result of the malfunctioning of an economy prone to regularly alternating cycles of prosperity and depression. For them the harsh Victorian Poor Law was the last resort.

The consolations of religion were, of course, abundantly available, and its dominant role in shaping the values of Victorian society warrants a very fat volume. It is worth recalling that the differences between the many versions of Christianity which were on offer, were often a divisive rather than a unifying force. Louis Billington's essay is a fascinating exploration of the influence of evangelism on non-conformist sects and popular culture. Especially relevant here is the recognition of a form of religious fundamentalism, in sharp contrast to which Sheelagh Strawbridge reminds us of Chesterton's remark that science was 'in the air of all that Victorian World'. In examining the impact of Darwin's thinking she questions the wisdom of Victorian and modern versions of 'scientism' – or the over enthusiastic veneration of science.

In the context of religion, one wonders how many parlour walls were graced with copies of a print entitled 'The Broad and Narrow Way', originally a German work with Bunyanesque overtones. The Picture was designed by Mrs Charlotte Reihlen and painted by Herr Schacher, of Stuttgart in 1862. A Dutch edition followed in 1866 and a copy was brought from Amsterdam to England by Mr Gavin Kirkham in 1868. He had lectured on it 'nearly a thousand times' before an English edition was produced in 1883 by Messrs Morgan and Scott of London. This is a reminder, as Asa Briggs suggests in his introductory essay, that it is wrong to think of Victorianism in purely British terms. The fundamental symbolism of the engraving is obvious, the broad highway, temptingly labelled 'Welcome' leading to the demon infested fiery pit. *En route* are the more obvious temptations, the Worldliness Tavern and Ballroom, a Gambling House and Loan Office, a Theatre, and, as the penultimate sin 'Sunday Trains'. The Narrow Way has its obvious perils offset by encouragements to the pilgrims on their way to a celestial reward. A more crudely deliniated version in an urban setting is much more explicit about the temptations to be encountered in one's journey along Great Pit Street, through the Flesh Market on the way to destruction. The Flesh Market carries a comprehensive bill of contents, 'Adultery, Fornication, Uncleanliness, Idolatry, Hatred, Wrath, Drunkenness and Such Like.' There are however, openings off Great Pit Street to ensnare the sinner. Lunacy Road and Grumbling Parade lead to the Workhouse and Prison, past Uncle and Co's pawnbroking shop, The Tippler's Friend. Self Will Road leads past Morality Chapel – Cushioned Seats to Vanity Fair which can also be approached along Good Intent Road on which stand a Museum Open on Sundays and a Freethinkers' Hall. Obvious temptations abound such as drinking Satan & Co.'s Hell Brand Rum at the Roaring Lion which also offers music, billiards and smoking. Less obvious but equally hazardous to the soul were the Emporium of Fashion on Pride Street; The Hall of Science and Vain Philosophy on Money Love Street; a Laundry and an establishment offering Cheap Funerals. The shop selling Excuses Made Up is clearly suspect but less so are the Almshouses for the Aged. Sunday Trains are again close to a vividly depicted Hell. How urgent a warning of the constant perils and pitfalls of life was this message on permanent display in some households, an ever present reminder which, with appropriate scriptural reference for each sin, exhorted the onlooker to be vigilant in following the path of righteousness. This stern message is a fundamental and powerful part of the array of Victorian values reminiscent of Mrs Thatcher's recollections of childhood

We had a very strict upbringing. We were never allowed to go to a cinema on a Sunday and were forbidden to play any games such as snakes and ladders. Although there were playing cards in the house, we were certainly never permitted to use them on that day. Of course my grandmother lived with us until she died when I was ten years old, and she was very, very Victorian and very, very strict.[6]

There were no Sunday cinemas available in Grantham when she was ten. I, however, can vouch for the utter boredom of Sundays spent under the deeply depressing set of prohibitions inherited from a not too distant Victorian age which certainly endured long past the death of the Queen.

In contrast to this generally gloomy picture of Victorian values, my own essay is intended to illustrate that the Victorians, of whom 'seriousness' is said to have been a main characteristic, were capable of laughing at themselves.

A volume of this kind cannot be anything other than incomplete in the range of topics offered. Hence the modesty of its title. Those who have responded so generously illustrate the complexity of the subject. Exploration seemed more appropriate as an objective, in an area where there is so much assertion and spurious generalisation on offer. The Victorians themselves were deeply beset with doubt which is never reflected in vulgarised versions of their supposed values. Increasingly the very bedrock of apparent success in industry and commerce was under attack from powerful emergent economies overseas. In the fields of religion, politics, art, notions of social justice, the relationships between the sexes, views of Empire, education – in fact over the whole range of interpretation of human endeavour there was questioning and doubt. To behave as though there were a set of Victorian values, fixed and immutable, commanding common assent is profoundly misleading. To preach a return to them is to counsel the impossible.

Notes

1 Between the delivery of the lectures and the appearance of this book, James Walvin, *Victorian Values,* Andre Deutsch, 1987, has been published as a companion volume to the series of programmes on Granada Television. Highly relevant also is Harvey J. Kaye, 'The use and abuse of the past; The New Right and the crisis in history', in R. Milliband, L. Panitch and J. Saville (eds.), *The Socialist Register 1987,* Merlin Press, pp. 332–64. Earlier there appeared a symposium of contributions on 'Victorian Values' in *New Statesman,* 27 May 1983.

2 M. Thatcher, Interview, Weekend World, 16 January 1982.
3 W. H. Greenleaf, *The British Political Tradition*, Methuen, 1983, Vol. II, p. 114.
4 E. J. Nell, in D. Bell and I. Kristol (eds.), *The Crisis in Economic Theory*, New York, 1981, p. 198.
5 A. Marshall, 'Economic chivalry', in *Memorials*, p. 336. Quoted by D. H. Macgregor, *Economic Thought and Policy*, Oxford, 1949, p. 69.
6 Quoted in Patricia Murray, *Margaret Thatcher; A Profile*, London, 1980.

1 *Asa Briggs*

Victorian values

I doubt whether there would be as much interest in Victorian values as there is during the 1980s if Mrs Thatcher had not proclaimed Victorian values. She has referred to them on several occasions, but the most complete proclamation of those values, if I can put it in that way, came in the course of a broadcast interview in April 1983 when she was prompted by her interviewer who used the term before she did. 'I was grateful to have been brought up by a Victorian grandmother,' Mrs Thatcher then explained. 'We were taught to work jolly hard; we were taught to prove ourselves; we were taught self-reliance; we were taught to live within our income.' And next Mrs Thatcher generalised about lessons taught in Victorian homes – 'You were taught that cleanliness is next to godliness; you were taught self-respect; you were taught always to give a hand to your neighbour; you were taught tremendous pride in your country.' For Mrs Thatcher these were not just Victorian values. They were perennial values, that is to say, values which were not dated in a particular period of time but 'values which are always relevant to the expression of the human spirit.'

It is interesting that Mrs Thatcher turned quickly to what the Victorians themselves thought of as 'nursery values' which were inculcated when children were very young, – cleanliness came first in the list – and that she ended with 'living within our income', a prescription for adults, although children could be taught 'take care of the pennies and the pounds will take care of themselves'. She had begun – and I think she was right in this respect – by locating, at the very core of that cluster of Victorian values with which she identified, the value of work, not just work in the factory – indeed, she had little to say of this – but voluntary work with a social purpose. If you were getting on yourself, you were *encouraged* to help others, not taxed to do so as part of a social policy.

Many, indeed most, of the necessary improvements in a rapidly changing economy and society were made voluntarily in those times; and while the scope of local government was extended, that of the State remained restricted. People built hospitals in scattered initiatives, and if they had not done so, there would have been even more bodies in the cemeteries which they also took pains to build and to adorn. They built schools too, for there were no completely public-financed schools until after 1870 and they were designed in the first instance 'to fill in the gaps'. The absence of such schools, which themselves attempted from the start to inculcate values, placed more weight before 1870 on education in the home and in the Sunday school, where the values were related in various fashions to texts from the Bible. These were made to sound very Victorian. 'If ye do not work, neither shall ye eat.' 'Which of you intending to build a tower, sitteth not down first and counteth the cost?'

It is usually suggested that in proclaiming Victorian values Mrs Thatcher was drawing a contrast for political purposes between a 'good' nineteenth century – at least for Britain, then at the height of its economic and political power – and a 'bad' twentieth century which she was seeking to put back on a proper direction. She seemed to have in mind her version of the 'permissive' 1960s rather than of the mid-Victorian 1860s and of the welfare state rather than of the strictly limited mid-Victorian state; and when she referred to 'tremendous pride in your country' she was thinking not of the Crimea but of the Falkland Islands. History was certainly being used, not explained – how did credit cards fit in? – and in this account it offered a very different picture of the Victorians, their motives and their activities, from that which most of Mrs Thatcher's twentieth-century Conservative predecessors had done. Indeed, a very recent Conservative Prime Minister, Harold Macmillan, had remarked only two years before Mrs Thatcher's interview that 'the Victorian age was simply an interruption in Britain's history.' Britain's first new Conservative Prime Minister of the twentieth century, A. J. Balfour, born in 1848, had been even more dismissive. 'The middle third of the nineteenth century does not, I acknowledge, appeal to me.' Nor did he hold any allegiance, he went on, to 'the intellectual dynasties which then held sway.'

In the light of such earlier Conservative comment, it is apparent that Mrs Thatcher, not herself a historian, was not just using history to illustrate an argument. She believed in the values that she was proclaiming, values that had more in common with the values of mid-Victorian liberalism of a radical persuasion than with the values of 'traditional' toryism – or of Disraeli's toryism – except in her emphasis on 'pride in your country', which radicals like Cobden and Bright and liberals like Gladstone, faced with Palmerston's foreign policy or Disraeli's, were loath to emphasise. Yet she was not alone in her approach within her own party. For a similar appraisal of Victorian values to that of Mrs Thatcher it is necessary only to turn to Sir Keith Joseph's introduction to an abridged edition of Samuel Smiles's *Self-Help* which appeared in 1986, although for Joseph, who represented a Leeds constituency, the main point of Smiles's book was not so much the gospel of work as the celebration in it of enterprise and of 'the *entrepreneur* and the virtues that make him what he is.' For that reason, he concluded, '*Self Help*, so deeply expressive of the spirit of its own times, is also a book for *our* times.'

Victorian *entrepreneurs*, including some who made their money after Smiles had ceased to be fashionable, have been celebrated recently in other places, not least for their ability to combine commercial success with belief in – and pressure for – social progress. This is the unifying theme of Ian Bradley's book about them, *Enlightened Entrepreneurs*, which starts with Thomas Holloway and ends with W. H. Lever. Yet Smiles was no unqualified exponent of success. He emerged from a radical background, describing his years in Leeds, when he edited the *Leeds Times* and was plunged into popular politics as 'the happiest and most fruitful years of my life'. Moreover, his impressive study of *The Lives of the Engineers*, 1861–62, is concerned not with *entrepreneurs* as such but with men of technical skill and vision. For him, as for Mrs Thatcher, it was work that lay at the very heart of the Victorian experience – very hard work, not least, for him, on the part of 'navvies' and dockers and moulders. Like Carlyle, he believed that work was good in itself. As one of Smiles's heroes, George Stephenson, the railway pioneer had put it – and Smiles himself for years was involved in railway management – 'Nothing that is of real worth can be achieved without courageous working. Man owes his growth to that active striving of the will, that encounter with difficulty, which he calls effort; and it is astonishing to find how often results apparently impracticable are then possible.'

Articulate Victorian belief in the 'will', 'indomitable will', and the relationship of that belief to their conception of law, 'inexorable law', demands fuller treatment. (Later, indeed, in Edwardian times, will and law were to clash.) So, too, however, does the Victorian concept of 'effort'. Charles Dickens once described the British people as 'the hardest worked people in the world', and it is significant that he said the 'hardest worked' people in the world and not the 'hardest working'. How we view 'work' depends on our experience of it. The very interesting collection of working-class autobiographies which was produced a few years ago, with John Burnett as editor, called *Useful Toil – Autobiographies of Working People from the 1820s to the 1920s* – describes views of work directly or indirectly as seen by the workers themselves. And there is one memorable passage in it which deals with some of the many different kinds of work which were performed by human-beings in Victorian times, many of which have become mechanised during the course of the last forty or fifty years – wheeling, dragging, hoisting, carrying, lifting, digging, tunnelling, draining, trenching, hedging and banking, blasting, braking, scouring, sawing, felling, reaping, mowing, picking, sifting and threshing. Many of these activities, agricultural activities, had been carried out by human-beings for centuries. Others were added in Victorian times – an age of steam – when as industrialisation was pursued and steam could relieve labour, heavy work was still being done manually by people. Bodies were strained more than nerves.

There was also a tremendous amount of work to which the term 'drudgery' can be applied – work in the home, particularly by the wife in the home, which subsequently, has been completely transformed – for example, black-leading of the fire-grate – in an age of electricity, plastics and detergents. Of course, in middle-class households much of this work was carried out by servants, so that the biggest single division in Victorian England was that between those families which had domestic servants and those families which did not. There were great value divides here at the very heart of Victorian England as the Victorians themselves saw it – only one of many divides – and given that the numbers of domestic servants were so large, and ultimately so dependent, it is not surprising that more than one American observer concluded that what was wrong with England was not that 'the working class' made so many claims but that 'the servile class' made so few. 'It never entered their heads that they might ever become ladies and gentlemen.'

Many Victorians themselves distinguished between work 'under orders', backed by disciplinary regulation, and 'creative work'. The classic account of the distinction was William Morris's 'Useful work versus useless toil', published in 1885. 'It is assumed by most people nowadays,' Morris wrote, 'that all work is useful, and by most well-to-do people that all work is desirable.' 'Let us grant first,' he went on, 'that the race of man must either labour or perish' and that 'Nature does not give us our livelihood gratis.' Nonetheless, 'there is some labour which is so far from being a blessing that it is a curse' and 'it would be better for the community and for the worker if the latter were to fold his hands and refuse to work, and either die or let us pack him off to the workhouse or the prison.' 'Useful work' was work illumined by 'hope', 'hope of rest, hope of product, hope of pleasure in the work itself.' The conditions of work in Victorian England, according to Morris, militated against all three kinds of hope. 'As things are now, between the waste of labour-power in mere idleness and its waste in unproductive work, it is clear that the world of civilisation is supported by a small part of its people.'

It is significant that Morris explicitly raised the issue of idleness just as in all his writings he raised the question of equality. There was an enormous amount of idleness in Victorian society at all levels. Whole sections of the working classes, whose labour was casual, were idle for long periods; for those sections where regular routines – only recently introduced – were maintained by discipline – in the last resort the threat of 'the sack' – there were obvious signs of wasting time and of other restrictive practices in industry even before there was talk of national economic decline. It is noteworthy that in the working-class autobiographies collected by Burnett none of the people who kept diaries carefully in the most difficult conditions said very much about their work at all. They talked about the other things that happened in their lives other than their work. They were, however, no different from middle-class diarists in this respect.

Moreover, examples of *aristocratic* idleness, and the pre-industrial values which went with it, like extravagance, even if it led to indebtedness, the opposite of thrift, were never lacking in Victorian England. Hunting and shooting, and racing and boxing, for example, depended on an alternative complex of values to the values associated in industry with work or with Smiles's 'prudence, frugality and good management'. Sport had participating patrons, not business sponsors, although by the end of Victoria's reign sport itself had changed in its rules, in its organisation and in its appeal. In this context the public school had played a key role, although by the end of the reign professional football under a different aegis had already established itself.

If you think of work, not leisure, as being at the centre of most Victorian experience, then before turning to such alternative clusters of values it is necessary to examine the other Victorian values which went with it. They included self-help, the title of Smiles's book which came out in 1859 – the term seems to have been invented earlier by Emerson – in the same year as Charles Darwin's *Origin of Species,* and John Stuart Mill's *Essay on Liberty.* Smiles wrote compellingly and in detail about three other related values – thrift, character and duty – and obviously believed in a fourth, cleanliness, which was picked out by Mrs Thatcher and which poses some of the same problems of interpretation as work. This was a period before the invention of most soaps and detergents, not to speak of toothpaste and deodorants – the first two came relatively late in the Victorian period with at least one great entrepreneur, W. H. Lever, recognising their business potential – and until then there was a great deal of scrubbing and scraping in the effort to keep clean. There were also 'clean' and 'dirty' parties, and a moral counterpart to the 'gospel of work', 'the sanitary idea', which caught the imagination of Victorians as different as Edwin Chadwick, Charles Kingsley and George Eliot. You could defeat Fate, they maintained, if you made lives longer and the environment more healthy. But you had to show 'will' here also, for *vis inertiae* was strong.

More important still, you had to consider the environment as well as the individual so long as the basic element in maintaining cleanliness, clean water, was sadly missing for many families, in some places for most families. It was not until a vast underworld of drains and sewers, largely provided out of rates and taxes, had been constructed under the influence of believers in 'the sanitary idea', perhaps the greatest of Victorian social achievements, that you could allow most of the Victorian values to triumph over pollution. Housing, however, was largely left to private enterprise, augmented by voluntary, philanthropic schemes, and in overcrowded rooms or noisy slums it was extremely difficult, though not impossible, to be guided by the so-called central Victorian values. Moreover, there were always immense problems, originating both behind the closed doors of private houses and openly in the noise and bustle of public streets, in communicating about human needs and moral values, problems more fully appreciated, perhaps, in Edwardian than in mid-Victorian or late-Victorian England, though obvious enough – and much commented upon – in the early years of Queen Victoria's reign during the 1830s and 1840s when class differences could never be ignored.

The idea of cleanliness was not built into the Victorian experience, as it were, as work was, for it was easier to mobilise factory workers than water babies. Health was always something that you had to put across as a kind of crusade. For the religious, cleanliness might come next to godliness, but you had to appeal to the irreligious also and to the indifferent, and even at the end of the century most people were probably far dirtier than they are today. Moreover, while the crusade was successful on limited fronts, the environment remained a dirty environment with a great deal of waste. Steam power was wasteful power, the new industrial towns and the cities were covered with smog, the rivers were polluted. Although cleanliness may in retrospect appear to be a Victorian virtue, therefore, there were always very real limits to cleanliness in practice in the

Victorian experience, well examined in private rather than public terms in Lawrence Wright's *Clean and Decent: The History of the Bath and the Loo,* 1980.

Like 'work' and 'cleanliness', individual 'self-help', whether fully believed in or not, was never a completely shared value. From the very beginnings of industrialisation, through the whole nineteenth century there was a considerable amount of emphasis on collective rather than on individual action. Sometimes such action was called mutual self-help, as in the case of friendly societies, but it was not always so described. In more militant terms the sense that 'union is strength' emerged during pre-Victorian stages of industrialisation, and the trade-union movement as it developed retained that sense, even when its leaders were extolling social harmony and advocating industrial conciliation procedures. It often rested on an alternative approach, not always systematic, to political economy.

When Robert Applegarth, Secretary of the Amalgamated Society of Carpenters and Joiners, told a Royal Commission in 1867 that he opposed piecework on the grounds that it led to the misuse of materials and overlong working hours, he was asked whether Praxiteles would have objected as he had done. 'We are not all Arkwrights, Brunels or Stephensons,' he replied. 'We have to make rules and regulations which will apply to workmen generally.' He was 'tired', he went on, 'of that system of individualism which gives Praxiteles his due and Arkwright, Brunel and Stephenson full scope for the exercise of their extraordinary skill' but 'leaves the thousands less skillful to scramble through a selfish world as best they can.'

Later trade-unionists would have made the same point in a different way. They knew that social mobility (although they did not call it such) was severely limited in Victorian England, more limited than it had been in the late-eighteenth century, and they had the feeling, too, rightly or wrongly, that it was becoming more limited as the century went by and new forms of business structure emerged. They knew also that as far as success was concerned – and Smiles was very uneasy on this point – much of it depended, not upon work, but upon luck. How could you fit luck (*Fortuna*) into the Victorian values cluster?

There were questions to ask also about 'thrift' and whether it was an adequate basis for individual living or national economic development, questions raised sharply by political economists like J. A. Hobson late in the reign when businessmen were complaining of 'economic depression'. Yet even in the middle years of the reign Smiles himself, in some of his most eloquent passages in his book *Thrift*, when he claimed the greatest possible merits attached to it, admitted that it came less naturally to working-class people, less used to restraint and to deferring, than it did to middle-class people. There were, in fact, wonderful 'sprees' when working-class families found themselves with more income than they usually had. They would go into places like Leeds market – Smiles knew that particular place very well – and spend as much as they could do and as quickly as possible on luxuries more than on necessities. Even in a very limited consumer goods society, where there were more shops than there ever had been and where people were talking more and more of 'things', there were all kinds of possibilities of spending money, so that the 'spree' is just as much a part of the Victorian experience as 'thrift'. Similarly, at a different level the many bankruptcies in the business world were just as much a part of the experience of that world as the successful new enterprises.

I have already talked about the complications of cleanliness as a shared value. What of 'helpfulness'? According to the verdict of their own contemporaries, there were many Victorians who were extremely unhelpful. Take one of the most interesting dichotomies in Victorian England, that between the respectable and the rough. It was a distinction that was very freely made. You had many people who were very rough, operating more in gangs than as individuals, and behaving in ways that were hostile and aggressive. You had also the respectable who behaved in ways that were extremely restrained and deferential, people who were felt to deserve help, although they did not always get it. Within each class the distinction between the rough and the respectable, on which in practice there was seldom complete agreement, lay at the very heart of Victorian experience, and it is impossible to understand that experience without pondering on the concept of 'respectability'.

Even the rough, however, might respond to the calls of duty – the Army depended upon them – and there was undoubtedly a strong sense of duty in Victorian England just as there was a strong sense of will. But it began to be clear, very frequently in local life and sometimes in national life, both that duty could be strained and that it might be expressed more in rhetoric than in action. It began to be clear also – before Ibsen dramatised the theme – that the activities of people who were thought of as 'the pillars of society' were driven by motives other than duty – including self-esteem, pride and display. Moreover, the best defences of duty were often made by people who had forged their own system of morality rather than borrowed it from traditional religion. Thus, George Eliot, who did not believe in God or immortality, believed in the inexorable demands of Duty. Again, the subject is a huge one, for traditional religion was challenged on more than one set of grounds, and it was the Victorians, not ourselves, who were first forced to confront the issue of how religion and morality were related to each other.

Pride of country was a point about which Mrs Thatcher made a great deal in the last part of her statement. But throughout the whole of Victorian Britain there was a debate about foreign policy, not a consensus on foreign policy. There were often very sharp differences between Liberals and Conservatives, particularly when Gladstone was on the stage, and there were very sharp differences within the Liberal Party itself even when he was not. Not least, there were always very sharp differences as to whether Empire was 'a good or a bad thing'. What Professor A. P. Thornton has called an 'argument' about Empire was continuous. It was only in moments like the Crimean War and the Boer War, when there were very powerful and eloquent dissenting opinions, that the need for shared values to bind rulers and ruled were much stressed outside the public house and the music hall, and they were discussed then, of course, by proponents of a strong sense of national interest who resorted to other means than argument to drown dissent.

To what extent did Victorian society as it actually was reflect Victorian values either in peace or war? It is difficult to generalise. There were sharp regional and local differences, including a sense of North and South, just as there were more general differences between rich and poor or rough and respectable. Enterprise was patchy both in business and in voluntary effort. Industry was often looked down upon. So, too, was new wealth. Shops were different institutions in Yorkshire and Sussex towns. The distribution of social institutions, like hospitals and schools, reflected different degrees of concern and effort as well as different levels of income. In neither case, however, was there a 'system', for there were gaps, duplications and ambiguities, with attendant waste. The environment itself, which was subject to very limited planning, could be a very wasteful and deteriorating environment, although it included features of which people were proud and houses and estates with order and beauty at one end of the scale and slums at the other. One favourite Victorian interpreter of the environment, John Ruskin, who was never short on values, encouraged people to look in order to understand, insisting that his fellow citizens would only get the architecture which they deserved in terms of the value by which they actually lived. There was little point in believing that you could put up a Gothic cathedral (or the Parthenon) in Bradford. The architecture of a society above all else reflected the values of the society.

Of course, the appearance of society, what you could actually see in Victorian England, was not just influenced by the set of values which were picked out by Mrs Thatcher as the main Victorian values. There remained a very strong feudal element in nineteenth-century Britain, as Richard Cobden, who knew both Manchester and Midhurst, was never tired of insisting. The country-house remained a dominant social institution. Even in the later part of the century, when there was decline in some of the traditional forms of agriculture, particularly cereal farming, the Victorians did not destroy the social power of the countryside or of its local leaders. And there was a conflict of values then between some of the people who were in possession in the countryside and some of the people who were in possession in the cities. But it was the people in the countryside who often played a very important part in the development of voluntary activities, not least in towns and cities, serving as patrons and presidents if only because they lent an air of aristocratic grandeur to bodies which otherwise might have seemed to be 'very ordinary'. No discussion of Victorian values in action can leave out the Seventh Earl of Shaftsbury, who, while guided by a firm Evangelical conviction, came from an hereditary aristocratic family and knew more at first hand of the countryside than of the city. He was a Tory, too, although his conservatism was radically different from that of Mrs Thatcher who represents an alternative inheritance.

The very strong emphasis in Victorian England on certain forms of leadership concentrated more on duty than on enterprise and on honour than on profit. The public school shaped it, and there were attempts to create other institutions which would be like the public school. The Army in Victorian England drew on it also, with both Tom Browns and Flashmans fighting far away on distant frontiers. At best the dreams were dreams not of work but of glory. Such dreams had little or no appeal to religious nonconformists, whether Quakers or Congregationalists. The term 'dissent', therefore, had a political as well as a religious connotation. So, too, did the 'Nonconformist conscience'.

A broader sense of conscience led even some of the early Victorians to spurn simple remedies, and it was W. Cooke Taylor, an eloquent proponent of the new factory system and the expanded role of industry, who wrote forthrightly in 1849 that 'we have found that morals are not, like bacon, to be cured by hanging; nor, like wine, to be improved by sea voyages; nor, like honey, to be preserved in cells.' During the middle years of the century the *Saturday Review* explored almost every divergence between moral standards and moral practices – there was no shortage of typical example in an age when 'scandal' was spotlit – while Smiles himself was devastating, not inspiring, when he complained in one of his most remarkable passages of 'the terrible Nobody' often more obviously present at the heart of Victorian society than Adam Smith's beneficient invisible hand:

> When typhus or cholera breaks out, they tell us that Nobody is to blame. That terrible Nobody! How much he has to answer for. More mischief is done by Nobody than by all the world besides. Nobody adulterates our food. Nobody poisons us with bad drink . . . Nobody leaves towns undrained. Nobody fills jails, penitentiaries, and convict stations. Nobody makes poachers, thieves, and drunkards. Nobody has a theory too – a dreadful theory. It is embodied in two words: *laissez-faire* – let alone. When people are poisoned with plaster of Paris mixed with flour, 'let alone' is the remedy . . . Let those who can, find out when they are cheated: *caveat emptor.* When people live in foul dwellings, let them alone, let wretchedness do its work: do not interfere with death.

There were clear limits, however, to public action. Thus, while emphasising the importance of controlling cellar dwellings locally and of enforcing building regulations, Smiles added in an interesting article of 1852 that 'here municipal or parochial authority stops; it can go no further; it cannot penetrate into the Home, and it is not necessary that it should do so.'

Within the middle-class home there was a sense of sanctuary, even of retreat from work and the cares that went with it. Hearth and home, therefore, represented different, if complementary values, to those of the workplace. Of course, precept and practice might radically diverge in the home as in the factory. Within the working-class home, too, there was a feeling that 'authority' in whatever form should, if at all possible, be kept out: the smallest cottage was a castle. 'Home sweet home' was sung by both middle-classes and working-classes, and the family was extolled as an institution even when it was far from the kind of 'happy family' depicted in the favourite parlour game with that name. It is interesting that when J. A. Banks re-examined 'the vital revolution' in family size in 1981, having written a pioneering book on the subject, *Prosperity and Parenthood* in 1954, he called it *Victorian Values*. Moreover, he came to relate the fall in family size after the 1870s to 'the failing hold of religion' more than to a rise in the standard of living and the pressures placed upon it. His books, which recognise the difficulty of explaining 'spontaneous changes in family belief systems', are of fundamental importance.

As far as 'personal morality' was concerned, it is clear from a wide range of Victorian evidence that 'the Victorian age', as Jeffrey Weeks has put it recently, 'was no golden age of sexual propriety'. In this case, too, indeed, the search in the nineteenth century for such an age 'tells us more about present confusion than past glories'. There were double standards, clearly noted at the time, for men and women – these were under increasing threat during the 1870s – and there was always an 'underworld' where prostitution and crime were obviously associated. A particularly brutal murder in Northumberland Avenue in the heart of London, in 1861 led the *Daily Telegraph* to identify what it called 'moral malaria'. Far from the scene of action there was always a vicarious Victorian market for sensational crime literature just as there was always a market for pornography.

And for those who stayed outside the market there was fear – and often guilt – about the presence of 'a wild beast within', as terrifying as the 'terrible Nobody' without.

Within this context, William Acton, author of *The Functions and Disorders of the Reproductive Organs in Youth, in Adult Age and in Advanced Life,* 1857, has been held up as the Samuel Smiles of continence. Yet just as Smiles did not believe that self-help or hard work came 'naturally' to people, so Acton could observe frankly that 'by any one acquainted with rural life, seduction of girls is a sport and a habit with vast numbers of men, married and single, placed above the ranks of labour.' And that was 'rural life'. 'Urban life' presented even greater 'perils', and they could start, as the Victorian autobiography *My Secret Life* shows, with the young domestic placed in the confines of 'home sweet home itself'. For the historian of morals, W. H. Lecky, 'the ultimate factor in human nature' seemed to be 'that the sensual side of our nature is the lower side and some degree of shame may appropriately be attached to it'.

There were, of course, marked changes in attitudes towards human relationships within the exceptionally long time span of Queen Victoria's reign, the longest reign in English history; and for this reason it is convenient, I believe, to divide it, like Gaul, into three parts, bearing in mind that to trace back the origins of Victorian values you have to go back well before the beginning of Victoria's reign to what has been called 'Victorianism before Queen Victoria'. There was certainly plenty of this during a long 'Victorian prelude'. For this reason 'Victorianism' – and Victoria is the only monarch who gave her name to an 'ism' as well as to an adjective – needs to be traced back to late eighteenth-century interchanges between Enlightenment ideas and the development of Evangelical religion within an increasingly industrial environment.

During the first part of the reign before the Great Exhibition of 1851, social and political conflicts spotlighted obvious differences of values, while during the middle years of the reign there was more emphasis on social harmonies. It may be then, indeed, that the conception of a cluster of Victorian values took shape. Yet it was then also that the Victorians proved that they were their own best critics. Take, for example, Arthur Hugh Clough's *The Latest Decalogue,* 1862, which includes the lines

No graven images may be
Worshipped, except the currency

and

Thou shalt not kill; but need'st not strive
Officiously to keep alive.

The best known lines came later:

Thou shalt not steal, an empty feat,
When it's so lucrative to cheat:
Bear not false witness; let the lie
Have time on its own wings to fly:
Thou shalt not covet; but tradition
Approves all forms of competition.

During the last part of Queen Victoria's reign there were many signs not only of criticism but of what has been described as a 'late-Victorian revolt', and it was during this period, when Queen Victoria was still on the throne, that nearly all the values that Mrs Thatcher picked out as favourite Victorian values, were values under challenge. Thus, there were people who claimed that it was just as morally rewarding to look at the story of failure as it was to look at the story of success and more urgent to study 'poverty in the midst of plenty' than plenty itself. Even Queen Victoria herself read Henry George. Why, people asked, had there still been so much poverty even during the 'prosperous' middle years of the century when society had become so much richer? Why had Henry Mayhew been able to write as he had of London's poor?

Moreover, the economy looked far less secure when Charles Booth took up his study of London's poor during the 1880s than it had done during the late 1860s, and respectability began to look far less convincing as a quality than it had done. For George Bernard Shaw – and for Oscar Wilde – if you really wanted to help people, you had to turn first to the unrespectable, not the respectable, because the respectable were perfectly capable of looking after themselves. You needed movement, not apathy. I have dealt in detail with some of these manifestations of change and of new convergences in the book which I wrote recently with Ann McCartney on Toynbee Hall, which celebrated its centenary in 1987, but I did not comment there on how much the very idea of earnestness was now being made fun of too in the 1890s. The world became a place of paradox, not of order.

Summing up, if you look at the history of Queen Victoria's reign, you will find that it does not follow one single line. There were varieties of reactions to value clusters, some of them far more difficult to trace than the three-fold division suggests, at different periods within the reign just as there were from one generation to another. And in order to explain why there were such varieties, you have to attempt a much deeper analysis than I have time to provide in a single lecture.

This, after all, is only an introduction to a series of lectures which will examine in more detail some of the themes upon which I have touched. Those general points must be made, however, at the outset. First, in looking back at 'the Victorian age' it is impossible not to be impressed by its energy even if at the same time being depressed by the waste that went with it. The age had the same qualities as the steam engine which was given its own gospel. Second, it would be unfortunate if in thinking and talking about Victorian values in late-twentieth century Britain we were to ignore the international context. Many of the values I have discussed were trans-Atlantic values: many, too, are still canvassed actively in the late-twentieth century in developing countries, and in China, where it is necessary to identify and to promote specific values – and encapsulate them in adages – in order to seek to achieve social goals.

Third, one of the genuine achievements of the Victorians was to motivate people in such a way that these values came to be thought of as 'inner directed', a term invented by the American sociologist, David Riesman. Victorians were often attacked at the time – by John Stuart Mill, for example – for their tendency to conform, to imitate each other. In retrospect, however, what stand out are their inner sources of strength. These have been given less attention than the adages and they command respect. Even in a late-twentieth-century British political context, therefore, it is completely misleading for Neil Kinnock to 'reply' to Mrs Thatcher with the statement that 'Victorian Britain was a place where a few got rich and where most got hell. The Victorian values were cruelty, misery, drudgery, squalor and ignorance.'

Fourth, we in Britain still depend for good and ill on a Victorian legacy almost a century later. We are both advantaged and handicapped by it. A controversial American report of 1974, the Hudson Report, concluded that many of Britain's problems 'are Victorian problems or stem from attempts to operate Victorian solutions in a society that exists in a late-twentieth century world.' A debate on this theme, which raises questions about intelligence and foresight, would be more immediately rewarding within the narrowly British context than the bigger debate, which must become philosophical, on Victorian values. Smiles was certainly grossly over-simplifying when he praised the old Norseman, who said that he believed 'neither in idols nor demons. I put my sole trust in the strength of my body and soul.' This remark, Smiles added, was an expression of 'the same sturdy independence and practical materialism which, to this day, distinguishes the descendants of the Norsemen.' Smiles was entirely at one with William Morris in this assessment. Both may well have been wrong.

2 *Allen McLaurin*

Reworking 'work' in some Victorian writing and visual art

'Victorian values' is a nicely alliterative phrase, all the more resonant for being vague and empty. It stands ready to be filled with whatever we will – with evocative words like 'work', 'family' and 'patriotism'. It is the very vagueness of the phrase which makes it so useful an item in political rhetoric. Although 'Victorian values' might equally conjure up images of exploitation, child labour and poverty, it now requires an effort of will to keep these in mind: it is the supposedly 'positive' images which have been triumphant in recent political discourse. The equivocal nature of the phrase should not lead us to doubt the very real effects of its employment as a guiding fiction and a justification for certain policies. The consequences are probably more important and have been more widely felt than were those which flowed from the comparable Victorian construction of a myth about a previous age, which involved the use of medieval images and the resurrection of what some Victorians supposed, or chose to pretend, were medieval values. Using the term 'neo-Gothic' as a linguistic model, it might be useful at the outset to make a distinction between 'Victorian values' and 'neo-Victorian values'.

The moral re-armament implied in neo-Victorian appeals to work, family and country was preceded by, and in an oblique way gained a kind of authority from, a revaluation of Victorian art and artefacts dating from around the 1960s and gaining momentum subsequently. This shift in taste, exemplified by the boom in Victoriana, helped to put back the warmth, attractiveness and profit in the word 'Victorian' after decades of rejection and scorn. This transformation took place after a long period of anti-Victorianism which before Victoria's death, in the works of Samuel Butler and others, was carried further in the attitudes of critics such as the Bloomsbury Group, whose weapons were all the sharper for having been forged in Victorian homes, and was not really challenged in any very visible way until recent years. A renewed interest in Victoriana of all kinds was one of the signs of this reversal of opinion, and we might say that the good ship 'Victorian values' which now seems to rule the waves was floated off on a tide of bric-a-brac.

An upturn in the market for things Victorian is a phenomenon which signals something more than a turn in the tide of taste and an examination of recent uses of nineteenth-century writings and visual works is important for our understanding of the process by which Victorian values are transformed into neo-Victorian values. One strategy in the construction of these values is the cutting free of images and words from their historical context. We can examine the way in which, uncoupled from their historical setting, they are reworked to form neo-Victorian values which might overlap but are not coterminous with the values of the Victorians. Any discussion of Victorian values must necessarily include a consideration of that essential item of the Victorian vocabulary, 'work'. Work itself of course is not a 'value', though it is presented as such by the neo-Victorians who advocate a return to 'Victorian' notions of hard work whilst surely being aware of the possibility that these had as much to do with such factors as the fear of unemployment as with any internal 'values' of the workers themselves. Further, 'work' cannot be dissociated from 'family' and 'country' in the Victorian values syndrome, and it will be the aim of this paper, if not to disentangle, then at least to describe this complex intertwining. The emphasis on works of art of various kinds is justified partly because questions relating to work were harnessed to aesthetics by some of the major nineteenth-century social thinkers, and one of the problems raised in this context was the question of what place could be found for the artist in the taxonomies of work which were so popular in the period.

To exemplify the reworking of Victorian words and images we can begin by examining the neo-Victorian version of Smiles' *Self-Help,* which was first published in 1859 and reissued as part of the Penguin Business Library in 1986 with an introduction by

Sir Keith Joseph, at that time Minister of State for Education. This edition brings into sharp relief the image of the isolated heroic self-made man, an aspect of the mythology of work which can be examined further by considering Howlett's familiar photograph of the engineer Brunel posing before the checking drum of the *Great Eastern.* One of the recurrent themes in the revaluation of the Victorians in recent years, even amongst those who, unlike Conservative ministers, have no obvious political axe to grind, has been an admiration of the Victorians for their *energy.* One of the images encountered most frequently in explicit or in silent confirmation of this notion of Victorian energy is Turner's *Rain, Steam and Speed,* so familiar on bookcovers or as an illustration in books on Victorian life that it has become part of that 'mental wallpaper' which accompanies our thoughts about the nineteenth century. This is at first sight a 'neutral' way of admiring the Victorians and their achievements, but by looking at the relationship between work and 'Nature' in Victorian art and literature it is possible to examine what it is that these celebrations of energy are in danger of obscuring. Victorian words and images which express the idea of work as being valuable in itself, which includes the idea of the 'dignity of labour', are often full of those ambiguities which truly reflect the complex nature of the issues involved in work, complexities which are resistant to, and ambiguities which undermine, the confident assertions of the neo-Victorians. Ford Madox Brown's painting *Work,* like the Turner picture mentioned earlier, is so familiar as an accompaniment of, and is often simply a decorative addition to, discussions of the Victorians. On closer examination it offers a much more complex comment on its subject than might appear at first sight. Finally, by looking at a late nineteenth-century work, Conrad's *Heart of Darkness,* we can see some of the 'underside' of that complex knot of thoughts and feelings involved in attitudes towards work and possibly gain an insight into the darkness from which those often frantic Victorian exhortations to work arose, and which is so falsified in the cosy appeals of the modern 'work, family and country' brigade.

When the neo-Victorians hark back to Victorian values they rarely name names. Who were the Victorians who supposedly held these values? There was a time when there was less reticence, when, for example, everyone seemed to claim Dickens as their ally. As Orwell pointed out in his 1939 essay on Dickens, for Catholics, Communists and others, 'Dickens is one of those writers who are well worth stealing'.[1] The neo-Victorians might well feel comfortable with some aspects of Dickens' work, but other images would jostle disconcertingly for attention. In *Dombey and Son,* for example, his image of a black cloud spreading from the inner city to the 'better portions' is one which the neo-Victorians would have to accommodate alongside the notion of the 'Family' (given supernatural credentials) which they would perhaps find more acceptable:

> Oh for a good spirit who would take the house-tops off, with a more potent and benignant hand than the lame demon in the tale, and show a Christian people what dark shapes issue from amidst their homes, to swell the retinue of the Destroying Angel as he moves forth among them! For only one night's view of the pale phantoms rising from the scenes of our too-long neglect; and from the thick and sullen air where Vice and Fever propagate together, raining the tremendous social retributions which are ever pouring down, and ever coming thicker! Bright and blest the morning that should rise on such a night: for men, delayed no more by stumbling-blocks of their own making, which are but specks of dust upon the path between them and eternity, would then apply themselves, like creatures of one common origin, owing one duty to the Father of one family, and tending to one common end, to make the world a better place![2]

The problem for the neo-Victorian is that the Victorians whom we have tended to value as writers and artists have often been, in a sense, 'anti-Victorian', or at least offer complex images which resist utilisation as purveyors of simple moral injunctions. In speaking of Victorian values the neo-Victorians perhaps have in mind those more or less forgotten nineteenth century folk (one thinks of minor clerics whose works clutter obscure corners of antiquarian bookshops in this context) – the sort of people who lost sleep worrying about the high birth rate of the 'lower orders', fearing the degeneration of the race by the 'swamping' of higher spirits. Were these the invisible presences whispering in Sir Keith Joseph's ear when he recommended that working class people should desist from having children? Investigation of nineteenth-century clerical opinion in Birmingham, where this speech was made, would almost certainly yield parallels. The moment a named figure of any interest is invoked difficulties arise, and need to be suppressed if the desired propaganda effect is to be achieved. This is the case even with Samuel Smiles, as we can see by examining the abridged (censored) edition of *Self-Help* published as a volume in the Penguin Business Library with an introduction by Sir Keith Joseph. Surely in Smiles, one would have thought, the neo-Victorians would be able to find a Victorian who in fact expressed the values which they wish to see established. If it is true that cliche is the mark of an ascendant ideology – as P. D. Anthony suggests in *The Ideology of Work*[3] – then the very high incidence of cliche in *Self-Help* suggests that we need look no further for a clear, perhaps even a 'raw' expression of Victorian values. The lapidary titles of some of Smiles' other works – *Character, Thrift* and *Duty* – seem to hold out the promise that here the neo-Victorians have found their man. But even here, with the title of *Self-Help* itself, arises a complexity which obstructs the use of the book for simple propaganda purposes. In the Preface to the 1886 edition of the work Smiles regrets the way in which the title had been misinterpreted in some quarters: 'In one respect the title of the book, which it is now too late to alter, has proved unfortunate, as it has led some, who have judged it merely by the title, to suppose that it consists of a eulogy of selfishness: the very opposite of what it really is – or at least of what the author intended it to be.' Smiles goes on to say that 'the duty of helping one's self in the highest sense involves the helping of one's neighbours'. There is little of this in Sir Keith Joseph's introduction, and in the abridged version of *Self-Help* itself there is a consistent effort to suppress and censor that element in Smiles' work. Smiles did believe that the young should 'rely upon their own efforts in life rather than depend upon the help or patronage of others', but this is very much modified in the actual biographies which Smiles presents. We need to ask why those responsible for the abridged version of *Self-Help* should feel it necessary to push this doctrine of individualism to the point of parody. A possible explanation is that the idea of helping others tends to contradict the competitive element in 'free enterprise', indeed, it is precisely because it is based upon competition and conflict that capitalism needs to construct an ideology of work. A further contradiction is that at the heart of the 'work ethic' as expressed in *Self-Help* is the idea of self-denial, an idea which runs counter to the notion of consumption which is described by Sir Keith Joseph in his Introduction to *Self-Help* as the key to the success of Capitalism. Here is one of the central contradictions which face us in examining work as a Victorian and a Neo-Victorian value.

There are many detailed issues which could be raised in relation to individual passages deleted from this 'Business' edition of *Self-Help* ('Revised Version' would perhaps convey better the status achieved by the book in the nineteenth century and which the Business Library wishes to restore). The following summary of cuts made indicates the general direction of the deletions and is intended to bring out the overall effect of the censored version in contrast with the original. The first thing to be said is that this new version underplays the casualties which occur in the process of self-help. Many aspects which complicate and deepen Smiles' account are removed in this way, such as the effect on wives and families of the single-minded pursuit of success. Smiles on a number of occasions alludes to the troubled relationship between family and work, and by suppressing this aspect of his book the 'work and family' constellation of neo-Victorian values can be kept free of conflict and contradiction. In one respect the potted biographies in the original text give us, in rudimentary form, some of the pleasures which we can obtain from reading a novel, in the sense that Smiles here and there hints at a complexity of motive in these self-helpers. This is eradicated in the Business version. The unkindest cuts of all occur in those parts of the book where Smiles acknowledges the co-operation needed for success in work. Passages are removed which run counter to the rampant individualism suggested in Sir Keith Joseph's Introduction and advocated more widely by like-minded politicians. In this way, many of Smiles' references to aid received from patrons, family, government funds and local authority grants are excluded. The lives of successful philanthropists are cut, as are the philanthropic works of those who have achieved their success elsewhere. Other incidental deletions, such as the removal of a side swipe at middle class complacency, are revealing but need less explanation than the other omissions which are being summarised here.

There is a more general issue at stake here than the simplifying and falsifying of Smiles' book. Very often he supports and enhances his examples with direct quotations and with anecdotes which make evident the difficulty for us as modern readers to draw simple lessons from the writings of another era. The neo-Victorian version denies this by suppressing those elements which mark the distance between Smiles and ourselves, so allowing Sir Keith Joseph to comment in his Introduction that *Self-Help* is 'a book for *our* times: the purveyor of a message that we, government and governed, employer and employee, in work and out of work, need to take to heart and keep in mind'. The 'Victorian values' movement is an attempt to bring the dead to life, not in all their complexity, but as zombies. By cutting the threads which bind them to their time and place they can be made to perform the will of those whose sense of the possibilities of human life seems in many instances so much less interesting than that of the Victorians themselves. This elaborate modern 'abridgement' of *Self-Help* is an indication of how difficult it is for the neo-Victorian to recruit under their banner even those Victorians who seem at first sight to be closest to their point of view.

One of the crucial moves in the re-writing of *Self-Help* is the exaggeration of the isolation of those heroes of work whom Smiles celebrates. In the abridged edition they are isolated from their families in a way which falsifies Smiles' presentation of the cost of self help. More importantly, the Business edition suggests a singular kind of spontaneous generation by deleting Smiles' references to the help which his self-helpers themselves received in their rise to success. In this, the neo-Victorians are simply exaggerating a feature present in a number of Victorian depictions of work. We can see this process of isolating the successful worker from suggestions of help or co-operation in one of the most well-known of Victorian images relating to work, Howlett's photograph of Brunel, dating from 1857, which shows him as a lone, top-hatted, cigar-smoking, muddy-booted figure framed by the huge chains intended to control the launch of the *Great Eastern.* Before examining a neo-Victorian use of this photograph a word needs to be said about the role of the engineer in nineteenth-century mythologies of work. Smiles himself believed that 'the character of our Engineers is a most signal and marked expression of British character', and this photograph is part of that romance of the engineer which is such a feature of many nineteenth century works.[4] The relationship of engineering to ideas about work is particularly interesting in this period, as engineers were becoming 'professionals', a transition in a sense encapsulated in this image of Brunel. (It is interesting to note that this metamorphosis from caterpillar tradesman to butterfly professional involved a self-denying ordinance on the part of engineers against the discussion of politics or wages at their meetings.)[5] A central plank of the work ethic, the valuing highly of the dilligent performance of menial tasks and physical labour is contradicted by this rush from 'trade' to 'profession' on the part of influential sections of society.

In his excellent analysis of this photograph of Brunel, Rob Powell examines the way in which an image of this kind can be detached from the historical circumstances of its making and become a free-floating icon ready to be used, for example, in an advertising campaign by a multinational company. Part of the caption read: 'IBM. As British as Brunel? . . . . You don't have to have British parents to contribute to Britain.'[6] As a multinational, IBM needs to soften the contradiction between pure self-help and the appeal to patriotism which is a necessary, but in a way antagonistic element in the neo-Victorian values syndrome. Images of and by the Victorians are used to represent 'our' past, our 'common heritage'. The Royal Family, perhaps with Victoria herself as a slightly absurd great great grannie, is part of this myth that we are all part of one great happy family. It is interesting that the family image contrived by IBM ('British parents') is firmly excluded from the doctored version of *Self Help,* where it would contradict the rampant individualism which is being promoted. Perhaps on board the SS *Great Britain* conflict and contradictions are not to be tolerated.

In *Rain, Steam and Speed* (1844), Turner has created one of the most popular and striking images of the Victorian period. In this painting the railway becomes a kind of natural phenomenon, an impression reinforced by the title. In this section I would like to examine the advocacy of supposed Victorian values which takes the minimal form which goes something like this: 'Yes, the Victorians had their faults and their problems, but for all that they had such energy and vitality!' This kind of argument needs to be treated with caution – especially when such comments are implicitly or explicitly supported by such dazzling images as *Rain, Steam and Speed.* The relationship between work, energy and Nature which we need to consider here can be seen more clearly if we consider a pair of earlier paintings by Turner, *Venice* (1834) and *Keelmen Heaving in Coals by Moonlight* (1835). The coal industry is, to say the least, a difficult subject for aesthetic presentation, and what we see in the latter picture is one aspect of that industry transformed into something rich and strange. The art critic of *New Society,* writing in 1983, had this to say about the painting:

> *Keelmen Heaving Coals by Moonlight,* however, did not only record the activity of coal heaving, or the appearance of piles of the stuff. In the illusory world of his picture, Turner enthused the activity and objects of the colliers' work with a dimension they could not possibly possess in reality. Some might say that such aesthetic transformations stand as a promise that reality, too, can be other than the way it is. At the very least, it seems to me that . . . we are entitled to ask our artists to provide us with consoling illusions.[7]

The writer is scornful of those who see any dangers in such 'illusions'. Another critic, Douglas Gray, who selected the Turner painting for an exhibition entitled British Mining in Art 1680–1980, sees in the work the essence of the power of coal, which held the key to so many crucial nineteenth-century developments.[8] This transformation of work, *Keelmen Heaving,* into an abstraction, power, or energy, or vitality, is a crucial move in many attempts to 'save' the Victorians. It does not falsify what Turner is about, but we might argue that it does too easily accept as unproblematic the Romantic subsuming of work under the category of 'forces of Nature'. (The matter goes beyond responses to Turner, of course. One might equally well look at Dickens's treatment of railway imagery in *Dombey,* for example, where once again certain problems and contradictions can be evaded by appeals to vitality and energy, by references to Romantic traditions, or even, if extremely desperate, to 'consoling illusions'.) The two modern accounts of *Keelmen* can be put in perspective by looking at two further contexts for the work – on the one hand its genesis and reception, and on the other the reality of the work which, according to its title, it depicts.

Certain assumptions about what were suitable subjects for treatment in a painting are evident in a review by the art critic of the Literary Gazette, writing in 1835: 'And such a night', he writes, 'a flood of glorious moonlight wasted upon dingy coal whippers, instead of conducting lovers to the appointed bower'.[9] Our idea of the strength of such prejudices is reinforced when we contrast that comment with the praise given a year earlier to 'Venice', in which the reviewer in the same journal discerned 'poetical imagination and splendid colouring.' That revulsion from the 'dingy coal whippers' can be related to the expectations about suitable subject matters for painting which obtained not only in the 1830s, but also much later in the century. As late as the 1860s there existed a strict hierarchy of subjects, beginning with 'High Art, sacred and secular' and 'subjects Poetic and Imaginative', running through 'Portraits and Scenes Domestic, Grave and Gay', and descending to 'Out-door figures, rude, rustic and refined' and 'Animals, Fruit and Flowers', finally reaching sea-level with 'Sea and Landscapes'. There is no place here for the depiction of industrial work. Measured by these expectations, Turner's decision to depict coal backers is a surprising one, and can be interpreted as one of the various, and variously-motivated, attempts to express the dignity of labour which were to become an important feature of nineteenth-century presentations of work. (There was a relatively slight financial penalty for Turner in this, though whether he felt it to be slight, I don't know, in that he was paid £350 for *Venice* but only £300 for his coal whippers.) Both paintings were bought, and possibly commissioned by Henry McConnell, a wealthy Manchester textile manufacturer. By considering the paintings as a pair, certain resonances can be perceived. For example, the connection between 'work' and patriotism' within the Victorian values syndrome is suggested. Here is sunlit, bustling beautiful Venice, but it is an indolent Southern civilisation, in decline. Set against this is the busy English river, an image of a powerful and prosperous civilisation, though when depicted by a great English artist, as beautiful as Venice. Even at night, in the moonlight, the place is active with business, even coal whipping can be beautiful. There is an alternative message, of course: that only distanced and bathed in moonlight could this activity be so obscured that it could conceivably be thought beautiful. And a quite different sense of the paintings is obtained if we set them in the context of some of Turner's other works, which suggest in their elegiac mood the decline and vanity of all Empires. One contemporary nineteenth-century reviewer, writing in *Frazer's Magazine* commented that 'The night is not night and the keelmen and the coals are any thing', a remark which gains credibility from the fact that at one point the painting was exhibited not as *Keelmen Heaving Coals By Moonlight*, but simply as *Moonlight.*

One escape from this moonshine might be to inquire about what such work was actually like. The relevant section of Mayhew's *London Labour and the London Poor,* contains the following statement from a coalbacker:

> I'll tell you what it is, Sir. Our work's harder than people guess at, and one must rest sometimes. Now if you sit down to rest without something to refresh you, the rest does you harm instead of good, for your joints seem to stiffen; but a good pull at a pot of beer backs up the rest, and we start lightsomer. Our work's very hard. I've worked till my head's ached like to split; and when I've got to bed, I've felt as if I've had the weight on my back still . . . feeling as if something was crushing my back flat to my chest. . . . Sometimes we put a bit of coal in our mouths to prevent our biting our tongues . . . but it's almost as bad as if you did bite your tongue, for when the strain comes heavier and heavier on you, you keep scrunching the coal to bits, and swallow some of it, and you're half choked.[10]

Perhaps when it comes to the experience of work it is the case that, as Lenin remarked, a participant is the only true observer. The subsuming of human labour within a larger entity – Nature, the landscape or riverscape perceived romantically and sublimely, has consequences of a contradictory kind. On the one hand it allow the artist, working against that traditional hierarchy of subjects, to make labour worthy of depiction and can convey a sense of the dignity of labour. On the other hand, work people can be reduced to being a kind of medium through which this natural force, work, operates ('the keelmen and the coals are any thing'). In this prespective a strike can be seen as an artifical, an unnatural damming up of this natural force of labour. The worker becomes, paradoxically, someone who can get in the way of this force, becoming in one recent extremist formulation, the 'enemy within'. Turner has created very powerful, impressive images – to see them simply as 'consoling illusions' is not just an inadequate, it is an irresponsible reaction.

In this section I would like to examine further that notion of the 'dignity of labour' which was touched upon in the discussion of Turner's work. No better starting point for a discussion of the ambiguities and complexities involved here can be found than Ford Madox Brown's *Work*. The painting is not just a compendium of representations of work, it exemplifies in its form the labour it appears to advocate: Brown sweated over it for a decade (1852–63) and its painstaking detail seems to be offered, like massive detail in so much Victorian art and literature, as a guarantee of excellence or worth. (We can see in this a formal similarity to Smiles' *Self-Help*, with its monumental heaping up of example after example of success gained through effort.) Biblical injunctions were incorporated in the frame of *Work*, reminding us that no discussion of Victorian values which ignores the religious dimensions makes any sense. One of these Biblical quotations in particular was echoed and re-echoed in nineteenth-century writings: 'I must work while it is day for the night cometh when no man can work'. This was the age of images of Christ the worker, for example in Millais's controversial *Christ in the House of his Parents* or Hunt's *The Shadow of Death*, again with its massive detail and its meticulous accuracy in the depiction of the tools of the carpenter's trade. One of the best known of all Victorian images, *The Light of the World*, was criticised at the time precisely because it did not portray Christ as a worker.

It is clear that Brown had absorbed some of the sociological thinking of his day, as he follows Mayhew's taxonomy of work quite closely in the composition of the picture, in which we find depicted those who will work, those who cannot work, those who will not work, and those who need not work. The genesis of the painting casts light on a crucial issue in considering 'work' in relation to the arts in the nineteenth century, that is to say the question of where the artist was to be placed in the world of work. Brown's original intention was to include a self-portrait in the painting to represent the 'artist as brainworker', thus complementing the manual labour which takes centre stage. He rejected this idea and substituted the social thinkers Carlyle and

Maurice as representatives of brainwork whilst 'invisibly' identifying himself, as artist, with the heroic manual labourer. It is interesting to note that immediately prior to this, with the writing of *Dombey and Son,* Dickens had in a sense moved in the opposite direction. Whereas Brown was attempting to equate painting with manual labour, Dickens was consciously trying to transform his work from being 'merely' popular writing to the status of an 'art'.

The 'message' of the painting is in some ways as confused as the scene which is being depicted. Mayhew's categories of workers and non-workers seem to fit, but then so does Morris's very different taxonomy: 'a class which does not even pretend to work, a class which pretends to work but which produces nothing, and a class which works, but is compelled by the other two classes to do work which is often unproductive.'[11] There are elements in the painting, and especially in Brown's own comments on it and more generally on his society, which harmonise with Morris's. Brown saw English society as 'internally a prey to snobbishness and the worship of gold and tinsel – a place chiefly for sneaks and lacqueys, and any who can fawn and clutch, or dress clean at church and connive'. Despite the influence and the pressure of Carlyle we must not assume that Brown is presenting us with that notion of the dignity of labour which is summed up in Morris's words as 'the semi-theological dogma that all labour, under any circumstances, is a blessing to the labourer'. But to see some kind of straightforward socialist message would be equally false. What the disunity which we can observe in the painting could indicate is that division of labour and division of class means that a unified notion of 'work' is impossible.

Although Brown depicts Carlyle the great advocate of work apparently lounging idly by, watching others engaged in strenuous labour, we need to resist the temptation to see this as some kind of simple irony. Brown was deeply affected by Carlyle's teaching and pored over *Past and Present,* a book whose vision of a medieval order of work in some ways parallels present day neo-Victorianism. Carlyle's writing was immensely influential on Victorian writing and visual art, and central to his philosophy was his advocacy of hard work. In Carlyle's overheated prose, work appears to be a 'semi-theological dogma' but also a desperate antidote to despair, and one suspects that his feeling lies behind many Victorian exhortations to work. To explore further the dark origins of such feverish Victorian commitments to work as a mission we can turn to a prose fiction text dating from the end of the Victorian period, Conrad's *Heart of Darkness.*

Nineteenth-century social thinkers and educationalists emphasised the idea of work as a mission, in the first instance to subdue nature, but also as part of the struggle waged by civilisation against barbarism. We have seen how ideas about work were connected with patriotic notions and with thoughts about the place of the family – often in an antagonistic relationship, but with the conflict of values hidden or suppressed. In addition, there were racist and imperialist overtones to some Victorian discussions of work. These are of special interest in relation to *Heart of Darkness,* but rather than these specialised aspsects of the debate about work I'd like here to look at the way in which Conrad's *Heart of Darkness* explores the darkness which generated appeals to work and from which work formed an escape. In this short novel Conrad traces the journey of his character Marlow from Europe, epitomised in the image of the Sepulchral City, to the heart of Africa. The tale had its origin in Conrad's own visit to the Congo. When the full horror of the place dawns on Marlow he plunges desperately into work, and like many a Victorian finds not just consolation and escape but a sense of identity to such an extent that he feels that work is the only thing which gives him a sense of his real self: 'I don't like work – no man does – but I like what is in the work – the chance to find yourself. Your own reality – for yourself, not for others – what no other man can ever know.'[12] This story forms a fitting conclusion to a discussion of Victorian and neo-Victorian values, not least because the Congo at this time is an image of ultimate privatisation, being the private possession of one man, King Leopold of the Belgians, whose idea of the 'mission' of work he expressed in the following way:

> The mission which the agents of the state have to accomplish on the Congo is a noble one. They have to continue the development of civilisation in the centre of Equatorial Africa, receiving their inspiration directly from Berlin and Brussels. Placed face to face with primitive

barbarism, grappling with sanguinary customs that date back thousands of years, they are obliged to reduce these gradually. They must accustom the population to general laws, of which the most needful and the most salutary is assuredly that of work.[13]

What I would like to emphasise here is not the irony of this comment when set alongside the quotation from *Heart of Darkness,* but the revelation of the real complexity of work which is revealed by such a juxtaposition. How misleading to see work as some kind of straightforward Victorian value which one can be asked to subscribe to! Not surprisingly Carlyle saw in Leopold a great saviour who rescued the Congo from 'cannibalism, savagery and despair'. 'Despair' sits very oddly with the other two 'problems', and it is the strangeness which gives us an insight into the darkness from which Victorian invocations of work arose.

Notes

1 George Orwell, 'Charles Dickens', reprinted in *The Collected Essays, Journalism and Letters of George Orwell,* Harmondsworth, 1970, Vol. 1, p. 454.

2 Charles Dickens, *Dombey and Son* (1848), Harmondsworth, 1970, p. 738.

3 P. D. Anthony, *The Ideology of Work,* London, 1977.

4 Quoted by Asa Briggs in *Victorian People,* 1954, rev. edn, Harmondsworth, 1965, p. 130.

5 See R. A. Buchanan, 'Gentlemen engineers: the making of a profession', *Victorian Studies,* 26, No. 4, Summer 1983, pp. 407–29.

6 The advertisement is reproduced in Rob Powell, *Brunel's Kingdom,* Bristol, 1985, p. 53.

7 P. Fuller, 'Black arts: coal and aesthetics', reprinted in *Images of God,* London, 1985.

8 Douglas Gray, 'Art and coal', *Coal, British Mining in Art 1680–1980,* Arts Council, 1982.

9 This and subsequent contemporary comments on Turner are taken from Martin Butlin & E. Joll, *The Paintings of J. M. W. Turner,* Yale University Press, 1977.

10 Quoted in J. F. C. Harrison, *Early Victorian Britain* (1977), London, 1979, p. 69.

11 William Morris, 'Useful work versus useless toil', 1885, reprinted in Asa Briggs (ed.), *William Morris, Selected Writings and Designs,* Harmondsworth, 1962.

12 Joseph Conrad, *Heart of Darkness* (1899), ed. R. Kimbrough, New York, 1971, p. 29.

13 Quoted in Kimbrough, *op. cit.,* p. 86.

3 *Ron Bellamy*

Victorian economic values

It is no mere trick of words that centres the economic values of the Victorian epoch around its Theory of Value – or more strictly, around its two diametrically opposed Theories of Value. For values embody the appraisal of, the approval or denunciation, the demand for the realisation or for the elimination, of some social phenomena. In the economic sphere the focus of values is upon the ability of existing institutions for the production and distribution of wealth to satisfy the interests of society as a whole or those of its different or conflicting social groups.

When society's material means of existence are produced through a division of its labour into specialised forms, possessed by individual owners who have the power to produce what they choose, no owners produce all – and most produce none – of the products they consume. The social institution which makes their choices mutually compatible, so that the aggregate of individual labours produces what society needs, is the network of markets in which the owners sell what they have produced and buy what they need. It is the ratios of exchange established in markets between the physical commodities produced, their (relative) exchange-values, which determine the distribution of the social product between their respective owners. If the value-in-exchange with which the market rewards the labours of each producer is less than he or she could have obtained from expending it on another product, then exchange-value acts as a signal of failure to maximise self-interest, and provides a stimulus to correct the mistake through reallocation of efforts. When the range of commodities extends beyond physical products to include labour-power itself, then the ratio of exchange in the labour market determines the distribution of the social product between buyers and sellers of labour-power, between the two classes, capitalist and workers. The theory which explains the determination of exchange ratios is the Theory of Value.

The development of economic ideas from the 1820s has been described by a celebrated modern textbook as a growing bifurcation of the theory of value inherited from the classical school of Adam Smith and David Ricardo. A mainstream trend, accepted by the establishment, increasingly rejected a crucial part of its inheritance from the classical school of Smith and Ricardo, the Labour Theory of Value, with all its underlying premisses and its conclusions. Yet it retained Smith's epoch-making conception of the existing order as a social system where the pursuit of individual self-interest was transmuted, as if by an 'invisible hand', into public benefits.

> A description of how the system worked *ipso facto* became a presumption as to how it should be allowed to work. True, classical political economy contained no final demonstration that *laisser-faire* produced the *optimum* result in human welfare. . . . The economists were quite content with the claim that (it) was superior as a condition for the production and increase of wealth; a claim that they were particularly concerned to demonstrate by contrast with State-aided monopolies or with State restrictions on foreign trade. There was every temptation to believe that a system which achieved an equilibrium by an internal coherence of its elements operated better left alone than when ignorantly interfered with. At any rate, it was a belief which inevitably found favour in an age when whatever exhibited the reign of natural law was implicitly held to be half divine.[1]

In the other direction, a socialist trend took as its explicit starting point the Labour Theory of Value, with its emphasis on labour in material production as the source of wealth, and on the production of a surplus which was appropriated by the capitalist class as profits. As this theory of value was the central arena of debate, let us examine it more closely in its most rigorously worked-out form, that of Ricardo's *Principles of Political Economy and Taxation* (1817). He starts from the accepted view that all commodities tend (in a position of rest, where those producers who can move don't want to, and those who want to cannot) to exchange in ratios which correspond to the ratios of their costs of production, measured in units (e.g. hours) of labour-time. Ricardo was of course well aware of the short-term deviations from this equilibrium, caused by temporary fluctuations in supply and demand. But no more than the entirely orthodox Alfred Marshall, who later in the century used the concept of long-run equilibrium prices determined by costs, was Ricardo numbered among those who (in the sardonic remark of Joan Robinson) 'think economics is about the momentary price of a cup of tea'.

What are the conditions required to establish and maintain these equilibrium ratios of exchange? They are that there shall be competition and mobility of resources. The first is guaranteed by the premise of self-interest, since all producers will move to produce that product whose price gives the highest rewards for an hour's labour, so increasing its supply and pulling down its price. The second is guaranteed by the equality of property of all producers, each of whom is possessed of all the resources required to enter any line of production, namely his or her own labour-power and the petty tools and materials of the trade. Now it is true that the picture above represents 'an early and crude state of society', one of self-employed handicraft producers. But competition and mobility of resources between different sectors of production can still be guaranteed, even if one changes the picture to one where the means of production are large enough to employ several wage-workers, and are owned by a separate class of capitalists, provided only that there is a large number of small capitalists of roughly equal size.

Let us now, with Ricardo, assume that the level of technique in society is sufficient (and it has been for thousands of years) for society's labour force to produce not only enough commodities to replace, during the process of personal consumption, the labour power expended in production, but to produce a surplus as well. The question is then: Who gets the surplus? Ricardo observed, as a question of fact, that the capitalists got it. But science requires an answer to the question: Why and how do they get it?

Consider the first case, of a pre-capitalist society of self-employed commodity producers – there are no private landowners. In this case there is clearly no other class who can receive the surplus. So by default it must all go to the self-employed producers. But in what proportions? Equally? Unequally? And by what mechanism?

Suppose some producers, moved by self-interest, begin to demand a price for their product greater than its cost of production. They will be giving in exchange to others commodities which cost less labour-time than those they receive in return. If initially they are the only ones to follow this course, they can, in principle, charge such a price that all the surplus would be appropriated by them. But others will quickly see what is happening and, moved likewise by self-interest, will either push up their own prices or alternatively move into the field where prices initially rose. In either case price ratios will begin to move back towards the ratio of costs. It is not difficult to see that an equilibrium will be reached in which the surplus is distributed in proportion to labour performed, or, if every producer performs the same amount of labour, the surplus will be equally distributed.

What is the guarantee of 'distribution of the surplus according to labour-time performed'? It is – and this is the most crucial point in our whole exposition – that each producer can move from being the seller of a low-priced commodity to being a buyer of it. To employ the term we shall use henceforth, '*he can cross to the other side of the market*'.

Consider now the second case – an economy of capitalists and workers. The exchange transaction between them is one in which means of subsistence (and the use-values they embody) are transferred from being the property of capitalists to become the property of workers and, as the *quid pro quo*, labour power (and the use values it embodies) is transferred from being the property of workers to become the property of capitalists. As before, it is the direct labour of the workers which produces the surplus, over and above what is necessary for subsistence. On the basis of the labour theory of value, the capitalists expend no labour (except possibly the labour of organisation and management, for which however they receive a wage, not profit) and therefore produce nothing. Yet, as Ricardo observed, it is they who receive the whole surplus product of society. How is this to be explained? For, surely, according to the theory outlined above, all the workers have got to do is to 'cross to the other side of the market', and become capitalist-buyers of labour power instead of worker-sellers of it. Then the number of capitalist buyers will rise, and even if the total surplus were fixed, it must be divided between a larger number of capitalists and the profit received by each will fall. But the total surplus is not given. As the number of workers falls the total surplus falls. Moreover, as more capitalist buyers compete for the shrinking labour force, the price of labour-power, i.e. the wage rate, rises. Profits are further squeezed. Where will the movement come to rest? According to the Labour Theory of Value, a continuous movement of wage workers to the capitalists' side of the market should go on until rewards of an hour's labour are the same on both sides of the market. But from the capitalists' side there comes no labour; they are not expending any energy of nerve and muscle which needs to be replaced. *Impasse*! The undoubted fact of capitalists' profits was something that Ricardo could not explain on the basis of a consistent and rigorous application of the Labour Theory of Value. But it is great tribute to his honesty as a scientist that he posed the dilemma so clearly.

When the post-Ricardian Socialists in England in the 1820s and 1830s began to resolve his dilemma by advancing theories of exploitation based on private property and to pose the question of a juster system based on social property, in the historical context of great hardship which gave rise to the mass trade unions of the 1830s and the Chartist movement of the 1840s, a watershed had come for the theory of value.

This challenge could be met only by counter-arguments which would show that profits were not a surplus created by the working class and appropriated by capital, but were a necessary – and therefore justified – payment by the rest of society to the capitalist class. In a simplified model of reality with only two classes, that meant a payment by workers to capitalists, via the margin of profit included in the price of the necessities of life which workers bought from capitalists. The source of this margin of profit was explained in a new theory of value. This new theory developed two different lines of argument, to be combined later in the century into a single synthesis.

All theories develop by transforming 'ideological material already to hand'. Had not Adam Smith, the prestigious discoverer of the operation of natural law in a *laisser-faire* society, left an ambiguous legacy in his theory of value. Since capitalists were observed to receive an income, could they not be presumed to be performing a service? Instead of starting from the end of costs, could one not start from services which contributed to what was after all the final aim of all economic activity, the production of commodities for consumption, the production of use-values, the production of 'utility'? Valuations now depend upon consumers' views of them, upon consumers' preferences. In this way emphasis is shifted away from costs measured objectively in labour-time hours, and reflecting the struggle of man against nature, towards utility, towards subjective feelings, towards human psychology – an emphasis reflected in the title of a famous theoretical work of this period, Professor Edgeworth's *Mathematical Psychics.* It was but a short step to give consumers an income in which to express their choices through money votes in the market, and one had a theory of demand. And was not demand (it was said, quite wrongly in fact) something the classical theory had simply ignored? Was not the new theory more general, and therefore more scientific? True, there were awkward corners. Did the millionaire's bid for a cigar reflect a greater 'utility' than the pauper's bid for a crust, or merely greater ability to pay? This objection was met by the more cautious, or more honest, economists by saying that one must of course assume equality in the distribution of incomes. But it is somewhat restrictive, indeed logically indefensible, that a theory which seeks to explain the distribution of income should start with the distribution already assumed. By comparison, it was no doubt a minor difficulty that the assumption hardly corresponded with the observable extremes of poverty and wealth.

Adam Smith had not needed any well-worked out argument that capitalism marked an advance in human welfare compared with the past. The growth in wealth spoke for itself. But once the first economic crisis had appeared as it did in 1825, and growth for a time faltered, as it faltered more acutely and chronically later, the system's ability to advance welfare could be called into question, and the awkward corners were harder to turn. None the less by the 1850s prosperity seemed more assured, and the new theory of value developed more assurance.

If capital is held to 'make a contribution' to output, it can be said to be 'productive'. This is the central proposition in the well-known theory of 'factors of production', in which output is attributed to the 'contributions of land, labour, and capital'.

Now no school of thought has ever doubted that production requires the use of land, the transformation of materials, the wear-and-tear of physical capital equipment, and the expenditure of human energy, in manual and mental labour, including the labour which organises coordination. Every school of thought, including socialist and marxist, believed that labour is more productive with more and better capital goods. They also believe that if the amount of labour is given, there may be some sense in which the extra output which results from labour using more and better capital goods can be said to be 'the product of the extra capital goods'. Indeed, in today's socialist countries a concept of 'the effectiveness of investment' is used to measure precisely that. But in phrases such as 'cooperating factors of production' there is an ambiguity. Co-operation is a characteristic of human beings, not of things. Physical capital goods and materials and land do not 'co-operate' with human labour. They are put into action by it. Is there not some sleight of hand here? If co-operation can take place only between human beings, then 'the co-operation of capital goods and labour power in production' really refers to the relations between their respective owners where the latter are different; in capitalist society, relations between wage workers and capitalists. And while there is a sense in which production cannot take place without the will of both, it is at least open to doubt whether the relation can be called one of co-operation.

As many economists have noted, the productivity theory contains a confusion: it endows a separate class of private owners of physical capital goods with attributes that properly belong to those goods. If those physical capital goods were owned by the individual labourers who worked with them (as in handicraft production) or if they were owned by the collective of labourers who worked with them (as in socialism), then there would be no special category of income called profit, belonging to a separate class. Profit, therefore seems to arise not out of productivity of capital goods, but out of their private ownership by a separate class.

The rebuttal of this argument began by emphasising the difference between land and physical capital goods. The former was a gift of nature, and had no cost to society. Arguably then rent arose simply out of private ownership of it. But capital goods were made. Now it is true, and was conceded under pressure, that in an economy where the capital stock is not growing, the capitalists are fully recompensed in payments for depreciation for all costs of production of the physical capital goods which comprise the capital stock. And unfortunately, with their passion to emphasise the harmonious and self-adjusting character of the economic system, economists were frequently tempted to abstract from the disharmony and disequilibrium introduced by growth and technical progress and postulate an economy without growth. But when they accepted the observable fact that economies grew and that the capital stock grew by the ploughing back of profits, they explained the reward to those who supplied the additional capital by the theory of 'abstinence' associated particularly with the name of Nassau Senior. The stock of capital goods had originally been built up by the thrift of pre-capitalist producers who consumed less than their income. Such thrift involved sacrifice, since everyone wants to consume. If society wants to have the extra output that comes from having a larger and technically better capital stock, then it must pay those who make society's sacrifices for it. Profits (in the broad definition of them which includes all payments to capitalists) are the payment necessary to call forth that sacrifice.

The sacrifice was conceived in psychological terms, as the utility sacrificed, the negative utility or disutility incurred, the pain of abstention felt as less consumer goods are enjoyed. The commonsense plausibility of the theory rested upon the partial truth that some at least of the early capitalists had become such by a process that involved considerable hardship. The present writer well remembers engravings which depicted the fireless grate, the beshawled wife and the hungry children of Richard Arkwright as he accumulated the small capital to begin exploitation of his invention. And Marx points to the meagre table of the small Manchester master seeking, on pain of extinction as a capitalist, to conform to the exacting 'law of Moses and the Prophets – Accumulate, accumulate, accumulate.' And if doubts might arise as to the existence of any such psychological law (was there no enjoyment to be gained from the thought of passing on riches to one's children?), the textbooks were not slow to universalise this 'human nature' by reference to a conveniently constructed (but entirely fictitious) primitive society in which our savage capitalist, previously catching fish with his hands, cuts consumption to build up a stock, and lives off it while he labours to construct a boat, or a net, or fishhook and line. He increases his productivity by accumulation, and lives better for the future, but at what a sacrifice. A sardonic critic remarked that such a savage, not yet hunting animals, had no clothes and must live in a warm climate. In such conditions the edibility of stored fish might be in doubt, even if one could telescope the centuries-long invention-process of real history into a few weeks.

Once this explanation of human behaviour, in terms of the subjective feelings of individuals, had been devised for consumers and for capitalists, it was but a short step to a final synthesis which applied it to manual and mental labour also. *The Principles of Economics* of Alfred Marshall which dominated the teaching of economics from 1890 well into the late 1920s did just that. True, he found it difficult to maintain the fiction that the third generation of inheritors of capital could seriously be supposed to undergo abstinence. But society still must pay them for 'waiting' i.e. not dispersing in luxury consumption the capital amassed by others. And with the subjective explanation of the supply of labour and capital firmly embraced, and the substance of Ricardo entirely rejected, Marshall could allow himself the luxury of going back to the classical principle that exchange ratios are determined in the long run by costs.

One final element was required to complete the picture. If petty abstinence out of wages were to make workers free to cross the labour market and become capitalists, small businesses must have a good chance of survival and growth. This logical implication of the theory is one factor in explaining the extraordinary tenacity with which mainstream economics adhered until the 1930s to the conception of 'perfect competition', in which firms were so small that none could influence the supply to, or the price in, any market. The other is that, after ridding themselves of the classical economists' 'erroneous labour theory of value', they could then draw authority from the traditional Smithian picture of a *laisser-faire* economy, of a self-correcting system which adapts smoothly, quickly and beneficially to changes in consumers' demand or in production techniques, provided only that state meddling does not prevent resources being fully used. Adam Smith's strictures on monopoly can be confined to trade unions. Nor did they seem unduly worried by the illogicality of asserting that firms plough back profits yet do not grow beyond a petty size, nor over the contradiction between the assumption of perfect competition and the growing fact of giant firms.

In summary, we can say that the mainstream theory of the Victorian epoch had three essential features. Capitalism was no transient social order: it was rooted in a psychology, a human nature, of eternal validity. Capitalists and workers had identical mainsprings of action, identical interests in maximising utility. Finally, if each actor sought his or her own interests, and was free to do so between no barriers to social movement existed, then Adam Smith's conclusions held. This was an order of harmony and beneficence.

Unfortunately for the theory, facts are 'chiels that wilna ging'. From the 1870s the privileged position of Britain in world trade was threatened by more efficient rivals. The twenty years of the Great Depression cast doubt on capacity of capitalism for self-adjustment to produce full employment and growth. The unskilled workers who flocked to the New Unionism were less disposed to acquiesce in concepts of harmony and common interest than had been the 'pompous and proud mechanics', their skilled forbears during what Engels had called 'the great sleep' of 1850–1870. In continental Europe, where large scale-industry had grown fast but without British privileges, the working class had formed powerful political parties based on the Marxism of *Capital* which had appeared in 1867. Britain was ripe for a return to the socialist ideas of the 1820s and the political radicalism of the 1830s and 1840s.

But this time the theories available to the working class were not the post-Ricardian Socialists' incomplete and vulnerable assertions of capitalist exploitation, combined with a purely Utopian vision of a new socialist order. Instead, there was the 'scientific' socialism, of Marx, which asserted that the 'laws of motion' of the capitalist system themselves created the two necessary and sufficient conditions for the transformation of capitalism into socialism. First, capitalism created the so-called 'objective' material conditions, in the form of large-scale production and micro-planning concentrated in a limited number of firms which together commanded the heights of the economy. Second, and by the very same process, capitalism had also created the 'subjective' conditions, the human agent – the 'gravediggers of capitalism', in Marx's graphic phrase – who had both the interest and the capacity to take political power and use it to transform private, capitalist ownership into social ownership of the means of production. This was the working class 'a class always increasing in numbers, and disciplined, united, organised by the very mechanism of the process of capitalist production itself'.[2]

As Samuelson's family tree suggested, Marx's theory started from the tradition of the classical school. He took over its emphasis on production as the starting point for all analysis of society, and developed it into a theory of social progress, the theory of historical materialism – which has a scope wider than our limited brief. He took over the Labour Theory of Value and developed it consistently, resolving the problem unresolved by Ricardo, and incompletely resolved by the post-Ricardian Socialists.

Ricardo, as we noted, saw clearly the fact that capitalist profits were a surplus produced by the working class, and appropriated by capitalists. But what made the fact inevitable, necessary? What was the logic of the process? Why did workers not cross to the other side of the market? Marx provided the logic essentially by specifying the social and historical changes in the sphere of production which had created a new class, direct producers to be sure, but direct producers who no longer worked with their own materials and instruments of production, their own 'means of production', to produce a commodity which was their own property and which they exchanged on a market with other producers working under the same conditions as themselves. This new class, the class of wage-workers, worked in factories owned by people other than themselves, by capitalists. They worked with means of production owned by people other than themselves, by capitalists. And the products of their labour belonged to, and were sold on the market, by people other than themselves, by capitalists.

Wage-workers enter into an exchange with capitalists in the

labour market. Having made their contract, they work in the capitalist's factory. First, they enter the process of exchange. Then they enter the process of production. *Post hoc, propter hoc.* Process of production *after* process of exchange. *Therefore* process of production *because* process of exchange. Is that right? Yes, says mainstream theory. The wage worker becomes a wage worker by choice. If he doesn't like the wages, or the conditions of work, he can go elsewhere. No, says Marx. You mistake appearance for essence. *Appearance*: a

> labour market ruled only by Freedom, Equality, Property and Bentham. Freedom, because both buyer and seller of a commodity, say labour power, are constrained only by their own free will. They contract as free agents, and the agreement they come to is but the form in which they give legal expression to their common will. Equality, because each enters into relations with the other as a simple owner of commodities, and they exchange equivalent for equivalent. Property, because each disposes of his own. And Bentham, because each looks only to himself . . . and no one troubles himself about the rest, and just because they do so, they all, in accordance with the pre-established harmony of things, or under the auspices of an all-shrewd providence, work together for their mutual advantage, for the common weal and in the interests of all.[3]

But what is the *essence* of the matter? It is that wage workers entered into *exchange* with the capitalists in the market for labour power because there was no other gateway through which they could enter into *production*. Denied that gateway, human beings are denied the possibility of expending the only resource given to them by nature for the production of their material means of life, namely their labour power. The capitalist class, having the monopoly of the means of production, is in a position to dictate its own terms for opening the gateway. Those terms are that the usefulness, the use-value, of the workers' labour power, its capacity to produce, shall become the capitalists property and that in return they shall pay through the market to its owners no more than 'exchange of equivalents' demands, namely its exchange value. And that means its cost of production. Since the use-value of labour power to the capitalists, as they consume it in production, is what it produces, and as it produces more than its own cost of production, the surplus accrues to the capitalists directly and immediately during production.

To escape from this necessity, to have Freedom of Choice of an alternative gateway into production, to cross over to the other side of the market, labourers would have to own means of production of their own. But it is just those which they do not have, dispossessed of them by an irreversible historical process. The wage-working class came into being precisely by a process of polarisation of petty owners, of self-employed farmers and handicraft workers, in which the large majority were dispossessed of their 'dwarfish' means of production, and only a small minority became capitalists. (For reasons of space we present only the abstract logic of development; the concrete historical process was a more complex one in which capitalists emerged by other routes as well.) This process is irreversible because once capitalists appropriate profits, competition forces them to 'abstain' and to reinvest them in the newest techniques, which requires in turn an increasing scale of production. The minimum size of capital required to survive rises historically, 'one capitalist kills many' smaller ones, with a growing concentration of capital in fewer centres of ownership and control. The growth and consolidation of stable trade unions is a recognition by the class of wage-workers of their irreversible status within the framework of capitalism.

Because the mainstream economists of the nineteenth century regarded capitalism as the end of human achievement and therefore as eternal, it is not surprising that they had so little to say about its negative sides, about periodic economic crises (in 1890 Marshall's book of 870 pages has three short references to unemployment, all treating it as fortuitous or the result of government interference), and above all about its long term dynamics (Schumpeter's Theory of Economic Development, the first major work of dynamics by a mainstream economist came only after the Victorian epoch had ended). For that reason we have confined our discussion of Marx primarily to his theory of value. Since this theory, unlike that of mainstream economics, was rooted in the social relations of production, it rested upon the anatomy of society which formed the matrix of its developing physiology. But that anatomy he saw not as eternal, but as historically transient, with a beginning, a maturity, and a death as its laws of motion created the necessity and prerequisites for socialism.

Notes

1 M. H. Dobb, *Political Economy and Capitalism*, 1937, p. 49.
2 K. Marx, *Capital*, London, Vol. 1, p. 789.
3 *Ibid.*, p. 155.

4 *Michael E. Rose*

The disappearing pauper: Victorian attitudes to the relief of the poor

Rattle his bones over the stones; he's only a pauper, whom nobody owns.[1]

Described by Steven Marcus as 'the first unperson in modern history', the pauper is a familiar figure to students of the Victorian period.[2] Confined in that grim institution, the workhouse, distinctly clothed and fed, he was divided even in death from other members of society by the sparse and hurried nature of the parish funeral.

Indeed the concept of the pauper, and his condition, that of pauperism, would appear to be a Victorian one, if the term can be stretched to cover the period from the late-eighteenth century to the early years of the twentieth. In the *Oxford English Dictionary*, most examples of the general use of the term are drawn from Victorian sources such as the works of Charles Dickens, Samuel Smiles, John Richard Green or the blind economist Henry Fawcett, whose course of lectures, *Pauperism: Its Causes and Remedies,* was delivered at Cambridge in the Michaelmas term of 1870.[3] With the death of Queen Victoria in 1901, use of the terms 'pauper' and 'pauperism' rapidly declined. By 1968, the Dean of the School of Social Work at UCLA could view them as 'a concept which by the middle of the twentieth century was largely one only of historic interest . . . the terms 'pauperism' and 'pauper' have little place in modern social thought'.[4]

To the Victorians, however, the concept was central to any discussion of the relief of poverty whether by private or public methods. Charles Booth might define paupers as 'all those . . . who have received any form of relief under the Poor Law within twelve months', but, in many Victorian minds, the term had a much wider, less clearly defined application.[5] Anyone dependent upon public relief or private charity was in danger of becoming a pauper and of falling into the state of pauperism. Poverty and pauperism were quite distinct. Poverty was the lot of most of the manual labouring classes, and was seen, at least until the latter years of the nineteenth century, as inevitable, natural and indeed necessary as a stimulus to hard work. By contrast, pauperism was the condition of a relatively small proportion of the population. It was a degenerate state in which the will to work was lost, the urge to self help was broken, and dependency and degradation were the results. 'Pauperism is the last stage in the downhill journey of manhood and when once reached, the victim is then and thenceforth *sans* pride, *sans* self respect and *sans* ambition', C. S. Watkins of Davenport, Iowa told a meeting of the National Conference of Charities and Correction in 1882.[6] Another American, Charles R. Henderson described the 'typical pauper' as 'a social parasite who attaches himself to others and, by living at their expense, suffers loss of energy and ability by disease and atrophy. Pauperism at this stage is a loathsome moral disease, more difficult to cure than crime'.[7]

This was the crux of the problem for socially concerned Victorians on both sides of the Atlantic. Pauperism appeared to them as a pathological condition. It was addictive, in that sufferers from it were likely to turn vicious if their sources of aid were cut off. More seriously, it was highly contagious. The independent, hard working poor might easily contract it from a few sufferers in their midst. Hence, in part, the need to isolate paupers as if they were the victims of cholera or smallpox. In a similar medical vein, Harriet Martineau described the pre-1834 poor law system as 'the great political gangrene of England which it was equally dangerous to meddle with or to let alone'.[8]

It was this pre-1834 poor law system, the so-called 'Old Poor Law', and the mode of relief associated with it in its latter years, the 'Speenhamland' or 'allowance' system, which was in large part responsible for the creation of the Victorian concept of the pauper. The system and the evils allegedly associated with it are familiar to most students of English social history.[9] During the inflationary, crisis-torn decade of the 1790s, parish overseers of the poor, usually with the sanction of the local JP, subsidised the low earnings of rural labourers out of the poor rates. Whilst the allowance system proper became less used after the end of the French wars in 1815 and the subsequent fall in food prices, other devices such as the 'labour rate' or the 'roundsman system' were adopted by overseers in parishes plagued by unemployment, often of a seasonal nature. Thus poor rates increased as farm profits fell. Land was said to be going out of cultivation whilst labourers, far from being appeased, seemed to become increasingly truculent and rebellious. The riots in East Anglia in 1815–16 or the more widespread 'Swing' riots of 1830–31 persuaded the ruling classes of the appalling consequences of creating a pauper class, dependent or semi-dependent upon public funds.[10]

The idea that rural England, particularly the southern counties, became 'pauperised' and demoralised by a wrong headed system of poor relief struck deep. The early historians of the Industrial Revolution, Arnold Toynbee, John and Barbara Hammond, Sidney and Beatrice Webb, G. D. H. Cole and Raymond Postgate, R. H. Tawney were all agreed as to the essentially evil nature of the Old Poor Law.[11] The 1834 reforms, though harsh, were seen by them as a cruel necessity, a cauterising of a wound without anaesthetic in order to stem the spreading 'political gangrene'. Only since the 1960s have historians, making more intensive analyses of local and regional sources, shown that the 'Speenhamland' system was far less serious and widespread than was maintained, and that it was a consequence rather than a cause of the ills afflicting rural society.[12]

For contemporaries, however, pauperism had become a threat, and, to the sound of scribbling pens in country rectories, a host of pamphlets propounding solutions burst upon the public in the first two decades of the century.[13] This wealth of good advice culminated in the appointment in 1832 of the Royal Commission on the Poor Laws, whose Report, published early in 1834, was designed to provide a final solution to the pauper problem.[14] The key feature of this lay in the adoption of the institution as a mode of relief. This device, as David Rothman has shown, was receiving a massive vote of confidence in this period from social reformers in both Europe and America.[15]

Outdoor relief to the able bodied applicant, the most dangerous type of pauper, was to be prohibited. Instead relief should be offered only in the institution, the 'well regulated workhouse'. Here the recipient would be separated from the rest of society and subjected to a disciplined regime of work, regular hours and plain food.[16]

The Poor Law Amendment Act, rushed through a grateful parliament in the summer of 1834, was intended to solve the problem. New local authorities for poor relief, under the direction of an expert central body, were empowered to establish or enlarge workhouses and concentrate relief in them.[17] Within a few years, as in Harriet Martineau's tale, the workhouse should have been empty and the workhouse master able to lock the empty building and throw away the key.[18] The 'paupers', an antique memory of the bad old days, would be replaced by an independent, thrifty, self-helping poor.

Unfortunately a theory of social reform rarely achieves its ideals in practice. The neat, self acting test which the workhouse seemed to provide to ideologues like Edwin Chadwick, Nassau Senior or the Reverend J. T. Becher, was fraught with contradictions and practical difficulties. In the first place, it was never made clear whether the model workhouse should be curative or preventitive. Should the institution welcome the potential pauper, and through education, training and discipline send him back into the world an independent man, or should it rather deter him from entry by threats of a punitive regime, thus forcing him to fend for himself and his family at all costs? If the latter were the case, should the orphan, the sick and the aged be subjected to the same harsh system as the able bodied?

Secondly, and on a practical level, it proved extremely difficult during the first two decades of the New Poor Law to persuade the new local authorities for poor relief, the boards of guardians, to incur the costs of building and staffing a new institution.[19] In some poor law unions, particularly those in the industrial north, it appeared cheaper and easier to maintain a system of small doles of out relief even at the risk of creating paupers.[20]

A third obstacle to the smooth working of the anti-pauper model lay in the fact that anyone reluctant to apply to a board of guardians and face the possibility of receiving an order of the workhouse could often turn instead to private philanthropy. In the anti-pauper model this was a desirable move, since private charities were conducive to self help through their support of thrift clubs or allotments schemes. The reality, however, especially in the larger towns, was a confused mass of rapidly growing and competing charities whose efforts might stimulate pauperism.[21]

Thus, by mid century, the pauper and the contagion of pauperism remained prominent in the public mind, although increasingly viewed as an urban rather than a rural phenomenon. In early industrial England's 'classic' city, Manchester, the Reverend Richard Parkinson described 'those wild beasts of prey which always infest the uncultivated wastes of humanity and prowl about the outskirts of civilization'.[22] Twenty years later, Henry Mayhew found amongst the vagrant poor 'no less than 100,000 individuals of the lowest, filthiest and most demoralised classes. In other words, there is a stream of vice and disease, a tide of iniquity and fever flowing from town to town, from one end of the land to the other'.[23]

In London, which by the 1860s had replaced Manchester as the 'shock city' of the age, Thomas Archer noted 'the slinking figures which one sees for a moment in doorways, round corners, at the threshold of the public house but seldom in it', an impression confirmed visually by the drawings of Gustave Doré.[24] Baldwyn Leighton, in his introduction to a collection of the letters of Edward Denison, pronounced pauperism and religion to be 'among the chief problems of our time' and that 'the next, if not the present generation, might suddenly demand their solution'.[25]

The public opinion which Leighton identified in 1872 had been roused in the 1860s by two events. Throughout the decade, much publicity was given to the existence of severe distress in East London, exacerbated by a series of harsh winters of which that of 1860–61 was the first.[26]

An inadequate poor relief system in this area was thought to have broken down, creating a vacuum into which flowed a mass of charitable effort from wealthy West London. Poor law reformers looked aghast at the 'Pauper Frankenstein' which they saw as having been created by the misguided efforts of soft hearted clergymen, amateur philanthropists and panic stricken magistrates.[27]

As Frankenstein's monster struggled to burst his chains in the East End, a potentially greater disaster occurred in the cotton towns of north west England. Disruption of the cotton industry caused by overproduction, speculation and the American Civil War threw thousands of factory employees out of work or on to short time.[28] As in East London, private charity rushed in to aid or replace an indequate and unwelcome poor law system. There were fears that the contagion of pauperism might spread in an area where it was little known, amongst the independent, thrifty, self helping cotton operatives of Lancashire, the pride of the British working class. This fear was increased by outbreaks of rioting in some cotton towns in 1863, a sign of increasing demoralisation.[29] Yet the cotton districts held firm, and, by the mid 1860s, trade began to revive to an almost audible sigh of relief from their governors.[30] Lancashire's salvation, it seemed, had been due not only to the sterling qualities of her workers, suffering silently in the cause of the American slave, but also to the stricter control of private relief in the area. In 1862, a central executive committee had been established to control the distribution of relief funds. Sitting in Manchester, it allocated funds to local relief committees and gave guidance on the way in which relief should be given.[31] Through the Poor Law Board's special commissioner in the area, Harry Burrard Farnall, himself a member of the committee, it was able to co-ordinate policy with the central poor law authority in London.[32]

The rescue of Lancashire from pauperism, and its continued threat in East London, brought with it, as Leighton argued, a growing determination to tackle the problem. The chief instrument for this task remained the institution. Outdoor relief to the able bodied must cease, and relief be given only in the workhouse. In the early 1870s, the new central authority for poor law matters, the Local Government Board, launched its 'crusade against out relief', a campaign supported by its zealous inspectorate and by some chairmen and vice chairmen of boards of guardians.[33] The institution of annual district and national poor law conferences from the early 1870s helped to publicise and to discuss the proposed new measures. Whitehall and the localities were no longer so far apart.[34]

The use of the institution as a defence against pauperism was, however, to be more discriminating and less simplistic than in the heady days of the early 1830s. An increased recognition of different types of potential pauper suggested a more complex institutional model. For the sick poor, there was to be a separation into discrete sick wards within the workhouse, or even into special asylums or hospitals particularly in London.[35] For the child, education in special schools or boarding out with working class families were remedies whose relative merits were fiercely debated from mid century.[36] All agreed, in theory at least, that children must not be left in workhouses exposed to the contagion of pauperism. For the aged, a continuation of out relief or the provision of improved and separate quarters within the workhouse were suggested, whilst the notion of old age pensions was being given serious consideration despite fears that these might pauperise.[37] If these categories of helpless poor could be aided elsewhere, then the full weight of the 'well regulated' or 'test' workhouse could be directed against the able bodied pauper thus ensuring his or her elimination.

In the war against pauperism, private charity was also to be re-organised so that it became an aid rather than an obstacle to 'dispauperisation', and worked in closer co-operation with the poor law system. The main thrust for reform here came from the Charity Organisation Society, founded in 1868. It saw its role as that of a clearing house for all applications for charitable relief. Charities would refer applicants to COS branches which would then send a trained visitor to the applicant's home. The needs of the individual and of the family would be assessed, and they would then be referred to the charity best able to help them back to independence and rescue them from falling into pauperism. If in the view of the visitor, the applicant was already pauperised and a member of the 'undeserving poor', no private aid would be given. Such an applicant would be referred to the board of guardians who would give relief only in the workhouse.[38]

As after 1834, this model did not function so perfectly in the real world, although the 'crusade against outdoor relief' saw the numbers of out relief fall sharply in the last quarter of the century.[39] As far as the COS was concerned, its practical influence on the poor law system seems to have been limited to a few London poor law unions and some rural ones like Atcham or Brixworth whose boards of guardians were chaired by COS doctrinaires like Albert Pell.[40] COS ideology however exercised a considerable influence on Victorian values in the realm of social policy. Its ideas of scientific philanthropy spread far and wide, whilst its individualistic, investigative approach to social problems stimulated scientific or pseudo-scientific research into the causes of pauperism.[41] Alexander MacDougall, a Manchester alderman and vice chairman of the board of guardians, carried out an investigation into pauperism in the city between 1883 and 1885. His final report purported to show that fifty one per cent of Manchester's pauperism was due to 'male and female drunkenness' although 'idleness' together with 'widowhood' and 'old age' also ranked amongst the ten causes listed.[42] Charles Booth investigating pauperism in Stepney in the early 1890s found that 'drink' accounted for less than thirteen per cent of pauperism, but was able to list twenty-two other causes including vice, early marriage (girl), laziness, pauper association, extravagance, temper (queer) and even ill luck.[43]

Studies like these, with their investigation of individual case histories, suggested that pauperism was not only a contagious disease but also a hereditary one. Booth described families like that founded by Martin Rooney and Eliza King of Stepney as being 'prolific in paupers'.[44] His Rooney family paralleled the horrendous 'Jukes' family whose history was recounted and analysed by R. L. Dugdale in a paper to the National Conference of Charities and Correction in 1877.[45] Although Dugdale's 'tentative' conclusions seemed to point towards environmental rather than hereditary factors as being most prominent in causing pauperism and MacDougall's study found only a low percentage of 'hereditary pauperism', the concept of 'pauper' and 'pauperism' were being given objective status and placed within a scientific framework of debate.[46]

Whether their findings stressed environment or heredity, these studies strengthened the case for isolating the pauper, and for placing him or her in a suitable institutional environment where they could be either cured of pauperism and restored to society, independent and self reliant, or kept there lest they infest the independent poor with their mischievous, licentious and socially dangerous ways. Booth, at the close of the Victorian age, like Chadwick at its opening, was confident that, with separate, specialist care for the sick in mind or body, the child or the aged, the full weight of the deterrent institution could be brought to bear upon the able bodied pauper and society be finally rid of the scourge of pauperism.[47]

The pauper and the condition of pauperism were thus defined as a threatening though remediable problem in Victorian England. It remains to enquire who were the paupers and whether they constituted the menacing group threatening social contagion which theory and investigation suggested. In numerical terms, this does not seem to be the case. Paupers, if one takes Charles Booth's technical definition of those in receipt of poor relief during the year, constituted a significant but ever decreasing minority. Numbering more than a million in the distressed 1840s, they were between that figure and 800,000 by mid century. From the mid 1870s, their numbers fell to 765,000 in 1879, then fluctuated between 750,000 and 800,000 for the next three decades, declining to 748,000 in 1914 and touching an all time low of 556,000 in 1919.[48] Given this fairly static absolute figure, they were continually falling as a percentage of the total population of England and Wales. In 1841–42, they were between eight and nine per cent, falling to four or five per cent in mid-century, to two and a half per cent by 1900 and to two per cent on the outbreak of the First World War.[49]

Within these overall totals, the old, the sick and the orphaned were always dominant. In the first quarter of 1845, J. R. McCulloch found that in the 585 poor law unions in England and Wales, 300,000 of those on relief were aged and infirm as against 280,000 adult able bodied paupers. Yet of this 280,000, 54,000 were widows, 141,000 were sick or had suffered an accident, 47,000 were unemployed or with insufficient earnings for maintenance, leaving 38,000 vagrants as perhaps the hard core of pauperism.[50] By the later nineteenth century, the aged increasingly dominated the poor relief statistics. On January 1st 1892, 269,000 over-sixty-fives were on relief, about twenty per cent of all those over sixty-five nationally. At that time only about two per cent of the total population of England and Wales was in receipt of relief. Numbering about twenty-five per cent of all those on relief in the 1840s, the aged were forty-five per cent by the 1890s and nearly fifty per cent in 1908, the year which saw the passage of the first Old Age Pensions Act.[51]

To penetrate this faceless wall of statistics and put flesh and bones on the lean figure of the pauper is no easy task. The figures that emerge rarely present any very menacing aspect. Those in receipt of the pauperising 'relief in aid of wages' would include Christopher Starkie and his wife, Mary Ann, from Barnoldswick in the West Riding of Yorkshire. Their weekly income of 8*s* 6*d* from handloom weaving was thought inadequate to maintain them and their six children, one of whom was crippled with rheumatic fever. They were granted 3*s* a week outdoor relief by the guardians.[52] Another candidate for inclusion in the pauper host was the old woman whom Mayhew found amongst his London street sellers. Living with her two daughters, one of whom was sick, in a leaky, nine foot square hovel, she received one shilling and two loaves a week from the poor law.[53] Even Booth's notorious Rooney family on examination seem scarcely likely to undermine the foundations of civilised society. Bad luck, insecurity and accident was a common feature of their story.[54] In the Ashley de la Zouch union, which Booth chose as a rural foil to his Stepney investigations, the most notorious pauper seems to have been an old fellow called Isaiah Heap, a professed shoemaker who sought refuge in the workhouse in winter and travelled around in summer selling pots. 'He quoted Scripture by the yard', reported Booth, 'and would argue about it for hours. He maintained the theory that the sun went round the earth.'[55]

In Brixworth, the Reverend Bury told the 1905–09 Royal Commission on the Poor Laws, those applying for relief included the 'partially disabled, hawkers, pedlars, women earning a little by charring and whom it will be so cheap (the guardians think) to relieve'.

These hardly seemed dangerous, but Bury, a strict COS advocate thought otherwise. He told the commissioners that in the elections after the 1894 Act, which removed the property qualifications for election to a board of guardians, 'the devil broke loose again' and the numbers on out relief rose from eighteen to 127 by 1907.[56]

These fortunate 127, Christopher Starkie, Mayhew's old woman and others were given small doles from the poor rates to enable them to muddle through. Although 'paupers' they were not clearly stigmatised as such. They remained in their own homes, or those of relatives, and in their own neighbourhoods where they were able to survive in the same hand to mouth fashion as were the 'independent' poor. A regular appearance before the board of guardians or its relief committee, visits from the relieving officer, relief in the form of loaves or clothing of a distinctly 'parish' variety might, of course, mark them out.[57] In addition house calls by visitors from the COS or its approved charities tempted the retort of the brickmaker to Mrs Pardiggle that they wanted 'an end of being drawed like a badger'.[58]

Those who were most deeply marked as paupers, however, were relief applicants compelled to accept the 'offer of the house', who comprised an increasing proportion of those on poor relief from the 1870s on. Entering a large imposing building, often sited far from their former homes, they were stripped, bathed and clad in workhouse uniform, with their own clothes and possessions being put in store. Families were separated, the men going to one ward, the women to another and children to a third, perhaps to await transfer to a separate institution. They slept in bare dormitories, roused and ordered to bed early. Their day was carefully timetabled, with periods of hard unpleasant work, stone breaking or oakum picking, for those able to perform it. They were fed institutional food at regular hours in carefully weighed and calculated amounts.[59] There were few breaks in this monotony. Occasionally outings were arranged for workhouse children or for the aged. At Christmas time, attention might be focussed on the workhouse in a rather sticky, sentimental fashion. Local newspapers would report the serving of a Christmas dinner or the erection of a Christmas tree, often paid for by the guardians themselves since poor law accounting forbade such frivolities.[60]

Of course the workhouse was not a prison. The adult, able bodied could demand release when they wished, although regulations were increasingly tightened to prevent the easy coming and going of vagrants.[61] If the accommodation provided was not comfortable, it was often cleaner and more spacious than its occupants could expect outside. The food too was often more substantial in quantity and regularity than that enjoyed by families of the 'independent' poor. From the 1860s, variety increased and more attention was given to the special needs of the young or the very old. There was something of a shift from the bread, cheese and gruel diets of the 1840s.[62] As a result the costs of poor relief rose as the number of its recipients fell.[63] For all this, the very separateness of the institution and its 'pauper' regime led the poor to avoid and fear it. Hippolyte Taine, visiting Manchester in the 1860s, was astounded that the able bodied refused to enter the new workhouse which was 'a palace compared with the kennels in which the poor dwell'.[64]

Notwithstanding this reluctance, both the political economist of the early nineteenth century and the scientific philanthropist of its later years thought it essential to separate the 'pauper' from society. Only by this means could the independent labourer be protected from 'pauperism', the potential 'pauper', particularly the child, be trained and educated to independence and the real 'pauper' be subjected to a disciplined regime which would encourage or frighten him into self reliance. Yet there remained the problem of identifying the real 'pauper'. The shiftless, able bodied idler always seemed on closer investigation to fade into a mass of orphans, widows, sick or aged, unemployed or exploited workers. Poor law officials, philanthropists, social investigators created the 'pauper' and his condition 'pauperism' in their own minds and then gave them objective status. There really existed only the poor, many of whom were foisted with the label of 'pauper' and treated accordingly. In their hunt for the chronic 'pauper', the Victorians resembled the person in the little jingle,

As I was going up the stair,
I met a man who wasn't there.
He wasn't there again today.
I wish, I wish he'd stay away.[65]

Notes

1 Thomas Noel, 1799–1861, 'Rhymes and roundelays (1841), the pauper's drive', *Oxford Dictionary of Quotations*, 3rd edn., Oxford, 1979, pp. 363–4.

2 Steven Marcus, *Engels, Manchester and the Working Class*, London, 1974, p. 236.

3 *Oxford English Dictionary*, Oxford, 1933, reprint 1978, VII, p. 569. Henry Fawcett, *Pauperism: Its Causes and Remedies*, London, 1871.

4 *Encyclopedia Americana*, XXI, 1968, p. 423.

5 Charles Booth, *Pauperism, A Picture and the Endowment of Old*

Age, An Argument, London, 1892, p. 6.

6 C. S. Watkins, 'Pauperism and its prevention', Committee on Pauperism, *National Conference of Charities and Correction*, 1882, p. 94. On the NCCC, see Frank J. Bruno, *Trends in Social Work 1875–1956*, New York, 1957.

7 Charles Richmond Henderson, *Introduction to the Study of the Dependent, Defective and Delinquent Classes and of their Social Treatment*, 2nd edn., Boston, 1901, p. 10. Charles Henderson (1848–1915) was Chaplain and Professor of Sociology at the University of Chicago.

8 Harriet Martineau, *History of England during the Thirty Years Peace, 1816–1846*, London, 1877, II, p. 487.

9 M. E. Rose, *The English Poor Law, 1780–1930*, Newton Abbot, 1971, Part I; J. D. Marshall, *The Old Poor Law, 1795–1834*, Studies in Economic and Social History, London, 1968.

10 E. J. Hobsbawm and G. Rudé, *Captain Swing*, London, 1969; A. J. Peacock, *Bread or Blood. The Agrarian Riots in East Anglia 1816*, London, 1965.

11 Arnold Toynbee, *Lectures on the Industrial Revolution*, London, 1884, pp. 111–12; J. L. and B. Hammond, *The Age of the Chartists, 1832–1854*, 1930, reprint, Hamden, Connecticut, 1962, p. 61; S. and B. Webb, *History of English Local Government, VIII, The Old Poor Law*, London, 1927, pp. 417–19; G. D. H. Cole and R. Postgate, *The Common People*, 2nd edn., London, 1946, p. 276; R. H. Tawney, 'The theory of pauperism', *Sociological Review*, II 1909, p. 367.

12 M. Blaug, 'The myth of the old poor law and the making of the new', *Journal of Economic History*, XXIII, 1963, pp. 151–83; *Ibid.*, 'The poor law report re-examined', *Journal of Economic History*, XXIV, 1964, pp. 229–45; M. Neuman, *The Speenhamland County. Poverty and the Poor Laws in Berkshire, 1782–1834*, New York and London, 1982, pp. 160–5; G. Boyer, 'The old poor law and the agricultural labour market in southern England. An empirical analysis', *Journal of Economic History*, XLVI, 1986, pp. 419–30.

13 J. R. Poynter, *Society and Pauperism: English Ideas on Poor Relief, 1795–1834*, London, 1969, pp. 223–71, 333–51; J. D. Marshall, 'The Nottinghamshire reformers and their contribution to the New Poor Law', *Economic History Review*, XIII, 1961, pp. 382–96.

14 S. and O. Checkland, eds., *The Poor Law Report of 1834*, Harmondsworth, 1974.

15 D. Rothman, *The Discovery of the Asylum: Social Order and Disorder in the New Republic*, Boston, 1971.

16 Checkland, *Poor Law Report*, pp. 374–5.

17 Rose, *English Poor Law*, pp. 95–100.

18 S. and B. Webb, *English Poor Law Policy*, London, 1910, reprint 1963, p. 86.

19 M. E. Rose, 'The New Poor Law in an industrial area', in R. M. Hartwell (ed.), *The Industrial Revolution*, pp. 121–43. Karel Williams disagrees with me here. I remain unrepentant; Karel Williams, *From*

Pauperism to Poverty, London, 1981, p. 82.

20 M. E. Rose, 'The allowance system under the New Poor Law', *Economic History Review*, XIX, 1966, pp. 607–20; Anne Digby, *Pauper Palaces*, London, 1978, pp. 105–22, 137.

21 D. Owen, *English Philanthropy, 1660–1960*, London, 1965, Chapters 5 and 6; F. Prochaska, *Women and Philanthropy in Nineteenth-Century England*, London, 1980.

22 Revd R. Parkinson, *On the Present Condition of the Labouring Poor with Hints for Improving It*, London and Manchester, 1841, p. 19. Although he noted that the poor gave more to each other than the rich gave to the poor, Parkinson argued that the poor were ignorant of each other and therefore 'cherish in their own bosoms a nest of idle or vicious outcasts', *ibid.*, p. 10.

23 Henry Mayhew, *London Labour and the London Poor*, 1851, reprint, London, 1967, Vol. III, p. 397.

24 Asa Briggs, *Victorian Cities*, Harmondsworth, 1968, pp. 55–6; Thomas Archer, *The Pauper, the Thief and the Convict*, London, 1865, p. 25. B. Jerrold and Gustave Doré, *London. A Pilgrimage*, London, 1872, reprint, 1978, pp. 30–1, 138–9.

25 B. Leighton, *Life and Letters of Edward Denison*, London, 1872, p. iv.

26 Gareth Stedman Jones, *Outcast London. A Study in the Relationship between Classes in Victorian Society*, London, 1971, reprint, 1984, pp. 241–61.

27 *Ibid.*, p. 246.

28 W. O. Henderson, *The Lancashire Cotton Famine, 1861–1865*, Manchester, 1934; D. A. Farnie, 'The cotton famine in Great Britain', in B. Radcliffe (ed.), *Great Britain and Her World, 1750–1914*, Manchester, 1975, pp. 153–78.

29 M. E. Rose, 'Rochdale Man and the Stalybridge Riot. The relief and control of the unemployed during the Lancashire cotton famine', in A. P. Donajgrodski (ed.), *Social Control in Nineteenth-Century Britain*, London, 1977, pp. 185–206.

30 Sir James Kay Shuttleworth, *Thoughts and Suggestions on Certain Social Problems*, London, 1873, pp. 22–3.

31 Henderson, *Cotton Famine*, pp. 75–7; R. A. Arnold, *History of the Cotton Famine*, London, 1865, pp. 82–3 Central Executive Committee, *Reports*, Manchester Central Reference Library, Political Tracts, p. 3339.

32 C. P. Villiers, President, Poor Law Board to H. B. Farnall, 21 May, 1862, PRO, MH32/24; H. B. Farnall, *Reports to Poor Law Commissioners on Distress in the Cotton Manufacturing Districts*, 1862, (413) XLIX. Appointed to the poor law inspectorate in 1848, Farnall had had oversight of poor law unions in the industrial districts of Lancashire and West Yorkshire in the early 1850s, and was later given charge of the metropolitan unions. This urban, industrial, experience qualified him to be the central authority's 'trouble shooter' in the Lancashire crisis of the early 1860s.

33 S. and B. Webb, *English Local Government. English Poor Law History Part II: The Last Hundred Years,* London, 1929, Vol. I, pp. 374–95. Local Government Board, *1st Annual Report, 1871–2,* pp. xv–xix.

34 Webb, *Poor Law Policy,* p. 151. The institution of these conferences, usually attended by chairmen and vice chairmen of boards of guardians, in the early 1870s, and the publication of their proceedings from 1875, was influential in disseminating new ideas on poor relief. Given that each board of guardians represented was entitled to a copy of the published proceedings, it seems curious that so few sets have survived. P. F. Aschrott, *The English Poor Law System,* 2nd ed., 1902, pp. 86–7.

35 M. A. Crowther, *The Workhouse System, 1834–1929,* London, 1981, pp. 88–9, see also Chapter 7.

36 Francis Drake, 'Pauper education', in Derek Fraser (ed.), *The New Poor Law in the Nineteenth Century,* London, 1976, pp. 67–86. Henrietta Synot, 'Little paupers', *Contemporary Review,* XXIV, 1874, pp. 954–72; Florence Hill, 'The family system for workhouse children', *Contemporary Review,* XV, 1871; William Chance, *Children under the Poor Law,* London, 1899.

37 Bentley B. Gilbert, *The Evolution of National Insurance in Great Britain: the Origins of the Welfare State,* London, 1966, Chapter 4. Jill Quadagno, *Work, Family and Social Policy in Nineteenth-Century England,* London, 1982, Chapter 4; Geoffrey Drage, *The Problem of the Aged Poor,* London, 1895.

38 C. L. Mowat, *The Charity Organisation Society, 1869–1913,* London, 1961; Kathleen Woodroofe, *From Charity to Social Work,* London, 1962, Chapter 2; Madeline Rooff, *A Hundred Years of Family Welfare,* London, 1972, Chapters 1–5; Helen Bosanquet, *Social Work in London, 1869–1912,* London, 1914. Despite its considerable influence on later Victorian (and present-day) attitudes to social policy, no modern academic study of its organisation and philosophy has been published.

39 Williams, *From Pauperism,* p. 164.

40 Mowat, *COS,* pp. 114–16. Bosanquet, *Social Work,* Chapters 3–4. On its relationships with a Board of Guardians in the north-east, see Keith Gregson, 'Poor law and organized charity: the relief of exceptional distress in N.E. England, 1870–1910', in M. E. Rose (ed., *The Poor and the City. The English Poor Law in Its Urban Context, 1834–1914,* Leicester, 1985, pp. 94–131.

41 Sir John Nicholls, *History of the English Poor Law,* 3rd edn., Thomas Mackay, reissue, London, 1904, pp. 517–61. On its introduction to, and rapid development in, the USA, see Bruno, *Trends in Social Work,* pp. 98–111.

42 Alexander MacDougall Jnr, *Enquiry into the Causes of Pauperism in the Township of Manchester,* Manchester, 1884, pp. 6–10.

43 Booth, *Pauperism,* pp. 10–13.

44 *Ibid.*, pp. 14–18.

45 R. L. Dugdale, 'Hereditary pauperism as illustrated in the Jukes Family', *National Conference of Charities and Corrections, 1877*, pp. 81–95. Dugdale was a member of the executive committee of the New York Prison Association.

46 *Ibid.*, pp. 94–5; MacDougall, *Enquiry*, p. 11.

47 'Withdraw old age; if it be possible withdraw the sick also and the problem at once becomes manageable . . . chronic pauperism would be confined to a ne'er do well class and might in the end be strictly regulated', Booth, *Pauperism*, p. 238. In the USA at the time Richard T. Ely thought pauperism to be 'for the most part a curable disease . . . the remedy is to break up these pauper and criminal bands and at the earliest age remove children from their poisonous atmosphere', R. T. Ely, 'Pauperism in the United States', *North American Review*, CLII, 1891, p. 399.

48 Williams, *From Pauperism*, pp. 156–66; Rose, *English Poor Law*, Graph I, p. 269.

49 Williams, *From Pauperism*, pp. 158–63; Local Government Board, *Thirty First Annual Report, 1901–02*, Appendix E; *ibid.*, *Report on Public Health and Social Conditions*, Cd. 4671, 1909, Section IV, Table I.

50 J. R. McCulloch, *A Descriptive and Statistical Account of the British Empire*, London, 1847, II, pp. 670–5.

51 Williams, *From Pauperism*, pp. 202–8; Booth, *Pauperism*, p. 164.

52 Union Clerk, Skipton to Poor Law Board, 22 Jan. 1853, PRO, MH 12/15515.

53 Mayhew, *London Labour*, I, p. 511.

54 Booth, *Pauperism*, pp. 14–18.

55 *Ibid.*, pp. 116–17.

56 *Royal Commission on the Poor Laws and the Relief of Distress, Minutes of Evidence*, IV, Cd. 4835, 1905, p. 511.

57 Arnold, *Cotton Famine*, pp. 101–6. On the varied experiences of a poor law relieving officer, see Pamela Horn (ed.), *Oxfordshire Village Life, the Diaries of George James Dew*, Abingdon, 1983.

58 Charles Dickens, *Bleak House*, 1853, Penguin edn, Harmondsworth, 1971, p. 158.

59 Rose, *English Poor Law*, pp. 160–77; Crowther, *Workhouse System*, Part II; James Greenwood, 'A night in the workhouse' in P. J. Keating (ed.), *Into Unknown England 1866–1913*, Manchester, 1976, pp. 33–54.

60 Norman Longmate, *The Workhouse*, London, 1974, pp. 221–31.

61 Rose, *Poor Law*, pp. 207–11; Longmate, *Workhouse*, pp. 232–50; R. Vorspan, 'Vagrancy and the New Poor Law in late Victorian and Edwardian England', *English Historical Review*, 92, 1977, pp. 59–81; Crowther, *Workhouse System*, pp. 245–66.

62 Rose, *Poor Law*, pp. 162–9; Crowther, *Workhouse System*, pp. 212–19.

63 Local Government Board, *Public Health*, Cd. 4671, 1909, section IV, Chart 10.

64 Hippolyte Taine, *Notes sur L'Angleterre,* Paris, 1923, edn., Vol. II, pp. 162–3.

65 Hughes Mearns, The Psychoed (Antigonish), *Oxford Dictionary of Quotations,* 3rd edn., Oxford, 1979, p. 336.

5 *David Foster*

Some Victorian concepts of crime

Such a title begs two questions – what is/was crime, and which Victorians are responsible for our view of criminal activity in the nineteenth century? This chapter therefore begins with a discussion of 'crime' as understood by historians and then considers the sources from which Victorian attitudes might be revealed. Given the breadth of the subject and the limitations of space, the essay then focuses on what may be termed 'general' as opposed to more specialised crime, such as political and industrial offences, and particular attention is given to the spatial and the environmental views held by Victorians.

Definitions and sources

In recent years, historians have come to accept modern definitions of criminal activity as a satisfactory base from which to study the subject in the past.

> Criminal behaviour is behaviour in violation of the criminal law. No matter what the degree of immorality, reprehensibility or indecency of an act, it is not a crime unless it is prohibited by the common law. The criminal law, in turn, is defined conventionally as a body of specific rules regarding human conduct which have been promulgated by authority, which apply uniformly to all members of classes to which the rules refer, and which are enforced by punishment administered by the state.[1]

This definition contains three important elements. Firstly, despite the fact that it advances a slightly circular argument, it is clear cut, referring not to what ought to be but to what is; secondly and consequently, crime does not describe offences against some moral imperative or absolute, laid down for all time and universally acceptable, but is relative to the norms and values of the society which has designated an action as a crime; and finally, to be considered a crime, an act so defined must have been recorded by the authorities and, if possible, prosecuted.

The sources

Students of Victorian crime have three main sources at their disposal. The annual statistical returns have been published as Parliamentary Papers since 1805; a wide range of contemporary literary sources offers comment on criminal behaviour and provides insight into Victorian concepts of crime; the formal records, first, of the courts of Assize and Quarter Sessions, which can often be supplemented by judicious use of local newspapers, are the official record of prosecutions brought, and second, of the local constabularies whose files offer further insights into official attitudes to crime.

Criminal statistics[2]

The annual statistical returns were significantly expanded and improved after their inception, particularly in the mid-1830s and the late 1850s. During the first thirty years of the nineteenth century, the figures related only to national commitals for indictable offences, but almost contemporaneously with the accession of Victoria, statistics at both national and county level were introduced for indictable and summary commitals. The County and Borough Police Act 1856 presented the statistics by police district, thus facilitating regional study, and improved them by introducing the category 'crimes known to the police', the nearest we come to a picture of total crime. A number of changes occurred in 1893, the most important of which was the change from a year ending on 29 September to one coincident with the calendar year.

However, particular administrative districts do not necessarily provide the most useful base from which to study crime. Many counties contain extremely varied social and economic characteristics which render the search for explanation difficult if not impractical. A recent work by Professor Rudé demonstrates the problems inherent in the county-cum-region approach. His study of crime and society in the first half of the nineteenth century is concerned with Sussex, Gloucestershire and Middlesex, a selection based on the claim that the two former counties are 'strictly rural counties, certainly when compared to London', a claim which is partially compromised when each is presented as having different regions, some based on geology and topography, others based on economic activity.[3]

In recent decades there has been an enthusiastic debate concerning the usefulness of the statistics to historians.[4] Chief amongst the difficulties involved are the categories used by the compilers which, even after 1857–58 when the category of 'crimes known to the police' was introduced, permit a picture of 'official' but not 'total' crime. Furthermore, the concept of 'official' crime is open to doubt since the decision to prosecute and to classify a case as indictable or summary, where the alternative existed, such as riot/breach of the peace, rested with the police; indeed, many statistics may have been the result of specific policing policies which temporarily distorted the trend for a given offence. A further difficulty arises from changes in the law which, at first sight can produce serious distortions in crime series. The introduction of the 1879 Summary Jurisdiction Act is one example of the tendency to move criminal offences between the indictable and summary categories; thus all juveniles under 16 consenting to be tried summarily for larceny and embezzlement and all adults pleading guilty to or willing to be tried summarily for the same offences if the property involved did not exceed forty shillings were removed from the court of indictable crimes.

In the light of these problems, it has been argued that the annual statistics are worthless for the study of criminal activity, though a strong case for their value as a source has been made. It seems clear that, with due attention paid to the difficulties inherent in the material and for the purpose of studying trends over sufficiently long periods of time and sufficiently populous areas so as not to distort the results, the annual statistics can be used to yield some valuable information about criminal activity in Victorian Britain.

Literary sources

In his introductory lecture to this series, Lord Briggs raised the question of the representativeness of various Victorian values; the same question can be addressed to the literary sources for the study of crime. Most of the overt conceptions of crime in Victorian England are 'official' and perhaps essentially middle-class views, with politicians, civil servants, clergymen, magistrates, and law officers predominating. Consequently, the literary sources offer a narrow and biased view of the problem. Furthermore, since law is created, and therefore crime defined, by the ruling elite, it can be argued that all law must reflect its prejudices and protect its privileges. On the other hand, our relative definition of crime suggests that behaviour which is deemed either criminal or acceptable reflects the attitudes of society. Clearly, this does not mean that the whole of any society, particularly one with a restricted franchise, concurred in the law which defined crime; legislation against trade unions and poaching are but two of the more obvious examples of class law, but it is a moot point as to whether legislation can run too far ahead of public opinion. To argue that all law was class-based is to ignore the uncomfortable facts that much of the crime of larceny, by far the most common offence throughout the Victorian age, was committed against members of the working classes, and that there was general, though in some places belated acceptance by the working classes of the protection offered them by the reformed police. However, despite these niceties of argument, this essay takes as its basic premise that Victorian concepts of crime are revealed by the legislation which gave it existence and are reflections of much wider values in Victorian society.

Court and police records

The principal courts involved in the prosecution of crime were the Court of Assize which dealt with the most serious indictable offences and was conducted by a circuit judge, and the Court of Quarter Sessions which consisted of the bench of magistrates in the counties and a professional barrister sitting as recorder in the larger incorporated boroughs. In all cases, it is normal to find registers of cases and the files associated with specific prosecutions. Increasingly during the century, the Court of Petty Sessions emerged to deal with minor offences at the local level, but they were not courts of record and the survival of any records is likely to be fortuitous.

The survival rate of local constabulary records varies, but, at their best they offer valuable insights into official attitudes to crime through chief constables' quarterly and annual reports to Quarter Sessions, the papers and minute books of Police Committees and the records of occurrence books.

Given that most, and from 1857–58, all of the statistical and official sources refer to local and regional units, much of the research has been carried out at that level. One of the most successful has combined the types of record from separate jurisdictions to produce a study of the Black Country in the mid-nineteenth century.[5] By judicious selection, the limitations of administrative structures have been overcome and the criminality of a specific socio-economic area has been studied.

Migratory crime

The Victorians had a keen sense of the spatial aspects of crime and high on their list of demonology was the migratory criminal who received massive coverage in the *First Report of the Commission appointed to inquire as to the best means of establishing an efficient Constabulary Force in the counties of England and Wales.*[6] Under the guidance of Edwin Chadwick, the report emphasised the importance of migratory crime through detailed descriptions of the criminal activities of the wandering poor which, in turn, encouraged many in authority to believe that local crime was generally committed by outsiders. Thus, in the 1830s, East Riding magistrates believed that 'a great proportion of the depredations are committed by vagrants and thieves from the West Riding of Yorkshire, Nottingham and London'; the worthies of Gloucester blamed the neighbouring cities of Hereford, Bristol, Cheltenham and even Birmingham for its crime; and Hull claimed to be invaded by metropolitan thieves who came by way of the North Sea.[7]

In the official view, beershops, public houses and common lodging houses were the focal points of migratory crime. In their replies to the Chadwick Commission in 1837–38, the magistrates of the East Riding were highly critical of beershops, released from licensing by an Act of 1830, as dens of wickedness and vice. The view of the 1839 Report, maintained throughout the century, was that tramps' lodging houses were the resort of beggars and common thieves; in rural districts they were referred to as 'flash-houses' which were alleged to be the most infamous brothels, and the places in which stolen goods were fenced and young people were schooled for delinquency.[8]

Recent work has shown that the migratory criminal was an illusory figure,[9] but he exercised a powerful force upon the Victorian imagination and was central to the campaign to extend reformed, professional police forces throughout the land. An important plank in the platform of the Chadwick Report of 1839 was the claim that criminals were driven out of the incorporated boroughs, which, under the 1835 Municipal Corporations Act, were required to modernise their police, into surrounding rural areas; therefore it was necessary to introduce professional police forces into the rural areas to control migratory crime. Faced with a range of political problems at home and abroad, the Whig government introduced adoptive rather than compulsory legislation in the form of the Rural Constabulary Act 1839 which was embraced by only one half of the counties of England and Wales during the subsequent decade.[10] Consequently, the 1853 Select Committee, established to consider a bill which sought to compel police reform in every authority, dominated by Chadwick, returned to the attack and made much capital from the opportunities afforded to thieves to commit crime in one reformed authority and then to escape with impunity to a neighbouring unreformed authority. The force of the argument was revealed by the enactment of the 1856 County and Borough Police Act which required all authorities to reform their police forces. However, later in the century, commentators still retained their faith in the migratory criminal as a fundamental explanation of crime. In 1876 L. O. Pike alleged that there was a direct correlation between high crime rates and high levels of immigration, contrasting Lancashire and Cheshire on the one hand with Cornwall, Devon, Somerset, Wiltshire and Dorset on the other, unintentionally undermining the earlier argument which implied that nation-wide professional police forces would resolve the problem of the migratory criminal.[11]

Urban rural character

Implicit in the migratory criminal thesis was the view that many criminals were essentially urban-based, a point emphasised by Colonel James Woodford, the first chief constable of Lancashire from 1839 to 1856, who claimed that even those boroughs with a reformed police were 'nurseries of crime'.[12] The perceived contrast between the villainy of urban and the purity of rural areas was much older than the Victorian period, and was captured graphically by Defoe's picture of London in the early eighteenth century in *Moll Flanders*, and confirmed by Patrick Colquhoun's description of London in the 1790s as a magnet for all kinds of criminal and dissolute.

The rapid spread of urbanisation during the nineteenth century alongside industrial transformation saw an extension of the association between crime and urban place from the metropolis to the provinces on a large scale. Despite numerous attempts to identify burgeoning industrialisation as the chief source of increasing criminal activity, doubtless encouraged by high-profile protest such as that of the Luddites and the Chartists, the more perceptive recognised that the important connection was between crime and urbanisation rather than industrialism. The Reverend J. Clay, chaplain to Preston gaol, noted in his 1849 report that crime and disorder were found principally in the large town; 'it is not manufacturing Manchester but multitudinous Manchester which gives birth to whatever criminality is attributable to it.'[13]

The corollary to this analysis was that the rural areas were largely crime-free, and this argument was used by many predominantly rural counties to reject the adoptive 1839 Rural Constabulary Act and to proclaim their vocal, though not actual, resistance to its 1856 compulsory successor. Obviously, the rural areas were not free of crime, nor was the majority of rural crime committed by urban thieves making nefarious excursions into the countryside. In fact, some crimes such as cattle-maiming and the destruction of fences, were almost exclusively rural, and arson was more widespread in the countryside than in the towns. Nonetheless, the dichotomy between patterns of urban and rural crime reflected the sociological study of community carried out by Tonnies at the end of the nineteenth century and the anomie produced by industrialisation and urbanisation.

The nineteenth-century analysis, based in part upon the distinctions which arose from local government boundaries, is too simplistic. The implication of two grand categories of countryside and town cannot be sustained. Counties varied considerably in population density and socio-economic composition, with some, such as Lancashire and the West Riding of Yorkshire, containing numerous industrial villages as well as idyllic hamlets, and many others containing contrasting villages based upon their 'open' or 'closed' character. Similarly towns, which varied from small market centres to large regional capitals were disparate and likely to have very different crime patterns. Thus, the urban-rural dichotomy only has value as an explanatory device when the categories are subjected to much closer analysis.

Criminal classes and residential patterns of crime

Throughout the nineteenth century, there was widespread belief in the existence of a criminal class which inhabited specific districts of the large towns.

The classic case is exhaustively described and classified by Henry Mayhew whose investigation of *London Labour and the Labouring Poor*, in the 1850s reinforced the prevailing belief in the criminal class, and emphasised its urban character by drawing attention to the ecological nature of the activity. In *Those That Will Not Work*, he produced graphic accounts of criminals who infested the centre of London, drawing a direct relationship between crime and neighbourhood.[14]

The ecological approach suggests a causal relationship between environment and crime, a view held by a number of Victorian writers. J. P. Kay, P. Gaskell and F. Engels, commenting on the industrial system of the 1830s and 1840s with special reference to south-east Lancashire, pointed to the concept of alienation as a cause of crime, noting the squalor and degradation of urban life which could only be relieved by excursions into drunkenness, prostitution and crime.[15] At the end of the century, the writings of the social explorers, Mearns, Booth and even Rowntree, are shot through with a belief in the existence of a criminal class located in specific areas of Victorian cities. As late as 1891, the Revd W. D. Morison, the chaplain of Wandsworth prison, commented that:

> There is a population of habitual criminals which forms a class by itself. Habitual criminals are not to be confused with the working or any other class; they are a set of persons who make crime the object and business of their lives; to commit crime is their trade; they deliberately scoff at honest ways of earning a living, and must accordingly be looked upon as a class of separate and distinct character from the rest of the community.[16]

However, not all later writers concurred. L. O. Pike rejected the view that crime was environmentally related and claimed that it was more the result of individual weakness; crime appeared to have declined at the time of Britain's most rapid urbanisation, and the difference between urban and rural, if it was valid, could be explained by the fact that towns attracted all kinds including those in 'whom the instincts of violence and rapine are apt to reappear upon the smallest provocation'.[17]

On balance, modern work is sceptical of the existence of a criminal class.[18] Whilst such a class of organised professional criminals may have existed in London, and there were undoubtedly criminal families in some of the towns of England and Wales, most crimes were committed by members of the general public, sometimes though not always under the spur of economic necessity.

Property

The extent to which law makers create or reflect the values of the society over which they rule is a moot point, particularly in democracies. Victorian England practised representative government and, although the basis of representation was widened through extension of the franchise during the nineteenth century, it was not until the end of the century that politicians began to produce the fore-runners of the modern manifesto and that Parliament became more inclined to legislate with the electorate in mind. Previously, much legislation had been constitutional and administrative, and that which exposed Victorian concepts of and attitudes towards crime tended to reflect the values of Parliamentarians who predominantly represented the landed classes.

It is no surprise, therefore, to find that the defence of property was paramount in Victorian England. The work of David Hay and Edward Thompson on eighteenth-century crime and society has familiarised us with the centrality of property in that period,[19] although the Victorians were spared that harsh view taken of property crimes by Peel's removal of the capital penalty from many trivial offences during the 1820s. Nonetheless, larceny was still an indictable crime until mid-century when, under certain circumstances, it could be tried summarily and, in one area at least, led to a major increase in the number of known offences. The interpretation of the evidence is fraught with difficulty. In addition to legislative changes in 1847, 1850, 1855 and 1879 which transferred a large number of property crimes from higher to lower courts, trends in specific crimes would vary according to the intensification of police activity, the willingness of the public to co-operate in the reporting of crime, and the propensity of victims, especially employers in industrial areas, to prosecute. Nonetheless, it is clear that, in all parts of the country, property crimes were far more common than any other type of indictable offence.[20]

The strength and determination with which the Victorians protected property can be seen through reference to the Game Laws.[21] Poaching was one of the most common offences in the nineteenth century, thought by some to have been the fastest growing offence in the second quarter and retaining a prominent role until the late century. The preservation of game and fish was both a status symbol and a commercial proposition for landowners, particularly since the 1831 Act which permitted the sale of game by anyone with a certificate, a right which they usually reserved to themselves. Thus, the Game Laws had enormous potential for fomenting class struggle in the countryside, particularly with the extension of the law through the 1842 Night Poaching Act and the 1862 Poaching Preservation Act. To the propertied classes, game lands were important breeding grounds for general crime and poaching was an art requiring some capital rather than a spasmodic response to poverty.

Vagrancy

In the minds of respectable Victorians, many of the offences against property, not least those which broke the Game Laws, were committed by vagrants. Accordingly, vagrancy was considered to be an evil. Attitudes towards vagrancy were foreshadowed in the 1824 Vagrancy Act which repealed all previous legislation on the subject and which remained the core of subsequent law. Described by one legal authority as 'a most potent form of social control',[22] this act retained the traditional distinction between the deserving and the undeserving poor and was generally used against begging, being a lewd or disorderly prostitute, sleeping in the open and having no visible means of subsistence, and being in enclosed spaces and frequenting places of public resort for illegal purposes. In the eyes of authority, the vagrant challenged the Victorian trinity of work, respectability and religion,[23] being physically repulsive destitute and of evil disposition. Thus the ready link between vagrancy and crime existed throughout Victorian England, given expression as early as 1839 by Chadwick who defined vagrancy as 'the habit of wandering abroad under colour either of distress or some other ostensible though illegal occupation, having claims on the sympathy of the uninformed constitutes one great cause of delinquency, especially juvenille delinquency'. Expanding the point, he noted that:

> The most prominent body of delinquents in the rural districts are the vagrants, and these vagrants appear to consist of two classes, first, the habitual depradators, house-breakers, horse-stealers and common thieves; secondly, of vagrants, properly so-called who seek alms as mendicants.[24]

The relationship between vagrancy and crime was widely accepted in the nineteenth century, and for many vagrancy and crime were the two ends of a slippery slope.

> That vagrancy is the nursery of crime, and that the habitual tramps are first the beggars, then the thieves, and, finally, the convicts of the country, the evidence of all parties goes to prove . . . [vagrants] constitute . . . the main source from which the criminals are continually recruited and augmented.[25]

A number of witnesses to the *Select Committee 1852–53 on Police*, advanced similar views, though in some cases they were little more than self-fulfilling prophecies – one example was Mr Swaby, a Buckinghamshire magistrate who noted that vagrancy, 'a great source of crime', had been dramatically reduced in counties which had introduced reformed police after the 1839 Act.[26]

Poverty

The problem with the Victorian attitude to vagrants was that it failed to distinguish sufficiently between the various types to be found on the roads of the country. Recent work has suggested that, in addition to the Irish immigrants associated principally with the potato famine of the 1840s there were four types of vagrant.[27] First were the travelling workers, including seasonal workers, whose mobility was important to the new industrial world; second were the unemployed, victims of the vagaries of the labour market and often on the road in search of employment; thirdly, the deserving poor who were theoretically provided for by the rigours of the New Poor Law; and finally the habitual vagrants and tramps who figured so prominently in the pages of the Chadwick Report of 1839.

The critics of the Chadwick Report and the subsequent legislation alleged that there was a clear relationship between the introduction of professional police forces and the enforcement of the New Poor Law; it was believed that the new police were to be introduced to protect property and to sweep the vagrants into the workhouses.[28] The tendency to treat vagrants as the outcasts of society, whatever their background, ensured that the Victorians denied that there was any relationship between crime and poverty. Early in the nineteenth century, there was some sympathy for the view that a direct causal relationship could be established between these two phenomena. Robert Owen, giving evidence to the *Selection Committee on Police 1816*, noted that 'if the poor cannot procure employment, and are not supported, they must commit crimes or starve'. But the search for efficiency in mid-nineteenth century, personified by Edwin Chadwick, soon dismissed such rubbish. In the 1839 Report, he revealed that 'the notion that any considerable proportion of the crimes against property are caused by blameless poverty or destitution we find disproved at every step'. It will come as no surprise to learn, therefore, that 'the whole [is] ascribable to one common cause, namely the temptations of the profit of a career of depredation, as compared with the profits of honest and even well-paid industry'.[29]

However, it would be wrong to suggest that this view went unchallenged or remained static throughout the Victorian period. As early as the 1830s, observers such as Gaskell and Kay noted the coincidence of poverty and crime in south-east Lancashire and fifty years later Charles Booth noted that the poorest districts of the capital were the haunts of beggars, prostitutes and thieves, another unholy Victorian trinity. Even in the rural districts, there were those who were prepared to concede the point – one nobleman admitted, in 1846, that 'there is comparatively little poaching when trade is good and a great deal when it is bad'.[30] But these observers did not reflect the intensely individualistic approach to society adopted by the Victorians who believed that poverty was a self-inflicted state which could be avoided by the correct attitudes towards work and independence.

Vagrancy and the existence of poverty was labelled as criminal because it challenged the related virtues of Victorian respectability, independence and the work ethic, and threatened the existence of an orderly civilised life. In a graphic phrase, one writer has seen the new professional police as 'domestic missionaries' created to 'act as an all-purpose lever of urban discipline'.[31] Thus by the control of leisure, particularly that centred on the public-house and the beershop, authority sought to compel social conformity throughout the country. The contrast between Victorian and contemporary views is very clearly illustrated in this context. In Victorian England poverty itself was the crime. In late twentieth-century Britain, the link between poverty and crime is well established, though the recent discovery by the political right of values that are alledgedly Victorian suggests that this connection is not universally espoused.[32]

Notes

1 E. H. Sutherland and D. Cressey, *Criminology*, 8th edn., New York, 1970, p. 4.

2 The best introduction to the statistics is V. A. C. Gattrell and T. B. Hadden, 'Criminal statistics and their interpretation', in E. A. Wrigley (ed.), *Nineteenth Century Society: Essays in the Use of Quantitative Methods for the Study of History*, Cambridge, 1972.

3 G. Rudé, *Criminal and Victim. Crime and Society in Early*

Nineteenth Century England, Oxford, 1985, p. 7f.

4 J. J. Tobias, *Crime and Industrial Society in the Nineteenth Century*, Harmondsworth, 1972, Chapter 2; D. Phillips, *Crime and Authority in Victorian England. The Black Country 1835–60*, London, 1977, Chapter 2; D. Jones, *Crime, Protest, Community and Police in Nineteenth Century Britain*, London, 1982, pp. 3–8.

5 D. Philips, *Crime and Authority.*

6 P. P. 1839, (169), xix. Hereinafter referred to as the *Chadwick Report.*

7 *Chadwick Report*, pp. 13–14.

8 *Chadwick Report*, p. 34.

9 J. Hart, 'Reform of the Borough Police 1835–56', *English Historical Review*, 70, 1955, pp. 411–27.

10 D. Foster, *The Rural Constabulary Act 1839*, London, 1982, pp. 13–18.

11 L. O. Pike, *A History of Crime in England*, London, 1876, Chapter 13.

12 *First Report of the Select Committee on Police with Minutes of Evidence*, P.P., 1852–53, (603), xxxvi, p. 98.

13 W. L. Clay, *The Prison Chaplain. A Memoir of the Rev. J. Clay B.D.*, Cambridge, 1861, pp. 517–18.

14 H. Mayhew, *London Labour and the Labouring Poor. Those That Will Not Work*, Vol. 4, London, 1967 reprint, pp. 2–27.

15 J. P. Kay, *The Moral and Physical Condition of the Working Classes Employed in the Cotton Industry in Manchester*, Didsbury, Manchester, 1832; P. Gaskell, *Artisans and Manchinery*, Manchester, 1836; F. Engels, *The Condition of the Working Classes in England*, translated and edited by W. O. Henderson and W. H. Chaloner, Manchester, 1958.

16 W. D. Morison, *Crime and Its Causes*, London, 1891, pp. 141–42.

17 L. O. Pike, *A History of Crime*, Chapter 13.

18 D. Philips, *Crime and Authority*, p. 287; V. A. Gattrell, 'The decline of theft and violence in Victorian and Edwardian England', in V. A. C. Gattrell, B. Lemon and G. Parker, *Crime and the Law. The Social History of Crime in Western Europe since 1500*, London, 1980, p. 265. But see J. J. Tobias, *Crime and Industrial Society*, p. 70 for a dissenting view.

19 D. Hay, P. Lindbaugh, J. G. Rule, E. P. Thompson and C. Winslow, *Albion's Fatal Tree*, Harmondsworth, 1977.

20 D. Philips, *Crime and Authority*, p. 190.

21 D. Jones, *Crime, Protest*, Chapter 3.

22 E. Manchester, *A Modern Legal History of England and Wales, 1750–1950*, London, 1980, p. 196.

23 D. Jones, *Crime, Protest*, p. 279.

24 *Chadwick Report*, pp. 30 and 31.

25 H. Mayhew quoted in J. J. Tobias, *Crime and Industrial Society*, p. 83.

26 *Select Committee On Police,* 1852–3, P.P.
27 D. Jones, *Crime, Protest,* pp. 183–86.
28 D. Foster, *The Rural Constabulary Act,* p. 24.
29 *Select Committee on the State of the Police of the Metropolis,* P.P., (510), v, 234; compare *Chadwick Report,* p. 73.
30 D. Jones, *Crime, Protest,* p. 69.
31 R. Storch, 'The policeman as domestic missionary. Urban discipline and popular culture in Northern England 1850–80', *Journal of Social History,* 9, 1976, p. 481.
32 Current attitudes are revealed in J. Benyon (ed.), *Scarman and After. Essays Reflecting on Lord Scarman's Report, the Riots and their Aftermath,* Oxford, 1984, and in *New Society,* 14 November 1986, pp. 3 and 5.

6 *William Stafford*

John Stuart Mill: critic of Victorian values?

In J. S. Mill we would expect to find a critic of Victorian values. Educated by his father, James Mill, and later the amanuensis of Jeremy Bentham, he was brought up in the atmosphere of philosophic radicalism, whose aim was to dig things up by the roots, examining the foundations of established beliefs and practices, campaigning against ignorance and prejudice. In the political crisis of 1831, Mill was uttering revolutionary sentiments in his private correspondence, and in the year of revolutions, 1848, he rewrote sections of his *Political Economy* so as to make the tenor of the work more favourable to socialism.[1] In terms of the spectrum of his day, he was on the left of British politics, eventually being elected in 1865 as a radical MP. Furthermore, Mill has at least a foothold in the philosophers' pantheon, as a classic authority in moral and political philosophy, perhaps also in the philosophy of mind and scientific method. This acceptance of Mill by academic philosophers results, for many of them, from the judgment that his thought is in some ways timeless – that is to say, not merely Victorian. Mill addresses the age-old philosophical problems and gives answers which are still relevant today. In this essay I want to examine and qualify this view of Mill as one who stood apart from Victorian values; and I shall do this by looking at two issues where Mill appears most radical and timeless: his feminism, and his defence of liberty.

Mill has justly been admired by feminists as an early and redoubtable campaigner for their cause. As an MP he moved an amendment to the 1866 reform bill which would have given women the vote on the same terms as men. His essay on the

Subjection of Women (1869) attacks the Victorian ideal of womanhood as degrading and hypocritical. He was well aware that to put women upon pedestals, to idealise them for their purity, goodness and gentleness, was also a strategy for denying them independence, power and opportunity.[2] He casts a critical eye on 'home sweet home' and family life:

> If the family in its best forms is, as it is often said to be, a school of sympathy, tenderness, and loving forgetfulness of self, it is still oftener, as respects its chief, a school of wilfulness, over-bearingness, unbounded self-indulgence, and a double-eyed and idealized selfishness.[3]

If it is the 'natural vocation' of women to be wives and mothers, he asks, then why is it necessary to force this role upon them by debarring them from other occupations? Mill has no time for assertions about what is 'natural' to women; they have had an entirely artificial character foisted upon them. Certain traits – those pleasing to men – have been stimulated and overdeveloped. Other capacities – those which would threaten male dominance – have been suffocated and suppressed.[4]

Mill believes that women, given opportunities, can equal men in all important attainments. They should be allowed to compete on equal terms for all jobs and professions; they should have the vote; they should be eligible for all public offices. The institution of marriage was a form of female servitude, and its laws should be drastically reformed. Women should be allowed to retain their rights over whatever property they had at the time of marriage and the possibility of separation should be readily available. Given these things, given career opportunities, wives would no longer be bondslaves; they would stay only if the marriage were eligible and agreeable.

Mill's essay *On Liberty* (1859) argues that men and women should be free from the pressures of some Victorian values. Those values he found repressive; and repression produced stunted, narrow-minded individuals. Mill thought that his contemporaries were hedged about by law and, more insidiously, by the pressure of public opinion, by the social stigma which attached to certain modes of thinking and conduct.[5] Such intense disapproval of the deviant led to a stifling and cramping of individual development:

In some such insidious form there is at present a strong tendency to this narrow theory of life, and to the pinched and hidebound type of human character which it patronizes. Many persons, no doubt, sincerely think that human beings thus cramped and dwarfed, are as their Maker designed them to be; just as many have thought that trees are a much finer thing when clipped into pollards, or cut out into figures of animals, than as nature made them.[6]

The pressure to conform militated against all robustness of character; it produced individuals who were so repressed that they were no longer capable of desiring anything strongly.[7] And it produced mediocrity; the general climate was not such as to encourage people to develop their unique talents.

Against conformism, Mill asserted his doctrine of liberty. Individuals should be free to perform any actions, unless they demonstrably harmed the interests of others. Society was not justified in interfering, either by law or by public opinion, with acts which harmed only the agents. Mill proceeded to unpack the implications of this principle. It sustains almost complete freedom of speech and publication. For example, individuals must not be made to suffer even for professing atheism; in an age of the revival of religion, Mill thought it important to insist on this. If a person chooses suicide, and persists in this choice, society should not interfere. We should be permitted to go to hell on heroin if we choose. There should be no interference with 'experiments in living'; and a clear implication of this is that any kind of sexual conduct between consenting adults should be tolerated. Mill's principle of liberty is abstract and general and therefore, in a sense, timeless; he worked out its implications for the Victorian period, but we can equally well work out its implications for today. Indeed it is constantly used as a starting-point in present-day discussions of liberty. In nervous, lucid prose, with sharp and devastating arguments, Mill used his principle to combat ancient prejudices, cutting swathes through Victorian piety and respectability. Our judgment today, that his essay is admirable and relevant, is undoubtedly justified.

So can we say that Mill's thought is timeless, not encapsulated by the framework of Victorian values? Or are there ways in which he is conditioned and limited by the assumptions of his age, by ways of framing the issues concerning women and liberty which are deeply embedded in the culture of the time? I want to show that he was not entirely liberated from Victorian values; and I propose to do this, not by measuring him against some supposed timeless standards, but by comparing him with two thinkers from the preceding epoch, thinkers who like him were radicals on the topics of women and liberty. I hope to show that the ways in which he differed from these thinkers mark him as a man of his age, of the Victorian age. His feminist predecessor was William Thompson, an Irish landowner, merchant and Owenite socialist, living in London. His *Appeal of One-half the Human Race, Women* (1825) is an interesting comparison with Mill's *Subjection of Women.* For Thompson and Mill came from the same stable; Thompson stayed with Bentham and imbibed his ideas.[8] And we know that Mill was acquainted with his work, because in his *Autobiography* he writes of 'a very estimable man, with whom I was well acquainted, Mr William Thompson of Cork, author of . . . an "Appeal in behalf of women" '.[9] The radical liberal with whom I propose to compare him is William Godwin, whose *Enquiry Concerning Political Justice* (1793) is at the extreme limits of liberalism, being a work of individualist anarchism. I cannot demonstrate that Mill had read it; but Godwin and his book were celebrated in radical circles, and it is unlikely that Mill would be unacquainted with it.

As a polemicist, Thompson is not as sharp and devastating, nor as persuasive as Mill; but in some ways he appears more feminist. He comes as one who thinks more highly of women than of men; for instance he speculates that the sexes may be specialised in such a way that, though men are stronger, women are naturally more intelligent.[10] There are also hints of a distaste for masculinity, and a preference for feminine characteristics; he observes that the tiger passions are cultivated in young men, they are indulged in cruelty and ferocity, and hence are unable to develop the higher intellectual faculties.[11] Mill by contrast thinks that women, conditioned to be weak, passive and emotional, have a tendency to pull their male companions down to a lower intellectual level.[12]

More striking, and more indicative of a Victorian turn of

thought on Mill's part, is the difference from Thompson on sexuality. Thompson, like many feminists this century, wants women to be sexually liberated. One aspect of male dominance is that women are strongly conditioned to be modest and chaste, to hide and repress their sexual desires:

> Woman must cast nature, or feign to cast it, from her breast. She is not permitted to feel, or desire. The whole of what is called her education training her to be the obedient instrument of man's sensual gratification, she is not permitted even to wish for any gratification for herself. She must have no desires: she must always yield, must submit as a matter of duty, not repose upon her equal for the sake of happiness: she must blush to own that she joys in his generous caresses, were such by chance ever given.[13]

Mill's essay by contrast lacks any open discussion of this topic. His few veiled references to it represent sexual desire as low and brutish.[14]

Though he thinks that jobs and professions should not be closed to women, Mill still believes that a woman's place, when she is married and has children, is the home. He takes it for granted that a decision to be a wife and mother is also a decision to have no other career, at least for the time being.[15] Here again, Thompson differs. He thinks it dreadful that women should be imprisoned in the home, with all the boredom of domestic routines. Nursery provision should liberate women to pursue other vocations at all stages of life.[16] This leads to a wider issue. What is needed to liberate women? Thompson goes further than Mill. He insists that legal and institutional changes by themselves will not give freedom and equality to women. In addition there must be sweeping economic and social changes. Private property and competition must go, to be replaced by common ownership and cooperation. For private property is the economic basis of the nuclear family which imprisons women in the home, rendering them the helpless dependents of their husbands. If a woman leaves her husband she is reduced to destitution. The removal of the bars which close certain professions to women does not mean that the ex-wife *will* be able to get a job and maintain her standard of living. But under a system of common ownership, where all draw from the shared pool according to need, this will be no problem. The competition of a free market is also disadvantageous to women. Often they cannot compete with men on equal terms; for on average they are less strong, and the periods when they cannot work because they are bearing or suckling children introduce disabling breaks into their career patterns.[17]

Twentieth-century feminists have criticised Mill's exclusively legal and institutional emphasis; they have agreed with Thompson that the liberation of women requires the further step of economic and social transformation.[18] Not only does Mill fail to take this further step; he actually takes a step back from the position Thompson had reached. Furthermore, this retrogression must have been deliberately chosen. As well as his essay on the *Subjection of Women* (1869) there is a shorter piece entitled *The Enfranchisement of Women* (1851) which appeared in the *Westminster Review.* The precise authorship of the earlier piece is uncertain, but it seems likely that it was written by Harriet Taylor, who became Mill's wife in that year, or that it was a joint production, or that Mill wrote it under Taylor's guidance.[19] It contains a passage which hints at the end of capitalism and competition as an epoch when the liberation of women will be facilitated.[20] We are entitled to say, therefore, that in the better-known essay of 1869, Mill chose to adopt a less unorthodox position.

Everybody reads Mill *On Liberty*: few read Godwin's *Political Justice.* There are good reasons for this. Mill is a better writer, sharper, better disciplined, less formal and repetitive, capable of memorable and striking phrases. His case for liberty is fuller and richer than Godwin's. Mill seems more modern; whereas Godwin often maintains that there is one perfect mode of human being and conduct, Mill allows for diversity. Godwin is visionary, therefore easy to dismiss; his case for absolute anarchy has found few supporters, then or since. Mill cannot be dismissed in this way. Mill and Godwin have much in common: both defend total freedom of thought and discussion, both have the same ideal of the completely autonomous human being, making her own rational choices without deference to custom, prejudice or authority. But Godwin's doctrine of freedom raises with great clarity and force an aspect of liberty which is only intermittently noticed by Mill, and not thought through by him.

The essential difference between Godwin and Mill is captured in the central terms they use when referring to the ideal of freedom. Mill uses above all 'liberty' and 'individuality'. Liberty is a word with long-standing and dominating political reference in Anglo-American culture; liberty means freedom from the state, from unwarranted government interference. Individuality is a newer word, and Mill uses it in a way influenced by romantic aesthetics, especially German romanticism. Individuality is to do with being an authentic self, growing and developing spontaneously, according to one's inner being; it is associated with diversity and genius. Liberty and individuality have respectively, therefore, political and psycho-cultural reference. Godwin's favoured word is 'independence'. Independence has both religious and social contexts of meaning. In the religious sphere, it means judging for oneself in matters of faith, without undue deference to priests and ecclesiastical establishments. In the social sphere, it means being free from social dependence, not standing as an inferior in relation to a superior, be he lord or patron; not needing to defer, not being beholden to another for one's livelihood and well-being. Independence is the ideal of freedom of the sturdy yeoman, manufacturer or tradesman, who wishes to stand on his own feet, not owing allegiance to lord or squire. In a revealing passage Godwin criticises Sunday schools, reflecting both the religious and social sides of independence: 'Even in the petty institution of Sunday schools, the chief lessons that are taught, are a superstitious veneration for the Church of England, and to bow to every man in a handsome coat.'[21] Godwin is aware that social and economic inequality hedge round and suffocate the freedom of those who are dependent. What is the value of political liberty to a man who depends upon his squire for employment, the roof over his head, the education of his children, and justice in the magistrate's court?[22] Dare such a man think for himself, and develop his individuality? Reverence for superiors is the death of free thought. All power over others is based upon inequality of wealth, which is deeply corrupting. Godwin goes so far as to say that it is a form of depravity to be, not only a servant, but even a hired labourer.[23] Utopian that he is, he wants a form of society in which no one will be compelled by want to sell himself into another's employment; where all will work under their own direction, by their own decision, for the common good. It is his clear conviction that liberty is impossible without equality.

There are passages in Mill's writings which argue that inequality is a threat to independence. The best of these is the chapter of his *Principles of Political Economy,* entitled 'Of the probable futurity of the labouring classes'. This denounces paternalism and dependence, and looks forward to the day when the relationship of employer to employee, master to servant, will be replaced by free co-operative associations of equals:

There can be little doubt that the *status* of hired labourers will gradually tend to confine itself to the description of workpeople whose low moral qualities render them unfit for anything more independent: and that the relation of masters and workpeople will be gradually superseded by partnership, in one of two forms: in some cases, association of the labourers with the capitalist; in others, and perhaps finally in all, association of labourers among themselves.[24]

In his autobiography, Mill tells us that the favourable account of socialism in the *Principles* was due to Harriet Taylor's influence, and that the aforementioned chapter contained her thoughts, often dictated by her own lips.[25] Like Godwin, she came from the culture of dissent. She was brought up a Unitarian, her first husband was one, and she had many Unitarian friends. But the linking of independence with equality can be found in writings Mill produced after her death. For example in the posthumously published *Chapters on Socialism* he reports the socialist doctrine that

No longer enslaved or made dependent by force of law, the great majority are so by force of poverty; they are still chained to a place, to an occupation, and to conformity with the will of an employer . . . That this is an evil equal to almost any of those against which mankind have hitherto struggled, the poor are not wrong in believing.[26]

Yet this insight has little impact on the discussion of socialism taken as a whole. The weight of the argument for socialism, as presented by Mill, has little to do with liberty; he concerns himself largely with questions of efficiency, motivation, and the promotion of moral qualities such as altruism and prudence. Mill has more to say about communism as a threat to liberty, than about equality as a condition of liberty. When we turn to the essay *On Liberty* itself, our puzzlement increases; for here there is no mention of the ways in which the economic inequalities of his own day might limit liberty. Mill certainly remarks on the way in which moral conformity is imposed by a ruling class, and gives examples:

> Wherever there is an ascendant class, a large portion of the morality of the country emanates from its class interests, and its feelings of class superiority. The morality between Spartans and Helots, between planters and negroes, between princes and subjects, between nobles and roturiers, between men and women.[27]

This is an interesting list, especially because it omits to mention the relationship between capitalist employers and their labourers. The liberty-limiting dependence upon employers is nowhere a topic in Mill's essay *On Liberty.* In the *Subjection of Women* he explicitly states that since the end of feudalism the rule of force and monopoly has ceased in the social sphere, with the single exception of the subordination of women to men.[28] In the last chapter of *On Liberty,* he expresses alarm at the prospects for freedom, if power should become concentrated in a large state bureaucracy:

> Every function superadded to those already exercised by the government, causes its influence over hopes and fears to be more widely diffused, and converts, more and more, the active and ambitious part of the public into hangers-on of the government . . . If the roads, the railways, the banks, the insurance offices, the great joint-stock companies, the universities, and the public charities, were all of them branches of the government; if, in addition, the municipal corporations and local boards . . . became departments of the central administration; if the employés of all these different enterprises were appointed and paid by the govermment, and looked to the government for every rise in life; not all the freedom of the press and popular constitution of the legislative would make this or any other country free otherwise than in name.[29]

This argument, while sound, clearly expresses the *political* orientation of the Anglo-American concept of liberty: but why should we not, with Godwin, be equally afraid for the fate of freedom at the hands of an economic elite of owners and managers, to whom the masses must look for livelihood and advancement?

Mill is for liberty, but not for equality. The earlier writers, Godwin and Thompson, were emphatic egalitarians. They believed that differences in intelligence and ability resulted not from inborn endowments but from education, conditioning and environment:

Examine the new-born son of a peer, and of a mechanic. Has nature designated in different lineaments their future fortune? Is one of them born with callous hands and an ungainly form? Can you trace in the other the early promise of genius and understanding, of virtue and honour? We have been told indeed 'that nature will break out', and that
'The eaglet of a valiant nest will quickly tower
Up to the region of his sire;'
and the tale was once believed. But mankind will not soon again be persuaded, that the birthright of one lineage of human creatures is beauty and virtue, and of another, dulness, grossness and deformity.[30]

Godwin and Thompson thought that inequalities of wealth, and inequalities of power, are alike corrupting, to be eliminated as far as possible. Mill by contrast is ambiguous. One of his arguments for liberty is that without it genius cannot flourish.[31] And the opening up of opportunities for women is justified on the grounds that there is always a shortage of really able people to do the important business of the world; hence it is stupid to debar able women.[32] He makes reference to 'persons of decided mental superiority',[33] and to the 'select few'.[34] In *On Liberty* he insists that the Many should let themselves be guided by the highly gifted and instructed One or Few.[35] This goes hand in hand with an often low view of the common herd; most men are little higher than brutes,[36] the tendency of the age is to produce mediocrity,[37] raising the low and lowering the high.[38] Mill's free society is not to be equal but competitive, with equality of opportunity, that is to say, opportunity to rise, to become unequal. The direction of progress has been away from societies such as the feudal in which men and women were born to their status and locked into it, towards societies in which status is achieved by individual effort.[39] Modern politicians who praise Victorian values certainly pay lip-service at least to this image of competitive striving.

Much of the time, Mill appears to be saying that the free market guarantees economic liberty for all. Hence for example he thinks it sufficient to remove the legal and conventional restrictions on women entering certain jobs and educational institutions; this accomplished, women will be able to compete on equal terms in the open market. He is critical of the marriage contract, which he rightly insists is not a free and equal one,[40] but he does not propose that the contract of employment between master and workman is essentially unfree or unequal. In wage bargaining masters and men are equally constrained by the laws of the market, especially by the relationship between the quantity of labour seeking employment, and the quantity of capital seeking investment opportunities. The main way in which the labouring class can increase its standards of living is by reducing the supply of labour, by breeding less. In his essay *On Liberty,* Mill is much troubled about the possibility of labourers organised in trade unions limiting the liberty of other labourers:

> It is known that the bad workmen who form the majority of the operatives in many branches of industry, are decidedly of the opinion that bad workmen ought to receive the same wages as good, and that no one ought to be allowed, through piecework or otherwise, to earn by superior skill or industry more than others can without it. And they employ a moral police, which occasionally becomes a physical one, to deter skilful workmen from receiving, and employers from giving, a larger remuneration for a more useful service.[41]

No doubt many would agree with Mill here; but it cannot be assumed that he is right without argument. After all, Mill's contemporary, Karl Marx, devoted his life's work to demonstrating that the free market is neither natural, nor free for the great majority. Even non-Marxists might feel that Marx has a point here. For why are we so repelled by Mill's suggestion that those married couples who are too poor adequately to support children should not be allowed to have any?[42] Surely in part it is because we do not regard poverty as an irremediable consequence of personal inadequacy and the nature of things. We feel that to an extent we are responsible for their poverty, responsible because we have created or maintained an economic order which allows them to be poor.

So it can be said that there is an important difference between the ways in which the liberty-limiting interferences of society are conceived by Mill and Godwin. Whereas Mill thinks of these interferences mainly operating in the political and cultural spheres, Godwin finds them equally in the economic and social. Mill's essay is written to defend the individual from the 'tyranny of the majority' – the majority organised in the democratic state, the majority expressing itself in the form of public opinion.

At present individuals are lost in the crowd. In politics it is almost a triviality to say that public opinion now rules the world. The only power deserving the name is that of masses, and of governments while they make themselves the organ of the tendencies and instincts of the masses.[43]

This is a revealing and question-begging way of framing the issue. All the emphasis is placed upon the great mass oppressing minorities; there is no suggestion that wealthy and privileged minorities might manipulate and control the mass. Mill is horrified by the narrow, stifling conformism promoted by newspapers, the so-called organs of public opinion; but he does not ask about the extent to which the proprietors of those newspapers mould public opinion. The thinking of the masses 'is done for them by men much like themselves, addressing them or speaking in their name, on the spur of the moment, through the newspapers'.[44] The wording here – 'men much like themselves', 'speaking in their name', 'on the spur of the moment' – implicitly rejects the idea that newspapers represent interests distinct from those of the mass of the people, and that they consciously set about the business of forming opinion.

To conclude, two radically different ways of thinking about freedom can be found unreconciled in Mill's writings. In some of his economic writings – the *Principles of Political Economy*, the *Chapters on Socialism* – Mill shows an awareness of the social and economic conditions of independence. But in his main work on the subject, the essay *On Liberty*, freedom is presented as the absence of political and cultural constraints. The ideal of freedom is severed in two, and this severance is of the utmost importance, philosophically and historically. How is it to be explained? The answer does not lie in setting J. S. Mill against Harriet Mill; it is not the case that she was the apostle of economic equality and independence, he of cultural and political liberty. The *Chapters on Socialism* were written long after her death; and the essay *On Liberty*, offered to a publisher immediately after she died was, Mill insists, more a joint production than anything else he wrote. Rather, the severance reflects a deep and persistent tendency in Anglo-American political thought, having its roots in the eighteenth-century struggles, in England and America, against the power of the executive, and in classical political economy. This severance has become a commonplace, to such an extent that liberty and equality are widely thought to be opposed rather than complementary. The severance has been unsuccessfully challenged by voices speaking as it were from outside; for example by Godwin from the outermost fringes of dissent, more influentially by continentally-inspired neo-Hegelianism and Marxism. Mill was not one of these critics. On this crucial issue he reflected and reinforced the mind-set of his age.

Notes

1 M. St John Packe, *The Life of John Stuart Mill,* London, 1954, p. 103.

2 J. S. Mill, *The Subjection of Women,* in H. T. Mill, *Enfranchisement of Women,* and J. S. Mill, *The Subjection of Women,* London, 1983, p. 142.

3 *Ibid.,* p. 66.

4 *Ibid.,* pp. 38–9.

5 J. S. Mill, *On Liberty,* in J. S. Mill, *On Liberty, Representative Government, The Subjection of Women,* London, 1912, p. 75.

6 *Ibid.,* p. 77.

7 *Ibid.,* p. 75.

8 R. Pankhurst, *William Thompson, Britain's Pioneer Socialist, Feminist and Co-Operator,* London, 1954.

9 J. S. Mill, *Autobiography* (1983), London, 1924, p. 105.

10 W. Thompson, *Appeal of one Half the Human Race, Women, Against the Pretensions of the Other Half, Men, to Retain Them in Political, and Thence in Civil and Domestic Slavery,* London, 1983, p. 127.

11 *Ibid.,* p. 209.

12 Mill, *Subjection,* pp. 166, 169, 175.

13 Thompson, *Appeal,* p. 64.

14 Mill, *Subjection,* p. 57.

15 *Ibid.,* p. 89.

16 Thompson, *Appeal,* pp. 179–81.

17 *Ibid.,* p. 155.

18 D. Spender, *Women of Ideas,* London, 1982, p. 394; S. M. Okin, *Women in Western Political Thought,* London, 1980, pp. 228–9.

19 A. S. Rossi (ed.), *Essays on Sex Equality by John Stuart Mill and Harriet Taylor Mill,* Chicago, 1970; Okin, *Women in Western Political Thought,* pp. 207–30.

20 H. T. Mill, *Enfranchisement of Women,* in Mill, *Enfranchisement,* and Mill, *Subjection,* pp. 21–2.

21 W. Godwin, *Enquiry Concerning Political Justice* (1798), 3rd edn., Toronto, 1946, II, p. 299.

22 The terrifying weight of social and economic power is the theme of Godwin's novel *Caleb Williams*.

23 Godwin, *Political Justice*, II, pp. 110–11, 463–4.

24 J. S. Mill, *Principles of Political Economy* (1871), ed. D. Winch, Harmondsworth, 1970, p. 129.

25 Mill, *Autobiography*, pp. 207–8, Mill's claim for Harriet Taylor's influence is backed up by Hayek in his careful study based on the correspondence. F. A. Hayek, *John Stuart Mill and Harriet Taylor*, London, 1951.

26 J. S. Mill, *Essays on Economics and Society*, ed. J. M. Robson, Toronto, 1967, p. 710.

27 Mill, *On Liberty*, p. 11.

28 Mill, *Subjection*, pp. 10–12.

29 Mill, *On Liberty*, p. 135.

30 Godwin, *Political Justice*, II, p. 86.

31 Mill, *On Liberty*, p. 80; but see p. 43.

32 Mill, *Subjection*, p. 34.

33 Mill, *On Liberty*, p. 83.

34 Mill, *Subjection*, pp. 154–5.

35 Mill, *On Liberty*, p. 82.

36 Mill, *Subjection*, p. 64.

37 Mill, *On Liberty*, p. 81.

38 *Ibid.*, p. 90.

39 Mill, *Subjection*, p. 29.

40 *Ibid.*, pp. 59, 89.

41 Mill, *On Liberty*, p. 108. But note that Mill defends trades unions and their activities in his *Thornton on Labour and Its Claims*, in *Essays on Economics*, pp. 634–68.

42 Mill, *On Liberty*, pp. 132–3.

43 *Ibid.*, p. 81.

44 *Ibid.*, p. 82.

7 *Sheelagh Strawbridge*

Darwin and Victorian social values

In his Foreword to the 6th edition of Darwin's *The Origin of Species*, George Gaylord Simpson wrote:

The book before you is one of the most important ever written. No other modern work has done so much to change man's conception of himself and of the universe in which he lives. . . . Here at last all the aspects of life are approached as natural phenomena to be explained by natural causes embodied in objectively testable theories.[1]

The publication of *The Origin* then, marked the birth of a truly scientific biology. It signified a final break with metaphysical and 'often frankly supernatural' explanations of the nature of life and the diversity of living things.

This essay raises questions about this and similar forms of judgement. It focuses on *The Origin of Species* and *The Descent of Man* and, whilst not doubting that Darwin was a revolutionary thinker in some respects, it is argued that he was very much a man of his time. His writings are more deeply imbued with contemporary attitudes and values than is compatible with the conventional image of science pursuing 'truth' in a disinterested way. Indeed, a study of Darwin illustrates well the close interrelationship, between science and social values, that has become widely recognised through recent work in the history and sociology of scientific knowledge. Such a recognition does not detract from the value of scientific knowledge as such. However, it does question the dangerously privileged status accorded to science as the standard against which all claims to knowledge must be judged. Furthermore, it may help to undermine the seemingly automatic, though often specious, authority bestowed on all kinds of social prejudices by their association with science. Social Darwinism can perhaps be seen in this light.

Social Darwinism is a term which has been used to refer to attempts to utilise Darwin's evolutionary theory both in describing human societies and in prescribing how they might best be constituted. It is, however, most frequently applied to a range of prescriptions including conservatism, militarism, racism, eugenics, *laissez-faire* economics, unfettered capitalism and the rejection of social welfare. It can be seen from the disparate range of views represented in this list that the precise nature of Social Darwinism is a complex question. It is, however, a question that has been widely discussed and it will not be pursued here. It will suffice to note, for the purposes of this essay, that all the views deemed to warrant the description Social Darwinist derive, in one way or another, from the belief that Darwin's theory of evolution is to be accepted and that the theory holds that there is a struggle for existence amongst animals and plants which results in evolutionary change. This same notion of a struggle for existence is, moreover, equally applicable to human individuals and/or human societies and the evolutionary change it brings about is to be regarded as developmental and progressive. As progress is a good thing, to be positively valued, evolutionary change should be cultivated and nurtured. Social Darwinists have tended to argue that this can be achieved by the more intense prosecution of the struggle for existence.

In 1958 Donald MacRae noted that:

> Racist theory is no responsibility of Darwin's and can be found long before him, whilst its bible – Gobineau's *Essai sur l'inegalité des races humaines* – first appeared in 1854–5. Nevertheless, the racists claimed in Darwin a scientific confirmation of their views which is still exploited in South Africa and the American South. The theory that public provision and private charity should not be bestowed on individuals or groups unable to take part in the social contest can be traced back to at least the sixteenth century, but here again Darwinism was, quite illegitimately, appropriated in order to hinder or to forbid charitable endeavour as being opposed to the best interests of a freely competitive economic order.[2]

Nevertheless, he could write as if the worst excesses of Social Darwinism were a thing of the past. Whilst in 1909, sociology, anthropology and the comparative study of religions were dominated by evolutionary theory, political science was under strong

Darwinian influence and eugenics was at its most fashionable,

Today the eugenics of that period, profoundly biased in terms of class and race, has ceased to count.[3]

and:

It is much to our advantage in the ordinary business of living, as well as in the pursuit of scientific knowledge about society, that the phrase the 'survival of the fittest' is seldom or never heard in the contemporary discussion of human affairs.[4]

Unfortunately we can no longer have the same confidence that Social Darwinist thinking is outmoded. Martin Barker analyses in detail its virulent modern form which draws on the neo-Darwinist theories of sociobiology for its scientific credentials.[5] He quotes the following illustrations of this new kind of argument:

Sociobiology is thus transforming our views of man and society. We are beginning to see that 'ethics' have an evolutionary origin, and that our biological nature may well explain why we make certain choices instead of others. Other types of behaviour operating according to these principles include communication, territorial defence behaviour and, of course, racialism.[6]

It has been said by Professor Darlington that man's faculty of reasoning has not destroyed the instinctive basis of his behaviour, but it has 'masked it and distorted it'. The great question of our time seems to be whether European man, the pinnacle of evolution, will destroy through the unnatural notions which are the modern forms of his intellect what his inherited instincts have striven through these eons of time to preserve.[7]

and:

Our genes, needing to prosper, turn man into an aggressive animal who will always seek to better himself at the expense of his peers. The sociobiologist's view of mankind is, of course, a bleak one . . . we are what we are, greedy, rapacious, self-serving individuals, out to get what we can for ourselves and Devil take the hindmost. If this is how we are, if this somewhat mordant description of mankind does exactly describe us, as the sociobiologists claim that it does, it is as foolish to condemn it as it is to condemn the fact that our noses are exterior rather than interior organs. . . . Science now seems to have caught up with Adam Smith. To support an economic lame-duck is not merely bad economics, but apparently is also against our deep-seated nature.

It will be a chilling thought to many, but it does begin to look as though we have a little bit of Maggie Thatcher in us all.[8]

Of course, the fact that such views claim the scientific support of sociobiology, does not demonstrate their derivation from sociobiological theory. The interrelationship is likely to be as complex as the interrelationship between Darwin's original theory and the views of earlier Social Darwinists. Despite their claims, it is clear that MacRae believed both Darwin's theory and Darwin himself to be innocent of any implication in Social Darwinism. Indeed, if there is such an implication, it is sufficiently ambiguous to have allowed writers and activists from the opposite end of the political spectrum – Marxists, Fabian Socialists and Anarchists – to find Darwin's theory quite compatible with their own differing analyses of human societies.

The interrelationships between scientific theories and other ideas and beliefs, such as social and moral values and political ideologies, are manifold and complex. Although it is beyond the scope of this essay to attempt any kind of exhaustive analysis, some exploration of those interrelationships in Darwin's case will serve to raise a number of issues which are still as relevant today.

When we talk of Social Darwinism the assumption is that the social ideas have been derived, or at least claim derivation, from the scientific theory. Whilst the particular derivation may be considered problematic, we are not uneasy about the general notion that scientific ideas may inform our views about society. On the other hand, the suggestion, that scientific theories are themselves influenced by the social context, including the broad web of beliefs and social values, within which they are formed, does tend to generate an uneasiness. It disturbs the conventional image of science, pursuing 'truth' in a disinterested way, untainted by social values and political ideals. Science should not be a prey to ideological fashion. However, Darwin, great scientist and revolutionary thinker though he was, was, nevertheless, very much a man of his time and was influenced, even in his scientific work, by the social values, ideas and beliefs of his time.

Although the belief in the fixity of natural species was still widespread in Darwin's day, theories of organic evolution were also the subject of much contemporary debate. Moreover, notions of social and cultural evolution dominated anthropological and sociological thinking, through, for example, the work of Edward Burnett Tylor, Auguste Comte and, of course, Herbert Spencer. So it was not the theory of evolution as such that was revolutionary in Darwin's work, if was, rather, his notion of 'natural selection' which was inspired by his reading of Malthus:

I happened to read for amusement *Malthus on Population*, and being well prepared to appreciate the struggle for existence which everywhere goes on, from long continued observation of the habits of animals and plants, it at once struck me that under these circumstances favourable variations would tend to be preserved, and unfavourable ones to be destroyed. The result of this would be the formation of new species.[9]

Malthus' argument concerned human populations and stated that:

1) Economic resources on which life is dependent cannot be multiplied indefinitely – nor at a very rapid rate.
2) Potential fecundity is such that populations grow without limit and at ever greater velocity unless somehow checked.
3) There are three checks to population growth: a) vice, b) misery and c) self restraint.

By vice Malthus meant such things as prostitution, corruption, 'unnatural passions' and improper arts – including birth control. By misery he meant poverty, malnutrition, exposure, disease, wars, infanticide, plague and famine.[10]

Darwin took up Malthus' theory, often seen as a response to the problems of early industrial capitalism, and applied it, together with the principle of evolutionary change, to animal and plant species. He argued:

A struggle for existence inevitably follows from the high rate at which all organic beings tend to increase . . . as more individuals are produced than can possibly survive, there must in every case be a struggle for existence, either one individual with another of the same species, or with the individuals of a different species, or with the physical conditions of life. It is the doctrine of Malthus applied with manifold force to the whole animal and vegetable kingdoms; for in this case there can be no artificial increase of food and no prudential restraint from marriage.[11]

Unlike Malthus, however, Darwin followed Spencer in asking which individuals would survive and he took his answer from Spencer who, in 1852, wrote that the survivors would be 'the select of their generation' or 'the fittest':

> Owing to this struggle, variations, however slight . . ., if they be in any degree profitable to the individuals of a species, will tend to the preservation of such individuals, and will generally be inherited by the offspring. The offspring, also, will thus have a better chance of surviving.
> I have called this principle, by the term Natural Selection, in order to mark its relation to man's power of selection. But the expression, often used by Mr Herbert Spencer of 'the survival of the fittest', is more accurate and is sometimes equally convenient.[12]

The principle of natural selection works upon chance variations and it was this element of chance which appears to have been one of the most disturbing aspects of the theory as far as Darwin's contemporaries and particularly his religious opponents were concerned. Indeed the idea of chance operating in the natural world was no less disturbing to Einstein over a hundred years after the publication of *The Origin of Species.* When confronted by the theory of quantum mechanics he is reputed to have said, 'I cannot believe that God plays dice with the cosmos'.[13]

Nevertheless, although natural selection works upon chance variations, which may be either beneficial or detrimental to individuals, it works to select those which are beneficial thus ensuring that evolutionary change implies progress:

> Although we have no good evidence of the existence in organic beings of an innate tendency towards progressive development, yet this necessarily follows . . . through the continued action of natural selection.[14]

> Modern forms ought, on the theory of natural selection, to stand higher than ancient forms. Is this the case? A large number of palaentologists would answer in the affirmative; and it seems that this answer must be admitted as true, though difficult of proof.[15]

and

> And as natural selection works solely by and for the good of each being, all corporeal and mental endowments will tend to progress towards perfection.[16]

Darwin lived in a period when European thinking in general was profoundly affected by the idea of progress and it would perhaps have been surprising for him to have escaped the influence of such a pervasive and powerful idea.[17] Certainly, in seeing progress as a process of improvement resulting from development through a series of finely graduated stages, Darwin was very much of his time, taking for granted a deeply rooted assumption of his culture.

In *The Origin of Species,* of course, Darwin was concerned with the evolutionary development of organic forms and his real scientific achievement must be assessed in relation to the contribution made by the notion of natural selection within this field of inquiry. He did, however, say that:

> In the future I see open fields for more important researchers. Psychology will be securely based on the foundation already well laid by Mr Herbert Spencer, that of the necessary acquirement of each mental power and capacity by gradation. Much light will be thrown on the origin of man and his history.[18]

Moreover, there is no doubt that the publication of *The Origin of Species* gave a powerful boost to social evolutionary thinking. Building on the tradition of British political economy Spencer had already stressed the importance of competitive struggle and the 'survival of the fittest' in social evolution and in the wake of the publication of *The Origin,* others, including Bagehot and Galton (Darwin's cousin), soon took up the idea.

Darwin was himself deeply influenced by this current of thought. He read Spencer, Bagehot and Galton with great approval and in 1871 he was moved to publish his own contribution to social evolutionary thinking in *The Descent of Man.* Had Darwin refrained from pursuing the notion of human evolution himself, he may have been justifiably acquitted of any charge that his writings gave explicit support to Social Darwinist ideas. Regrettably perhaps, he did not.

Darwin made no first hand study of human societies and cultures (apart from his quite limited enquiries concerning *The Expression of the Emotions in Man and Animals*[19] and whilst *The Origin* can be seen as a significant contribution to the theory of organic evolution, *The Descent,* is for the most part derivative. As Kenneth Bock convincingly demonstrates it strongly reflects the conventional wisdom of the time and relies heavily on contemporary social anthropology and sociology.[20] Moreover, Darwin is less circumspect than, for example, Tylor, upon whose work he draws, in his quite uncritical acceptance of European culture as the latest and highest product of human history. For Darwin there was simply no question that the western nations of Europe stand 'at the summit of civilisation' and that amongst these nations the Anglo-Saxons excel.[21] Non-European tribal peoples, on the other hand, were described as savages, devoid of any real religion, incapable of enjoying true beauty and judging by the 'hideous ornaments and equally hideous music admired by most savages' as having their aesthetic faculty less developed than that of birds.[22] Furthermore, Darwin held them to have poorly developed reasoning powers and to be licentious and given to unnatural crimes.

In *The Origin* Darwin was concerned with the operation of natural selection upon organic characteristics. However, he believed that mental and moral capacities and dispositions were also heritable and this belief was greatly strengthened by his reading of Galton's essay on 'Hereditary Talent and Character' (1865).[23] He was convinced that natural selection had acted upon them through history in the competition between individuals, tribes, nations and races. On the other hand, it had operated to strengthen social and sympathetic feelings amongst men but, in turn, these feelings had inhibited effective natural selection in civilised societies thereby posing a threat to continued progress and a dilemma for the eugenicists. Darwin shared their concern and wrestled with the problem in *The Descent* without achieving a solution.

Like the sociologists and social anthropologists of his day, Darwin used the 'comparative method' to build his cultural developmental series which, as Bock notes, moves from apes to civilised man and includes idiots, infants, savages, women in civilised societies and boys in civilised societies. The comparative method entails treating contemporary forms as reflecting historical stages and rests on assumption of progress. Darwin had already used this somewhat dubious method in *The Origin* but there it was at least supplemented by reference to the fossil record. The application of the comparative method to human cultures resulted in their ordering according to their degree of similarity to European culture – the summit of civilisation and obviously the best that evolution had produced.

The cultural succession is not precisely defined in *The Descent* but the general pattern connects apes, negroes and civilised man by gradations and Darwin details a great range of examples in its support. Bock notes a number of these, for instance,: the sense of smell, important in many animals, is more highly developed in the dark races of man than in white civilised races; the human foot gradually loses its prehensile power and this is less the case amongst savages; idiots are curiously fond of climbing furniture and trees – boys delight in climbing trees; idiots snarl savagely and snarling is probably more common amongst savages than civilised races; civilised adult males are less emotionally demonstrative than savages – they weep less, even amongst civilised Europeans Englishmen rarely cry whereas some continentals shed tears freely; and:

A savage will risk his own life to save a member of his own community but will be wholly indifferent about a stranger; a young and timid mother urged by the material instinct will, without a moments hesitation, run the greatest danger for her own infant, but not for a mere fellow creature. Nevertheless, many a civilised man, who never before risked his life for another, but full of courage and sympathy, has disregarded the instinct of self-preservation, and plunged at once into a torrent to save a drowning man – though a stranger.[24]

The effects of social institutions and other cultural factors on human capacities and behaviour are given scant attention in *The Descent.* Darwin displays none of the sensitivity and perception of John Stuart and Harriet Taylor Mill, for example, who argued in *The Subjection of Women* (1869) that it was simply not possible at that time, to determine the innate relative mental capacities of men and women, due to the differences in the social circumstances to which they were subjected. Darwin merely asserts that we should expect men and women to differ as the bull from the cow, the boar from the sow, the stallion from the mare and the males of the larger apes from the females. 'Man', he claimed: 'is more courageous, pugnacious and energetic than woman, and has a more inventive genius'.[25] Whilst women excel in tenderness, unselfishness, intuition and powers of rapid perception and imitation, we should bear in mind that at least some of these qualities are characteristic of the 'lower races' and, therefore, of a past and lower state of civilisation. In anything requiring deep thought, reason or imagination – or merely the use of the senses and the hands, men are preeminent. Thus:

If two lists were made of the most eminent men and women in poetry, painting, sculpture, music, history, science and philosophy with half a dozen names under each subject, the two lists would not bear comparison.[26]

As Oldroyd comments, Darwin, in *The Descent,* clearly displays 'the prevailing social attitudes of the well-to-do Victorian gentleman'.[27] It can be said with little fear of contradiction that the work makes scant contribution to any real understanding of cultural differences let alone cultural development.

Darwin was then, in some respects a revolutionary thinker, but he was also very much a man of his time reflecting the dominant values of his culture. Science and ideology are more intimately intertwined than we may wish to believe. Darwin's conception of organic evolution was profoundly influenced by his belief in progress and defended using the 'comparative method', itself dependent on the same belief. His central notion of 'natural selection' was inspired by his reading of the social theories of Malthus and Spencer and his own work in turn added weight to current social theories. If *The Origin* can be seen as innocent of giving explicit support to Social Darwinism, *The Descent* certainly cannot.

Nevertheless, perhaps because it is the achievement of *The Origin* which is seen as central to Darwinism, Darwin is frequently dissociated from Social Darwinism. Indeed it is true that many prominent Social Darwinists looked more directly to Spencer than Darwin and this is not so surprising when we realise just how derivative Darwin's own social ideas were from Spencer, Galton, Tylor and the like. Why then do we not hear of Social Spencerism?

The foregoing argument has attempted to demonstrate, by way of Darwin, something of the interrelationship between scientific theories and their cultural context, something of the interplay between scientific ideas and current ideology. It remains to indicate the importance of recognising this interrelationship by considering the ideological force of science itself.

From the time of its birth, modern science has had a powerful ideological impact. Bacon and Descartes felt the need to try to assure the Church and the State that there was nothing to fear from 'the new philosophy' whereas Voltaire and Tom Paine argued the reverse. Auguste Comte proclaimed the coming of a positive order in which scientists rather than priests would be canonised and social scientists in general, inspired by the achievements of the natural sciences, have for long aspired to mimic them.

To regard a set of ideas or theories as scientific is to confer upon them great authority. Social Darwinism was a set of social and political doctrines rendered 'scientific' by association with Darwin's theory of natural selection. It is arguable that we have Social Darwinism and not Social Spencerism because of the authority bestowed by this association. In Darwin's age, as in our own, there was a widespread veneration of science. W. H. Greenleaf argues that:

> In many minds indeed the possibilities of science replaced the slowly waning certainties of religion . . . Natural science became increasingly one of the dominant spiritual forces of the time, the key to solve as well all the practical problems of life: it was, as Chesterton wrote, 'in the air of all that Victorian world'.[28]

Everything had to be justified by reference to science. Chadwick, for example, referred to the 'New Poor Law' as the 'first piece of legislation based upon scientific or economical principles'. Science became and remains the model for all rational thought. Greenleaf refers to this as scientism:

> Scientism is a convenient word to describe all these many and varied forms of belief resting on the notion that the only effective method of thinking and analysis is that deriving from, or deemed characteristic of, the inquiries of modern natural science and technology . . . what is not thus scientifically grounded is either merely subjective or . . . no more than vain philosophy, speculative metaphysics – to be cast into the flames. The implication of this position is that scientific method (as variously conceived) is the only means to ensure effective understanding of any aspect of human or natural experience and that genuine knowledge of man and society can only be acquired in the same way that mastery of nature is achieved.[29]

By thus ousting all other forms of reasoning and inquiry, scientism contends for the status of the metaphysics of the modern world and is ideally suited to the ideological functions it is called upon to perform.

Because the use of scientific categories is taken as the mark of sound and progressive thought, all kinds of ideas and prejudices cast in this form became more acceptable and persuasive. The authority of Darwin's science added weight to Victorian notions of racial superiority and helped to justify imperialism. Today new forms of racism, based on notions of a natural motivation to form groups, defend territory and prevent 'swamping' by strangers, justify anti-immigration laws as well as the more extreme policies of the National Front. These notions gain strength by association with the neo-Darwinist theories of ethologists and sociobiologists.[30] A clearer conception of the interplay between scientific ideas and social values can help to counter, amongst other things, such claims to 'scientific racialism'.

As well as the specific use of certain scientific ideas to provide spurious justifications for social prejudices and policies based upon those prejudices, there is a broader danger inherent in 'scientism'. This danger must seem particularly acute to those of us today working in humanities and social science departments in our beleaguered educational institutions. The danger lies in scientific thinking and scientific training being promoted at the expense of everything else. As Peter Scott has argued recently, the intellectual system which has nurtured the knowledge which has produced the bomb has failed to produce the moral categories which permit such knowledge to be civilised in the service of man.[31]

> Our culture élites are often in bondage to technocratic and scientific knowledge. We can best describe technocratic thought by the discrepancy between its claims and its consequences. It claims to be a full description of reality but its consequences frequently entail a systematic inhibition of the moral imagination.[32]

We live in an age which Habermas has depicted as one dominated by 'technological rationality' in which the development of the social system seems to be determined by the internal logic of scientific and technological progress.[33] We find it difficult enough to ask where we are going let alone why we are going there. Our age has become, as Max Weber foretold, an age of 'Specialists without spirit, sensualists without heart; this nullity imagines that it has attained a level of civilisation never before achieved.'[34]

Science may and does throw up moral problems, it cannot, however, solve them. Moral reasoning is outside its scope. Indeed, the very existence of science depends on the prior acceptance of an ethic, including such principles as truth telling and abstaining from fraud, attending to evidence and respecting the discoveries of others, which cannot be justified scientifically. The danger is, that in this climate of 'scientism', it is easy to believe that because moral principles and social ends are not amenable to scientific reason they cannot be reasoned about at all. Lacking a strong value framework legitimated by religion, our culture, even more than Darwin's, falls too easily under the influence of the ideology of science and eschews serious inquiry into or debate about values which can be sold, pre-packed and unexamined, as a 'lucky bag' from a former age, or simply dismissed as mere matters of opinion. The disciplines of social and political theory which might have helped develop the intellectual tools of such debate have striven so assiduously to become 'scientific' themselves that they have, until recently, neglected the task. Even philosophy, for too long, under the spell of science, cast itself in the role of 'under-labourer in the garden of knowledge', turned from substantive questions and limited itself to conceptual clarification.

These disciplines are now under fierce attack, no doubt facilitated by their own seduction by scientism. They are to be sacrificed in the name of economic necessity and scientific progress. However, an age which has experienced the moral degeneration which made genocide thinkable and which has harnessed the power of global self-destruction, cannot afford to neglect the question of its values and their justification. It is imperative that science, whilst being respected for what it can do, is demystified. The metaphysical pretensions of scientism must be undermined and it may be hoped that a clearer understanding of the interrelationships between science and its social context will contribute to this urgent task.

Notes

1 G. G. Simpson, 'Foreword', in C. Darwin, *The Origin of Species*, 6th edn., Collier Books, New York, 1962, p. 5.

2 D. G. MacRae, 'Darwinism and the social sciences', in S. A. Barnett (ed.), *A Century of Darwin*, Heinemann, London, 1958, p. 301.

3 *Ibid.*, p. 298.

4 *Ibid.*, p. 301.

5 M. Barker, *The New Racism*, Junction Books, London, 1981.

6 *Ibid.*, p. 153.

7 *Ibid.*, p. 153.

8 *Ibid.*, p. 146.

9 See D. G. MacRae, *op. cit.*, p. 296, quoted from C. F. Darwin, *The Life and Letters of Charles Darwin*, 1887.

10 *Ibid.*, p. 297.

11 C. Darwin, *The Origin*, 6th edn., p. 78.

12 *Ibid.*, p. 76.
13 *Observer*, 'Sayings of the week', 5th April, 1954.
14 C. Darwin, *op. cit.*, p. 213.
15 *Ibid.*, p. 355.
16 *Ibid.*, p. 484.
17 See for example, J. B. Bury, *The Idea of Progress*, Macmillan, London, 1928.
18 C. Darwin, *op. cit.*, p. 483.
19 Published in 1872, after *The Descent of Man*.
20 K. Bock, *Human Nature and History: A Response to Sociobiology*, Columbia University Press, New York, 1980.
21 *Ibid.*, p. 46.
22 *Ibid.*, p. 46.
23 See J. C. Greene, *Science, Ideology and World View*, University of California Press, Berkeley, 1981, p. 104.
24 K. Bock, *op. cit.*, pp. 44–45.
25 *Ibid.*, p. 50.
26 *Ibid.*, p. 50.
27 D. R. Oldroyd, *Darwinism Impacts*, 2nd edn., Open University Press, Milton Keynes, 1983, p. 150.
28 W. H. Greenleaf, *The British Political Tradition*, Vol. 1: 'The rise of collectivism', Methuen, London, 1983, p. 238.
29 *Ibid.*, p. 239.
30 See M. Barker, *op. cit.*
31 P. Scott, *The Times Higher Education Supplement*, Editorial: 'The year of the bomb', January, 1983.
32 *Ibid.*
33 See, for example, J. Habermas, *Toward a Rational Society*, Heinemann, London, 1971, Chapter 6, 'Technology and science as ideology'.
34 M. Weber, *The Protestant Ethic and the Spirit of Captialism*, Unwin University Books, London, 1974, p. 182.

8 *Rosamund Billington*

The dominant values of Victorian feminism

We deny the right of any portion of the species to decide for another portion, or any individual for another individual, what is and what is not their 'proper sphere'. The proper sphere for all human beings is the largest and highest which they are able to attain to. What this is cannot be ascertained without complete liberty of choice.[1]

In this passage by Harriet Taylor Mill we have a clear statement of the liberal utilitarianism for which her husband, John Stuart Mill, was a spokesperson. But the passage is taken from Harriet Mill's anonymously published essay (1851), 'The enfranchisement of women'. In this she argued *against* the prevailing view that women had a different sphere of activity and influence from men, and *for* women's enfranchisement as a step towards taking an equal place with men in society. This juxtaposition of one of the most influential and ultimately conservative ideologies of the nineteenth century – liberal utilitarianism – with the radical idea of equality for women, tells us a great deal about Victorian values and about the values underlying the movement for women's emancipation.

The term Victorian values may be taken to mean that there was a consensus of values in the nineteenth century. But if that had been the case, how would we be able to explain the enormous social changes which took place, including those which affected women, since consensus implies stability and lack of social change? It is difficult indeed, to show that at any period in history there has ever been a consensus of values. Far more convincing, is the notion that there are dominant values maintained by the hegemony of powerful or ruling groups, a dominant ideology, and that conflicting with this are alternative values, beliefs, ideologies, which are those of other, subordinate groups. It can then be argued that this conflict of values is a cause of social change, indeed, that this is a continuous process, at some times more drastic than others. However, we cannot attribute social change and social movements simply to ideological conflict, but must acknowledge the real material base which underlies such a conflict of values, though we may wish to argue that ideology does not 'reflect' the material conflicts of society in any simple way. Nineteenth-century bourgeois feminism was both an expression of complex ideological conflict and of the economic and social contradictions of women's existence, but it is the *ideas* of nineteenth-century bourgeois feminism that I want to discuss here, rather than the material base from which they sprang.

I began by pointing out what appears to be a contradiction between Harriet Taylor Mill's use of the inherently conservative ideas of utilitarianism and her use of more radical notions concerning women's rights to equality with men. But incorporation of ideas from a dominant ideology to articulate the interests of a subordinate group should not surprise us, if we remember that part of the way in which ideology dominates is that it forms the prevailing langauge and symbols, the ideas and beliefs in which people commonly express themselves. It is this aspect of ideological hegemony that some modern feminists have failed to appreciate when criticising organised nineteenth-century feminism for its lack of radicalism and its bourgeois character.[2] Feminists utilised the dominant theories and discourses of the culture and society in which they lived. Apart from the fact that these were most easily available to them, it is also possible to argue that by using this set of Victorian values they were able to develop a critique of the prevailing situation of women which influenced many other women and men, simply because it *was* phrased in terms of dominant values. We need to remember also, particularly with reference to the mainsteam women's education and suffrage movements, that an ideological framework which they shared with bourgeois men gave middle-class women access to male dominated channels of communication and organisation without which they were powerless, and which of course, were unavailable to proletarian women.[3]

The nineteenth-century women's movement had many strands and many contradictions. Organisations aimed at a particular reform (e.g. education, employment, property laws, prostitution) developed specific arguments to forward that cause, but we can distinguish a dominant set of ideas which underlay the whole movement and it is these I shall discuss first.[4] Many feminist activists came from Dissenting and Non-Conformist groups, like other reformers whose radicalism and liberalism stemmed from the earlier struggles of these groups for equal rights and status before the law. Quakers and Unitarians were particularly vociferous in demanding the abolition of civil disabilities and looked towards a society based on reason and individual freedom.[5] Middle-class feminists applied these ideas to women as a group, in the same way that they had applied them to argue for the abolition of negro slavery in the British Colonies and America. In the essay already mentioned, Harriet Mill quoted the American Declaration of Independence, pointing out that the 'inalienable rights' of all individuals, referred to in that Declaration, applied equally to men and women. She saw the struggle for women's emancipation as part of the democratic revolution which included the abolition of slavery. This theme was an important one in the ideology of the women's suffrage movement and will be returned to later.

The women's movement shared with other nineteenth-century reform movements a 'social evangelicalism', or what one historian has described as 'a common faith in reform as a law of nature. Particular reforms were of less importance than recognition of the universal duty to strive for social and individual betterment.'[6] Feminists too, argued that 'God sent all human beings into the world for the purpose of forwarding . . . the progress of the world', and women must be allowed to take their share of this work.[7] But women's precise role in such progress was unclear until they had been educated to develop and utilise their full capacities as human beings:

> We must also and even in the first place set before them the highest aim by which humanity can be urged to exertion – the full development of our being in accordance with the design of our Creator, a development . . . women have not yet reached . . . Time and conditions only are required to shew, that *of whatever women are capable, for that they were intended.*[8]

Despite the conventional view embodied in this statement from the *English Woman's Journal*, – of human beings designed to carry out God's will – it also includes a direct challenge to conventional views that women had very limited capacities for work in the world. The leader of the women's education movement, Emily Davies, put the matter in similar terms: 'who shall say for another – much more, who shall say for half the human race – this, or this, is the measure of your capacity; this and no other is the work you are qualified to perform?' Although agreeing that 'women's work was helping work', Emily Davies pointed out that practical answers were still needed to the question 'Whom are they to help and how?',[9] and like many other spokeswomen for the movement, she felt that women still needed to develop whatever their real capacities were.

The women's education movement was particularly important in practically demonstrating women's capacity for learning and academic performance, the development of intellectual capacities without the destruction of 'natural femininity' and therefore proving women's capacity for entering the professions and the public sphere. This movement also shows very clearly how feminists understood the strength of dominant values surrounding the position of women, while at the same time subverting these for their own purposes. As Josephine Butler stated:

> Education was what the slave-owners most dreaded for their slaves, for they knew it to be the sure way to emancipation. It is to education that we must first look for the emancipation of women from the industrial restrictions of a bye gone age.[10]

Mainstream Victorian feminism offered no radical alternative to the Victorian family, or to the relationship of men and women within it. Rather, feminism aimed at perfecting and reforming the institutions of marriage and family, while at the same time stressing women's freedom and capacities as individuals. Poorly educated women with no political and legal rights were unfit to be the moral guardians of society through fulfilling the roles of wife and mother, when marriage was an economic necessity rather than a moral ideal. Feminists argued that not only were women prevented from helping in the work of social progress, but that marriage had become degraded – a trade. Maria Grey, one of the more conservative spokeswomen of the ıt was especially critical of the mercenary nature of Girls were '*not* educated to be wives, but to get hus-

> What they are educated for is to come up to a certain conventional standard accepted in the class to which they belong, to adorn (if they can) the best parlours or the drawing room . . . to gratify a mother's vanity, to amuse a father's leisure hours, above all, to get married.[11]

Although Mrs Grey thought women the 'Heaven-appointed guardians' of the home and family she also thought that women should be educated for 'self-dependence', based on what she called the '*spiritual* equality of all human beings'. Only when this equality was recognised would marriage become truly Christian, rather than an institution in which girls sold themselves 'for the comforts or luxuries of life'.[12] Marriage was an economic necessity for middle-class women because they had no means of earning an independent living without losing their social status as 'ladies'. The women's movement argued that adequate education for all women and later training facilities would enable the many women who did not marry (because of the surplus number of women in the population) to become financially self-sufficient. By implication, of course, this gave women a choice between marriage or a career and many notable Victorian women deliberately chose to remain single, including Florence Nightingale, Dorothea Beale and Frances Buss.

Given the importance of the family and marriage as ideals in Victorian values, women's roles as wives and mothers were seen also to give them more moral authority than men. If most of the evils of society were moral ones, it was women's duty to instil moral values into children, particularly male ones, and to make men 'willing to strive, and instil the right motives for action'.[13] Millicent Fawcett summarised this viewpoint: 'how vastly important for national welfare it is that mothers of children should be persons of large, liberal and cultural minds'.[14] Feminists criticised the superficial and unsystematic nature of girls' and women's education, a criticism given legitimacy by the Report of the Schools Inquiry Commission in 1868. This criticism was essentially a utilitarian one and feminists stressed the harm which frivolity and idleness caused: it encouraged 'a trifling habit of mind, injurious not only to the women who indulge in it, but to everyone with whom they have to do'.[15] Dorothea Beale, one of the pioneer Victorian Headmistresses, stressed the function of education in enabling girls to perform their traditional role:

> moral training is the end, education the means; the habits and obedience to duty, of self-restraint . . . [and] humility . . . should be specially cultivated in a woman, that she may wear the true woman's ornament of a meek and quiet spirit . . . [W]e shall find the results . . . to be gentleness of manner, unselfishness, humility, and a more cheerful and entire obedience to rightful authority.[16]

In fact, many ex-pupils of Miss Beale and similar headmistresses went on to be active in the women's suffrage movement, did not display a 'meek and quiet spirit' and certainly disputed the rightful authority of an all-male political system! Clearly, this emphasis on women's traditional role labels the women's education movement as part of the dominant value system, but we must remember also feminists' belief in social evangelicalism discussed earlier. On the one hand, as Emily Davies stated, the purpose of education was to enable the individual to develop 'a formed and disciplined character, able to stand alone, and to follow steadily a predetermined course, without fear of punishment, or hope of reward', but on the other hand, the 'existence of capacities is in itself an indication that they are intended for some good purpose'.[17] She actually used the term 'calling' to indicate how human capacities should be utilised. It was in the open-endedness of such capacities and the duty to put them to good use that feminists found legitimacy for their claim for better and equal educational facilities for women:

> As the daughters of Deity, as part of humanity common to both sexes, women, besides being created for wives and mothers, are also created for themselves, and for that Deity, [but] . . . only by great and long continued efforts can they hope to gain the position of workers in the world's affairs, instead of the idlers they have been hitherto.[18]

Although in general supporting the prevailing ideology that the natural sphere of women was the private one of home and family, at many points, feminists challenged dominant views of the biological and mental inferiority of women, which were the rationalisations for their economic, legal and social inequality. Spokeswomen for the movement refused to discuss in detail the supposed differences between women and men, but in general terms indicated that many of the supposed differences could be accounted for by social arrangements, not innate characteristics. Emily Davies argued, for example, that whatever differences there were, there was also 'a deep and broad basis of likeness', and if women were educated like men this would bring the two sexes closer together in intellectual matters.[19] Feminists pointed out that if femininity was given by nature and therefore immutable, this nature could only be enhanced by encouraging women to develop all their human capacities:

> the more fully and freely a girl is allowed to develop her whole being, the more distinctly marked will her feminine characteristics become. They are deeply rooted in her very nature; there is no need to cripple her for fear of destroying.[20]

It should have become clear by now that the ideas contained within the dominant Victorian value system were open to several 'readings', that they were complex and also not necessarily consistent with each other. Also, it is difficult to decide the extent to which feminists really subscribed to the dominant ideology and the extent to which they deliberately represented their propaganda in the terms that they knew would be accepted. An important factor here, is the particular set of constraints surrounding middle-class women's public behaviour. The emphasis of the movement on appearing 'ladylike' and 'respectable' was an acknowledgement of the power of the dominant ideology rather than a demonstration of belief in it. There is insufficient space to discuss this adequately here and one example must suffice.[21] That Girton College for women was built some distance from the men's colleges tends to be seen today as an indication of how conservative its feminist founders were. But Emily Davies and her committee deliberately built the college at this distance in order to allow the women students relative freedom. The nearer they were to young men, the more chaperonage and protection respectable society would have required. Emily Davies expressed it thus: the main aim of the movement was

> that of giving to women an opportunity of laying out their own lives, in circumstances which may help them to lay them out wisely. Women have plenty of practice in submitting to little rules. We want to give

them the discipline of deciding for themselves and acting upon their own responsibility.

What she wanted to protect women students from most was 'the morning calls and the dropping in and the servants coming with notes to wait for an answer and the general victimisation by idle ladies'.[22]

A comparison of the dominant ideas of the women's suffrage movement with those of the education movement is instructive. Although firmly rooted in the dominant liberal democratic ideas of the day, many of the arguments for women's suffrage challenged the dominant ideology concerning the position of women more directly than those of the mainstream women's education movement. The following statement clearly indicates the strength of the opposition to feminism and the potentially radical implications of granting women the right to vote in parliamentary elections. In 1865, when it was first proposed to set up a women's suffrage committee, Emily Davies wrote to a friend: 'I don't see much use in talking about the Franchise till first principles have made more way. The scoffers don't see how much is involved in improved education, but they are wide awake about the Franchise.'[23] Davies, like Butler, quoted earlier, clearly recognised the long term radical implications of educating women, even if more conservative supporters of the movement did not. But Davies also understood that giving women political power was generally perceived as more radical because of the importance placed on the formal parliamentary political system in the Victorian period.

More than a century later it is perhaps difficult to appreciate why feminists fought so hard and so long for the vote and why they met such prolonged opposition for over fifty years. But we must try to understand the high value placed by Victorians on the parliamentary franchise. It was both the tool and the symbol of liberal democracy, empowering and legitimising the new bourgeoisie. The Reform Bill of 1832 had begun the process of enfranchising and incorporating the bourgeoisie into the formal political process (although not without violence), and later reform bills gradually extended the franchise to include more of the bourgeoisie and eventually some working men. Although the process was not completed until this century, widening of the electorate increased the number of radical MPs and it was amongst radicals and liberals that women suffragists looked for support.

One historian has argued that 'the mid-Victorian liberal consensus was most clearly distilled in the life and works of John Stuart Mill'.[24] Certainly, Mill's intellectual influence on liberalism was important and his liberalism included the enfranchisement of women (as another contributor to this volume has shown). J. S. Mill and other spokespeople for liberal democracy drew a parallel between women as a group and unenfranchised slaves and the working classes. Enfranchisement was necessary for all these groups, to ensure the removal of legal, social and educational disabilities, and would be a recognition of their common humanity and rights to citizenship:

> The suffrage is the turning point of women's cause; it alone will ensure them an equal hearing and fair play. With it they cannot long be denied any just right . . . without it their interests and feelings will always be a secondary consideration, and it will be thought of little consequence how much their sphere is circumscribed or how many modes of using their faculties are denied to them.[25]

It is this ideology which formed the basis of feminist arguments. But at least as important, in the feminist articulation of pro-suffrage arguments, was the discourse previously mentioned, concerning the requirement that women's public behaviour, including their speeches and feminist propaganda, should be such that their status and femininity was preserved, and their credibility as serious reformers and politicians maintained. Once again, it is instructive to quote Emily Davies, because of her shrewd understanding of this discourse and its importance in allowing women to work for their own emancipation through the 'cultural space' it created. Commenting on a rather 'bohemian' female friend's proposed speech on women's suffrage she advised as follows:

> I don't think it quite does to call the arguments on the other side 'foolish'. Of course they *are,* but it does not seem quite polite to say so. I should like to omit the paragraph about outlawry. You see, the enemy always maintains that the disabilities imposed upon women are not penal but solely intended for their good, and I find nothing irritates men so much as to attribute tyranny to them. I believe many of them do

really mean well, and . . . it seems fair to admit it and to show them that their well intentioned efforts are a *mistake,* not a crime.[26]

This statement shows a careful balance between conformity to and subversion of dominant values. The cautious attitude expressed by leaders of the suffrage movement was an acknowledgement of the situation in which women needed the support of powerful men. As Christabel Pankhurst, the suffragette leader, commented, nearly half a century later, women needed the vote to get the vote. Similarly, their political powerlessness led feminists to demand enfranchisement on the same terms as men, thus seeming to accept the property basis of the franchise which remained throughout the century, and losing the sympathy of working class activists who aimed at adult suffrage. Acceptance of the property qualification for enfranchisement excluded married women from suffragists' demands (married women could not hold property in their own right and to enfranchise them as joint owners was seen as 'double counting') and there was a major division within the movement on the issue of excluding married women.

In order to gain maximum parliamentary support, feminists argued that women's suffrage was not a party political issue, but although support did cut across party lines, most came from Liberals. Many women suffragists made the property basis of the franchise a positive justification for their demands, stating that it was unjust that men of little competence and education could vote because they owned property, while many able and competent women who owned at least as much property were excluded. Some Conservative suffragists thought middle-class women should be enfranchised as a hedge against runaway democracy and the dangers of an ill-educated working class male electorate.[27] We can clearly see here, an uneasy and contradictory alliance between democratic and élitist ideas.

More generally, the propaganda for women's suffrage was couched in the terms of the liberal individualism already discussed in the context of the women's education movement. For example, Helen Taylor, daughter of Harriet Taylor Mill (and beloved step-daughter of J. S. Mill), speaking at a public meeting in 1875 claimed that:

As the breath of political liberty stirs among the nation, it touches . . . women too with something of its glow. As a sense of justice, – . . . the noble ambition to do, to be, to live and to dare – thrills through a people, it awakes an answering chord from . . . women's hearts; as a possibility of a freer and larger and higher life is opened out . . . for men, the women too, . . . hope that they may enter in.[28]

Similarly, Jane Taylor claimed for every woman, through enfranchisement,

the right to belong to herself, as a self-contained individual . . . [and] the right that every soul stamped with the divine image, has a striving to perfect itself by the free exercise of its own faculties: the right to refuse submission to the sovereign rule of a fellow creature . . . the right to perfect liberty in fulfilling her duties in the world in accordance with nature's teachings and her own convictions.[29]

It was not simply as an abstract matter of justice that women demanded the vote, but because 'women have interests as a class which they themselves must defend when once they are aroused', because legislators had consistently ignored their interests. Arabella Shore stated this very clearly: women, she said,

have a right to a livelihood, a fair day's wages for a fair day's work . . . the means to live decently and with sufficient comfort to bring up a family decently . . . a right to just and equal laws, to have their interests, their persons and their property as well protected . . . as those of men are.[30]

Women suffragists argued that man-made laws, such as those which regulated prostitution (the Contagious Diseases Act), merely upheld the double moral standard and were 'an arbitrary flagrant violation of . . . the sacred right of human beings to the absolute sovereignty over their own persons'.[31] (Only prostitutes, not their male clients, were liable to compulsory medical examination under the CD Acts.) This claim by middle-class women for all women to have control over their own bodies not only has a modern ring to it, but then, as now, was an attack on the male dominated sexual exploitation of women. Although publicly condemned, the double moral standard – the belief that men's sexual desires were urgent and had to be indulged but that women must remain chaste – was part of the dominant value system. Feminists challenged this. Once enfranchised, they argued, middle-class women would have a duty to ensure legislation preventing the sexual and economic exploitation of their working class sisters.

The concern of middle-class women for the rights of lower class women was a genuine one, even if it was articulated as part of the patronising class relationships of the time. Although the concept of sisterhood belongs to modern, twentieth-century feminism, some consciousness of the sisterhood of all women and their common oppression by men, was expressed by nineteenth-century feminists, in contradiction to the dominant discourse of class and liberal individualism. Speaking in 1880, in a hall built on the site of the Peterloo massacre, Jessie Craigen reminded her audience that underlying the demand for women's enfranchisement was

> the unity of womanhood . . . We are separated by many barriers of caste, creed and education . . . but they do not separate the hearts of womanhood that beat in unity, nor the sunlight of God's justice that shines down upon rich and poor alike. In the name of this common womanhood we are gathered here . . . to raise our voices altogether to ask for justice.[32]

The overwhelmingly bourgeois nature of the ideology of the women's suffrage movement must be acknowledged. Like those of the women's education movement, the ideas were part of the ideological hegemony of Victorian values, yet at the same time they involved a critique of many of these values and the social and economic structures they supported. Despite the ultimate conservatism of liberal individualism, the use of this ideology by bourgeois feminists allowed them to claim rights for women as free individuals in terms of a dominant discourse easily understood. They were able too, from this standpoint, to criticise other aspects of the dominant ideology which contradicted the emphasis of liberal utilitarianism on the development of individual capacities and freedom, and at the same time argue that women were under-utilised in the important business of encouraging social progress.

Having established that granting women the rights and freedom they demanded would generally lead to social improvement, feminists were critical of politics itself, and of many of the injustices which were part of Victorian society. Victorian feminists who worked for improvements in women's education and for the enfranchisement of women hoped that the greater involvement of women in public life would result in a more prosperous, peaceful and humane society. More than a century after feminists were able to prove the intellectual capacities of women and a half century after the enfranchisement of women, it does not appear that such a society has been achieved. Despite the achievements of Victorian feminism, the continuing injustices of life in Britain in the 1980s should make us question the adequacy and analytical power of the dominant Victorian values they utilised.

Notes

All letters, pamphlets and suffrage society reports cited are located in the Fawcett Library, London, unless indicated otherwise.

1 Harriet Taylor Mill, 'The enfranchisement of women', in Alice S. Rossi (ed.), *John Stuart Mill and Harriet Taylor Mill: Essays on Sex Equality*, Chicago, 1970, p. 100.

2 Carol Dyhouse, *Girls Growing Up in Late Victorian and Edwardian England*, London, 1981, Chapter 5, is critical of the movement in this way. For studies which show both the strength of the dominant ideology and the challenge of feminism see Sara Delamont & Lorna Duffin (eds.), *The Nineteenth Century Woman: Her Cultural and Physical World*, London, 1978; Joan Burstyn, *Victorian Education and the Ideal of Womanhood*, London, 1980; and Martha Vicinus, *Independent Women: Work and Community for Single Women, 1850–1920, especially Chapter 4.*

3 For working class feminism see Barbara Taylor, *Eve and the New Jerusalem: Socialism and Feminism in the Nineteenth Century*, London, 1983, and Jill Liddington & Jill Norris, *One Hand Tied Behind Us: The Rise of the Women's Suffrage Movement*, London, 1978.

4 Although there was clearly not a consensus within the women's education movement, it is possible to discern the dominant ideas of the organised movement, as expressed by the leaders and in the published pamphlets, books, articles and addresses designed to gain public support.

5 Raymond V. Holt, *The Unitarian Contribution to Social Progress in England*, London, 1938; Frank R. Salter, *Dissenters and Public Affairs in Mid-Victorian England*, London, 1967; Torben Christensen, *Origin and History of Christian Socialism, 1848–54*, Aarhus, 1962, especially p. 11.

6 J. F. C. Harrison, *Living and Learning 1790–1960: A Study in the History of the English Adult Education Movement*, London, 1961, p. 145ff.

7 Barbara Leigh Smith (later Bodichon), *Women and Work*, London, 1857, p. 6.

8 *English Woman's Journal*, I, 1858, p. 362 (emphasis in the original).

9 Emily Davies, *The Higher Education of Women*, London, 1866, pp. 171–2.

10 Josephine Butler, *The Education and Employment of Women*, London, 1868, p. 16.

11 Maria Georgina Grey, *On the Education of Women: A Paper . . . Read at . . . the Society of Arts, May 31st 1871*, 2nd edn., London, 1871, p. 16 (emphasis in the original).

12 Maria Georgina Grey & Emily Shirreff, *Thoughts on Self Culture Addressed to Women*, London, 1850, 2 v., I, pp. 2 & 27–8 (emphasis in the original).

13 Grey & Shirreff, *Thoughts on Self-Culture*, I, p. 38.

14 Millicent Fawcett, 'The schools inquiry commissioners on the education of girls' (reprinted from *Fortnightly Review*, November 1868), in Henry Fawcett & Millicent Fawcett, *Essays and Lectures*, London, 1872, pp. 202–3.

15 Emily Davies, *Thoughts on Some Questions Relating to Women 1860–1908*, Cambridge, 1910, p. 6.

16 Dorothea Beale, 'On the education of girls', *Transactions of the National Association for the Protection of Social Science*, 1865, pp. 285–6.

17 Davies, *Higher Education*, pp. 56–8.

18 *English Woman's Journal*, I, 1858, p. 362.

19 Davies, *Higher Education*, pp. 95, 170. In a private letter she wrote: 'we scarcely know yet what occupations are really, and what only conventionally appropriate [for women]', also, 'as regards fitness. . . . It is difficult to see why, apart from habit, it should be good for girls to learn German and not good for them to learn Greek', Emily Davies to Thomas Dyke Acland, 28 December 1864, Autograph Collection of letters on the education of women.

20 *English Woman's Journal*, III, 1859, p. 319.

21 See Rosamund Billington, 'Ideology and feminism: why the suffragettes were "Wild Women" ', *Women's Studies International Forum*, V, 1982, pp. 663–74 for other examples.

22 Emily Davies to Henry Sidgwick, 31 December 1870, quoted in Barbara Stephen, *Emily Davies and Girton College*, London, 1927, pp. 252–3. Also quoted in the same volume, p. 248, see Emily Davies to Anna Richardson [12 January], 1870, 'you can scarcely understand how disturbing it would be to have 2,000 undergraduates, most of them idle and pleasure loving, close to your doors. . . . I do not say that will always be so. I am only speaking of English human nature as it has been made by social habits and by the system of separating boys and girls from childhood'.

23 Emily Davies to H. R. Tomkinson, 14 November 1865, quoted in Stephen, *Emily Davies*, p. 109.

24 R. K. Webb, *Modern England From the 18th Century to the Present*, London, 1969, Chapters 4–8, quotation p. 295. On Mill's influence also see John Vincent, *The Formation of the Liberal Party, 1857–1868*, London, 1966, 183 ff, and John Stuart Mill, *A Logical*

Critique of Sociology, ed. Ronald Fletcher, London, 1971, pp. 16–20, Fletcher's introduction.

25 National Society for Women's Suffrage, *Report*, 1869, p. 13.

26 Emily Davies to Mme Bodichon, 14 November 1865, quoted in Stephen, *Emily Davies*, p. 108.

27 Constance Rover, *Women's Suffrage and Party Politics in Britain 1866–1914*, London, 1966; David Morgan, *Suffragists and Liberals: The Politics of Woman Suffrage in Britain*, Oxford, 1975. Also see Rosamund Billington, 'The women's education and suffrage movements, 1850–1914: innovation and institutionalisation', unpublished Ph.D thesis, Hull University, 1976, for the major suffrage movement sources, which detail the ideas of and divisions within the movement.

28 *Miss Helen Taylor. Speech at a Public Meeting . . .*, Manchester, 1875, leaflet in *Women's Suffrage Publications*, 1875–1878, bound pamphlets.

29 Edinburgh Women's Suffrage Society, *Report*, 1872, p. 15.

30 Arabella Shore, *What Women Have A Right To: A Lecture*, London, [1879], pp. 3, 9, in *Women's Suffrage Publications*, 1871–1880 bound pamphlets.

31 William Count, *Electoral Reform*, Bristol & London, 1880, p. 14, in *Women's Suffrage Pamphlets*, 1871–1880, Library. Count was the general secretary of the National Union of Working Women.

32 *Miss Jessie Craigen on Women Suffrage*, in *Women's Suffrage Pamphlets*, 1871–1880.

9 *Joan Bellamy*

Barriers of silence; women in Victorian fiction

The constraints on women in Victorian society are familiar to any student of the period. These constraints operated in every area of political, social, economic and legal rights. They were upheld by a complex structure of morality, ideas and theories which found powerful expression in the art and literature of the period, as well as in theology and philosophy.

The many and far-reaching changes in Victorian society could not leave women's conditions and aspirations static and immobile and inevitably tensions developed around demands for change in their position in society and the powerful systems that had hitherto established their subordination and even their acquiescence.

In 1837 when Queen Victoria came to the throne, married women had no property rights, not even in the proceeds of their own earnings, they had no rights to the custody of their own children, divorce from a husband was practically impossible, they had no vote, they were utterly excluded from the universities and the professions, except the teaching of the very young and of older girls.

One significant change resulted from the rapid expansion of the Victorian publishing industry and the reading public which included a large proportion of women. It offered to a small but significant section of women of the expanding middle classes opportunities for earning a living by writing, instead of teaching, sewing or remaining dependent on the charity of relatives. Writing for this new public did not require the sort of education reserved for boys intending to enter the learned professions which were closed to women, but it did offer to some few bolder spirits avenues for self-expression, intellectual activity and economic independence.

For most women of the propertyless classes faced with the necessity of working outside the home for a living, there was generally hard toil in badly paid jobs, in unprotected conditions, in domestic service, sewing, industry, the mines and agriculture. Limited legal measures achieved throughout the rest of the century ameliorated some aspects of women's conditions, but progress was slow and complicated and nowhere more so than in the field of ideas. Demands for reforms in most spheres of women's social life generated debate about the very 'nature' of women, their role and function.

To what extent did the Victorian novel participate, explicitly or indirectly in that debate? How far did it express women's desire to break through the barrier of silence surrounding their aspirations, concealing the quality of their lives, or how far did it collude in the preservation of that barrier, against which women had to clamour and protest?

While Victorian novels are not to be regarded as simple tracts they did enter the field of the social, moral and ideological debates of the time including those bearing on women's lives.

Novels were widely read by women, often read aloud in the family circle. They are generally concerned with individual development, moral crisis and personal relationships, love and marriage, in a recognisable historical and social setting.

There was an acknowledged commitment from many nineteenth-century artists to the view of the powerful moral influence of art and the correspondingly serious moral responsibility of the artist.

In *Adam Bede* George Eliot declares to her readers: 'I aspire to give no more than a faithful account of men and things as they have mirrored themselves in my mind. The mirror is doubtless defective, the outlines will sometimes be disturbed, the reflection faint or confused: but I feel as much bound to tell you as precisely as I can what that reflection is, as if I were in the witness box narrating my experience on oath.' On another occasion she stated 'I am content to tell my simple story, without trying to make things seem better than they are; dreading nothing indeed but falsity, which, in spite of one's best efforts, there is reason to dread.'[1]

Eliot seems here to express a theory of art as reflection
she must have been acutely aware through her actual practic
novel writing that she was engaged in a work of *constructing* a literary artefact, in inventing, imagining, selecting, deciding to emphasise one thing rather than another. She was, like all writers, alert to the power of the publishers, who in turn operated with an eye on the circulating libraries and their *de facto* censorship in catering for the middle-class reader.

Given the conviction about the moral influence of literature and the assumption that females were sensitive, even frail and easily lead, it was no wonder that some publishers were reluctant to allow their writers to acknowledge sexuality even within marriage, and certainly it was rare for it to be dealt with outside it; for the most part women's sexuality was ignored, even denied. The sensibilities of the conventional reader tended to dominate the literary scene.

Sexually experienced women outside marriage, if treated at all, were depicted as fallen women, required in the end to die, preferably redeemed through an act of self-sacrifice – Nancy in *Oliver Twist* for example, though as Patricia Thompson points out Nancy's profession as a prostitute is so indirectly suggested that many readers remain unaware of her moral status.[2]

The unmarried mother also had to be treated with great caution, even if she 'falls' through ignorance, as Hetty does in George Eliot's *Adam Bede,* and Ruth in the novel of the same name by Elizabeth Gaskell. Ruth lives an agonised life of guilt and self-sacrificing devotion to her illegitimate child and dies. Hetty commits infanticide and is hanged. Lady Deadlock in Dickens' *Bleak House* having successfully guarded her guilty secret for years, dies nevertheless. With *Ruth* Elizabeth Gaskell at least in 1853 opened up a challenge to concealment which Hardy in *Tess of the D'Urbervilles* was to take up more boldly in 1891, though not without meeting the shock of outraged protest.

The unmarried woman, too old to be regarded as any longer in the marriage market, is unlikely to be the heroine of a novel though sometimes an admirable secondary character.

So-called 'surplus' women were regarded as a problem in Victorian times. There were articles in the serious press encouraging the organisation of their mass emigration to the colonies where there were 'surplus' men. These attitudes deplored the idea of the independent, forceful woman, (the term 'strong-minded' was pejorative). The destiny of the true heroine was to marry and it is with a declaration of love, or the proposal that the nineteenth-century novel generally ends.

But despite the efforts to suppress and to enforce conformity to a particular stereotype, novelists did raise discomfiting questions and enter into aspects of the prevailing debates at the same time as women reformers were demanding new rights and opportunities.

The nineteenth-century novel's concerns, particularly with family relationships, love and marriage, the views about its function in moral life, combine to offer a particularly rich field of investigation into the connections between literature and women's position in society and concepts about their social and moral function.

They offer a picture of women within a specific social world which they create for us. The destinies they work out for their heroines, the nature of the language, imagery, narrative comment and plot they create and what this reveals about the writer's and reader's assumptions, explicit or implicit, help us to develop an imaginative grasp of the ideologies of the period relating to women's place in society.

A basic work of Victorian ideology is Samuel Smiles's *Self-Help.* It assumes an expanding world of economic opportunities and upward social mobility for the energetic and ambitious man. Smiles does not seem to have considered that these opportunities were available for women and indeed as the middle-classes expanded in Victorian society in number and prosperity, their women's lives, paradoxically, contracted. No longer engaged in the economic activity of the family, women were cut off from other forms of productive labour outside the home. Excluded from the new professions they were confined to the home and family life, as wives, mothers, carers. Their approved role was now to exercise a pure, self-sacrificial moral influence. This was not some specifically male point of view. It was held and advocated by many women including writers who resisted their more liberated sisters' demands for change.

Sarah Stickney Ellis, writing in 1850 in *The Daughters of England* declared:

Can it be a subject of regret that she is called upon, so much as a man, to calculate, to compete, to struggle, but rather to occupy a sphere in which the elements of discord cannot with propriety be admitted – in which beauty and order are expected to denote her presence, and where the exercise of benevolence is the duty she is most frequently called upon to perform?[3]

Objections to such a prescription for women's lives arise as much from Stickney's lack of realism about how women actually lived as from its advocacy of life denying passivity.

As Stickney was writing, women were beginning to campaign for rights regarding property and divorce, developing more professional philanthropic organisations, seeking new areas of employment for working women, raising the demand for higher education, and for the vote. The debate was launched.

In that context of challenge and resistance we examine four outstanding novels in the nineteenth-century English canon, *Jane Eyre,* 1847, *Great Expectations,* 1860, *Middlemarch,* 1870, and finally *Tess of the D'Urbervilles,* 1891. How did they engage with some of the issues of this debate? Even when they were not directly operating in the field of the debate, in which direction they did seem consciously or not to be leading the reader?

Jane Eyre was in many ways a new kind of heroine, self-supporting and typical in being a teacher. She is in many ways characteristic of the nineteenth-century Romantic movement. Alienated from society, despising hypocrisy and self-deception, identifying with nature and above all yearning for freedom and self-realisation, she is in the grip of the contradiction between the spontaneous romantic needs of her individual personality and the pressures of the 'real' world of work and social convention.

After leaving Lowood School to be a governess at Thornfield Hall she still aspires to 'other and more vivid kinds of goodness' and excuses herself as follows:

It is in vain to say human beings ought to be satisfied with tranquillity: they must have action; and they will make it if they cannot find it. Millions are condemned to a stiller doom than mine, and millions are in silent revolt against their lot. Nobody knows how many rebellions besides political rebellions ferment in the masses of life which people earth. Women are supposed to be very calm generally; but women feel just as men feel; they need exercise for their faculties, and a field for their efforts as much as their brothers do; they suffer from too rigid a restraint, too absolute a stagnation, precisely as men would suffer; and it is narrow-minded in their more privileged fellow-creatures to say that they ought to confine themselves to making puddings and knitting stockings, to playing on the piano and embroidering bags. It is thoughtless to condemn them, or laugh at them, if they seek to do more or learn more than custom has pronounced necessary for their sex.[4]

Rochester longing for a loving and intellectual relationship, and having 'won' Jane Eyre, reverts to type treating the bride-to-be as an object of conspicuous consumption.

The hour spent at Millcote was a somewhat harassing one to me. Mr Rochester obliged me to go to a certain silk warehouse: there I was ordered to choose half a dozen dresses. I hated the business, I begged leave to defer it: no – it should be gone through now. By dint of entreaties expressed in energetic whispers, I reduced the half-dozen to two: these, however, he vowed he would select himself. With anxiety I watched his eye rove over the gay stores: he fixed on a rich silk of the most brilliant amethyst dye, and a superb pink satin. I told him in a new series of whispers, that he might buy me a gold gown and a silver bonnet. With infinite difficulty, for he was stubborn as a stone, I persuaded him to make an exchange in favour of a sober black satin and pearl-grey silk. 'It might pass for the present', he said, 'but he would yet see me glittering like a parterre.'[5]

At this distance from 1847 it is perhaps not easy to grasp the radical, rebellious quality and tone of a novel in which the heroine passionately loves and physically desires her own employer. Jane is governess to Rochester's 'ward', probably his illegitimate daughter. She accepts his proposal of marriage only to discover, literally, at the altar his intention of committing bigamy: his wife, hopelessly mad, is incarcerated in the turret at the top of the house!

It would be easy to develop a conventional ending to such a plot. Surely Brontë should have her heroine spurn the detestable villain, find true love with a noble hero who would love and cherish her, etc., etc. Jane Eyre, on the contrary, persists in loving Rochester passionately, tearing herself away from the overwhelming temptation to become his mistress. she later refuses another offer of marriage and mysteriously, is recalled to Rochester. It is, however, at this point that Brontë 'conforms'. Rochester is blinded and maimed as a result of the fire caused by the mad wife, who conveniently for the purposes of the plot and a conventional happy ending dies in the conflagration. We have here not the fallen woman redeemed through suffering but the fallen man. To be worthy of the heroine, Rochester must purge his moral guilt symbolised by physical maiming.

At the close of the book therefore Brontë reverts to the powerful formal convention of the nineteenth-century novel ending happily in the marriage of the heroine. The final chapter of the novel opens with the now famous words, 'Reader, I married him', the conventional order is reversed; not 'Dear Reader, he married me'. Jane Eyre at the close is still an active agent! Charlotte Bronte was not a sympathiser of the women's movement, but she joined issue in the debate on women's nature and women's right to self realisation and expression through her art.

The critical reception of the book provoked defence of convention and hostility.

> We cannot wonder that the hypothesis of a male author should have been started; (Brontë published under the non-de-plume Currer Bell) or ladies especially should still be rather determined to uphold it. For a book more unfeminine, both in its excellence and its defects, it would be hard to find in the annals of female authorship. Throughout there is masculine power, breadth and shrewdness, combined with masculine hardness, coarseness and freedom of expression. Slang is not rare. The humour is frequently produced by a use of Scripture at which one is rather sorry to have smiled. The love-scenes glow with a fire as fierce as that of Sappho, and somewhat more fulginous. There is an intimate acquaintance with the worst parts of human nature, a practised sagacity in discovering the latent ulcer, and a ruthless rigour in exposing it, which must command our admiration, but are almost startling in one of the softer sex. *Jane Eyre* professes to be an autobiography, and we think it is likely that in some essential respects it is so. If the authoress has not been, like her heroine, an oppressed orphan, a starved and bullied charity-school girl, and a despised and slighted governess (and the intensity of feeling which she shows in speaking of the wrongs of this last class seems to prove that they have been her own), at all events we fear she is one of whom the world has not been kind. And, assuredly, never has unkindness been more cordially repaid. Never was there a better hater. Every page burns with moral Jacobinism. 'Unjust, unjust', is the burden of every reflection upon the things and powers that be. All virtue is but well-masked vice, all religious profession and conduct is but the whitening of the sepulchre, all self-denial is but deeper selfishness.[6]

Brontë was stung to defend herself and remained defiant. She went on to explore still further the theme of the young woman searching for ways of living a more vivid and satisfying and independent life in a world which resisted her ambitions.

The autobiographical form of Jane Eyre was a typical narrative mode of nineteenth-century Romanticism. *Great Expectations* by Charles Dickens is the story of the hero recounted by himself and describing in particular his own complex, moral development when, as a boy of humble origins, he yearns to become a 'gentleman' in order to marry his social superior, Estella.

Pip is befriended by his lawyer's clerk Wemmick. The ideal of the nineteenth-century middle-class home, a retreat from the struggles and temptations of life in the harsh world outside is embodied, humorously and vividly but not critically, in Dickens' picture of Wemmick's house at Walworth. As he leaves the world of Jaggers, of crime and punishment, Wemmick's wooden impassivity progressively relaxes, he becomes genial and benevolent. His home is an idiosyncratic mock fortress designed by himself with turrets, drawbridge, a moat, even a cannon. It symbolises a place of refuge and isolation from the grim world outside.

> After I have crossed this bridge I hoist it up . . . so . . and cut off the communication.[7]

Great Expectations traces the moral decline and redemption of a young man, but his fate and values are influenced by women, Estella and Miss Havisham; the one cold, proud and unloving, the other bent on wreaking revenge on men. It is a commonplace of Dickens criticism that he seems incapable of depicting women characters convincingly, 'in the round'. They are either vapid heroines, who conform to the stereotype of women as passive, dependent, patient and pure on the one hand, or on the other active but dangerous. In this novel, Biddy notwithstanding, Dickens has created mainly dangerous women. They have to be tamed.

Pip achieves redemption through his growing sympathy for Magwitch, the convict, his generous help to Herbert, his friend. His near-fatal illness in which he is nursed by Joe, the gentle blacksmith and surrogate father, symbolises his passage to moral salvation. Miss Havisham in her turn repents but redemption for her is symbolised by the fire in which she meets her death. Estella with 'a saddened softened light of the once proud eyes' becomes finally capable of loving through suffering at the hands of the brutal Drummle. The termagent, Mrs Joe is violently assaulted by Orlick, struck down by the handcuffs which shackled Magwitch. She is reduced to virtual imbecility and when finally Orlick is brought to confront her 'there was an air of humble propitiation in all she did such as I have seen pervade the bearing of a child towards a hard master'.

The word 'master' recurs in the scene where Jaggers, as the young men look on, displays his housekeeper's powerful wrists and hands and his ability to keep her tame.

> Her entrapped hand was on the table, but she had already put her other hand behind her waist. 'Master', she said in a low voice with her eyes attentively and entreatingly fixed upon him, 'don't'.
> 'I'll show you a wrist', repeated Mr Jaggers, with immovable determination to show it. 'Molly, let them see your wrists.' 'Master', she again murmured, 'Please'.
> 'Molly', said Mr Jaggers, not looking at her but obstinately looking at the opposite side of the room, 'let them see both your wrists. Show them. Come'.[8]

Jaggers, whose motivation beneath his bullying manner is humane, has saved Estella's mother from the scaffold and he treats her still as a wild beast; 'he kept down the old, wild, violent nature whenever he saw an inkling of its breaking out, by asserting his power over her in the old way'.[9]

In *Great Expectations* men are the centres of moral force and power. Women who seek to usurp that power like Miss Havisham, like Mrs Joe, or who, like Estella, deny women's essential nature as loving, caring and dependent, or who wreak actual violence, like Estella's mother, are to be crushed, tamed, even destroyed. Powerfully criticial as Dickens was on a wide range of social evils, his vision did not include the emancipated woman. Insofar as they connect at all with that particular debate his novels reinforce the *status quo*.

In *Middlemarch* (1870) George Eliot undertook a powerful and ambitious novel which seeks to deal with the complex interconnections between individual character and fate and the general movement of social life in a provincial town in the Midlands around the years 1829–32, during the period of agitation for Parliamentary reform.

In Dorothea Brooke, one of the two central characters, Eliot takes up the familiar theme of the young woman chafing at the constraints of a life without purpose, frustrated by lack of useful knowledge and opportunity. Her limitations and possibilities are summarised in the epigraph to the first chapter;

> Since I can do no good because a woman, reach constantly at something that is near it.

Already we are being warned of an outcome for Dorothea that will rest firmly within the bounds of the social possibility which corresponds to the England of the 1830s, not of Eliot's own 1870s.

Dorothea's seriousness and piety, her contempt for social frivolity mark her out as different from both the gentlewomen of her own class and the wives and daughters of the prosperous bourgeois of Middlemarch. She is seen as unpredictable and consequently possibly something of a risk in marriage. Proof of her oddness is her determination to marry the elderly Casaubon under the illusion that he will lead her into a world of expanding knowledge and purposive intellectual activity. He is in fact emotionally frigid, and an unsuccessful scholar toiling fruitlessly in an outdated area of research. Dorothea's first marriage is predictably unhappy and frustrating. It is through her second marriage following Casaubon's death that she reaches out to the limited good foreshadowed in the epigraph. This marriage, too, defies public opinion. It takes her into a class socially lower than her own, but for all the unconventionality it offers no possibility of independent action and identity, only the prospect of being the helpmeet of Ladislaw now able to embark on a political career in the aftermath of the Reform Bill.

It is through marriage that Lydgate, the young doctor is destroyed. With his false views, which he shares with the generality of society, of a wife merely as solace for the tired husband, passive and dependent in every way, he marries the beautful Rosamund Vincey, the perfect product of education for the marriage market. Though Eliot is critical of Dorothea's wilfulness and egoism, she represents her essentially as a victim of the pettiness of women's education and moves her through a series of trials from which she emerges with enhanced moral force, sympathy for, and knowledge of, others. For Rosamund, Eliot offers no excuses; she is seen not as victim but as a threat, 'a pot of basil feeding on men's brains'. On only one occasion does she act selflessly and positively for good.

The two genuinely educated women in the novel are Mary Garth and her mother. Balanced, shrewd, morally strong and more sensible than their menfolk, they nevertheless engage in subterfuge to maintain the myth of male authority and superiority.

Middlemarch engages with a great many intellectual and social issues of Eliot's own times, even though it is set some forty years earlier and it is necessary to be aware of the risk of distortion in the discussion of one particular aspect of the work in isolation. However, while women's position, their education and their social influence are not the *only* concern of the book, they are an important element in it. How could a realist novel aiming to be a study of a whole network of social relations not be concerned with women and engage with aspects of contemporary views of that situation? Eliot was in fact deeply interested in women's education and in the question of women's rights. As she became famous, different sections of the women's movement were naturally anxious to enlist her support even though she avoided publicity herself, living as she did out of wedlock with George Henry Lewes who was married to someone else.

As early as 1855 she had written an article which included discussion of Mary Wollstonecraft's *The Vindication of the Rights of Woman,* of 1792 and from which she quoted the following.

> Women, in particular, all want to be ladies, which is simply to have nothing to do, but listlessly to go they scarcely care where, for they cannot tell what. But what have women to do in society? I may be asked, but to loiter with easy grace, surely you would not condemn them all to suckle fools and chronicle small beer. No. Women might certainly study the art of healing and may be physicians as well as nurses. Business of various kinds they might likewise pursue, if they were educated in a more orderly manner. Women would not then marry for support, as men accept of places under government, and neglect the implied duties.[10]

Eliot develops this characteristically rationalist argument. She argues that such wives as Mary Wollstonecraft describes are a burden to men, ignorant and silly and are consequently dangerous partners. She foreshadows Lydgate's fate. Certainly the Garths' virtues are seen as a function of their superior education.

As Eliot grew older and more socially respectable she seems to have modified her views on women's rights. She supported the establishment of Girton College but hoped that higher education would be used not to challenge men in their professions but to make women more effective in their philanthropic duties. In 1866 she refused to support the petition for extension of the franchise to women on the grounds that women's harder lot ought to be 'the basis for a sublimer resignation in woman and a more regenerating tenderness in man'.[11]

Though writing *Middlemarch* more than twenty years later than Charlotte Brontë's *Jane Eyre*, and a novel deeply concerned with marriage, Eliot never emulated her in depicting the power of sexual passion in women. Dorothea's sexual frustration and misery on her honeymoon is presented extremely indirectly. In love scenes the characters are reduced to sentimental infantilism. Mary's and Fred's love is simply an extension of their childhood affection, Rosamund precipitates Lydgate's proposal as she weeps for self-pity and she is described 'as natural as she had ever been when she was five years old',[12] Dorothea and Ladislaw declaring their love 'stood with their hands clasped, like two children',[13] and Dorothea speaks 'in a sobbing childlike way'. All this is worlds away from one bitter debate in progress when the novel appeared. The Ladies National Association for the Repeal of the Contagious Diseases Act were seeking to protect women prostitutes from the threat of arbitrary arrest and detention and the establishment of licensed brothels. The ladies of the Association were attacked, accused of immorality and coarseness in a storm of outrage and abuse. True ladies were not supposed to know about prostitution and venereal disease. Given the ferocity of this debate, and others like it, in relation to women's rights it is no wonder that publishers and authors were still reluctant to challenge sexual convention. George Eliot does not take up the cudgels directly for any women's cause in *Middlemarch* but neither does she, so far as Lydgate and Dorothea are concerned, collude with sentimental, idealised happy endings. Dorothea marries and contributes in but a modest way to a possible growing stream of good. Lydgate defeated by Rosamund, becomes a fashionable doctor and dies young and disappointed. In Eliot's later novel *Daniel Deronda,* there are more challenging elements: a discarded mistress and illegitimate children; the heroine does not marry the hero, but is left seeking to work out her own independent destiny. Once more the stereotypes were coming under challenge.

Leslie Stephen (father of Virginia Woolf and Vanessa Bell), editor of the Cornhill magazine, was preparing to publish Thomas Hardy's novel *Far From the Madding Crowd.* He was very uneasy about one of the key situations. Fanny Robbins, not the heroine of the novel, bears an illegitimate child; she suffers terribly and along with the baby dies, a conventional enough outcome. Stephens, however, was writing to Hardy, 'I should somehow be glad to omit the baby'.[14] Stephen's plea went unheeded and seventeen years on Hardy offered in *Tess of the d'Urbervilles,* seduction, illegitimate baby and the mother as heroine, moreover a working class woman. To describe Tess as 'A pure woman' was to lob a powerful explosive into the very centre of a system of values whose moral basis rests on the notion of female chastity, denial of women's sexuality before marriage, and a virtual market price on virginity. It is a system which equates chastity with purity. The subtitle succinctly proposes new meanings for purity, Tess's qualities of honesty, spontaneity and capacity for love.

Hardy creates a world of continuously conflicting moral systems and values which engage his characters not only in conflicts with each other but within their own divided selves. In Tess's world women work to keep themselves, they support each other in innumerable acts of solidarity, they drink, they fight, and they feel, are even destroyed by, sexual passion, but for the most part, they operate shrewdly within the male dominated system to avoid destruction. (Joan Darbeyfield is not so much outraged by Tess's seduction or by Angel's rejection to her, as by her daughter's apparent incompetence in getting from men what seems to be due to her.)

It is not her companions in the harvest field who point the finger at Tess, as she suckles her baby, on the contrary, it is Tess, with her divided self, who induces her own sense of shame and guilt. 'Most of the misery had been generated by her conventional aspect, and not by her innate sensations', writes Hardy.[15]

The burden of guilt that Tess carries seems to be the consequence of her own modernity, her schooling, cutting her off from organic instinctual life and it is her sense of shame and inadequacy, as well as her romantic illusions about Angel, which disarm her in face of his rejection of her. She accepts his view of her; 'The punishment you have measured out to me is deserved – I do know that – well deserved – and you are right and just to be angry with me.'[16] Angel for all his self-congratulatory modern enlightenment about Christian belief and dogma, is unable to challenge the powerful and sexual conventions of the middle-class pious world from which he springs. Tess murders her seducer. Tess's tragedy is not that 'Justice is done' and she dies, but ironically that living she has become more deeply divided than ever within herself. 'But he (Angel) had a vague consciousness of one thing, though it was not clear to him till later; that this original Tess had spiritually ceased to recognise the body before him as hers – allowing it to drift, like a corpse upon the current, in a direction dissociated from its living will.'[17]

In the preface of the fifth edition of *Tess,* Hardy mentions 'a spirited public and private criticism', which attacked the novel's attitudes to religion, its style, and, of course, the fact that it is one 'wherein the great campaign of the heroine begins after an event in her experience which has usually been treated as fatal to her part of protagonist, or at least as the virtual ending of her enterprises and hopes'. Put more simply Tess, not a virgin, is unqualified as a heroine of a conventional novel.

While he insisted that 'a novel is an impression, not an argument',[18] Hardy did not seek to minimise the importance of its effect. 'So densely is the world thronged that any shifting of positions, even the best warranted advance, galls somebody's kibe. Such shiftings often begin in sentiment, and such sentiment sometimes begins in a novel.'[19]

So Hardy declares his conviction in the power and influence of the novel and his view of the novelists' responsibility to persist in challenging the upholders of false, oppressive conventions which stereotype women and reinforce their oppression.

Although the debate about woman's nature and her place in

society was shifting in the direction of change, it was still somewhat easier for a male author to carry forward the challenge than for a woman writer: Virginia Woolf writing after the end of Queen Victoria's reign still testified to that and indicated the distances yet to be travelled.

Notes

1 George Eliot, ed. Stephen Gill, *Adam Bede,* Penguin English Library, Harmondsworth, 1980, p. 121.

2 Patricia Thomson, *The Victorian Heroine, A Changing Ideal 1837,* London, 1956, p. 120.

3 Sarah Stickney Ellis, 'The Daughters of England, 1850', in C. Bauer and L. Ritt (eds.), *Free and Ennobled,* Oxford, 1979, pp. 13–14.

4 Charlotte Bronte, *Jane Eyre,* ed. Q. D. Leavis, Penguin English Library, Harmondsworth, 1966, p. 141.

5 *Ibid.,* p. 296.

6 'Christian Remembrance', April 1848, cited Cicely Havely, *Study Companion to 'Jane Eyre',* An Arts Foundation Course, The Open University, Milton Keynes, 1978.

7 Charles Dickens, *Great Expectations,* introduction by Angus Calder, Penguin English Library, 1972, p. 229.

8 *Ibid.,* p. 236.

9 *Ibid.,* p. 425.

10 *Essays of George Eliot,* ed. Thomas Pinney, London, 1962, p. 204.

11 Letter to John Morley, cited Gordon S. Haight, *George Eliot, a Biography,* Oxford, 1978, p. 396.

12 George Eliot, *Middlemarch,* ed. W. J. Harvey, Penguin English Library, Harmondsworth, 1972, p. 335.

13 *Ibid.,* p. 868.

14 For a more detailed discussion of this correspondence see Patricia Stubbs, *Women and Fiction,* Harvester, Brighton, 1979, p. 21.

15 Thomas Hardy, *Tess of the d'Urbervilles,* introduction by P. N. Furbank, New Wessex edition, Macmillan, London, 1974, p. 127.

16 *Ibid.,* p. 383.

17 *Ibid.,* p. 429.

18 *Ibid.,* p. 30.

19 *Ibid.,* p. 31.

A further reading list

Patricia Stubbs, *Women and Fiction,* The Harvester Press, 1979.

Mary Jacobus (ed.), *Women Writing and Writing about Women,* London, 1979.

Jenni Calder, *Women and Marriage in Victorian Fiction,* London, 1976.

Virginia Woolf, *A Room of One's Own*, Penguin, 1945.
Elaine Showalter, *A Literature of Their Own*, London, 1978.
Ellen Moers, *Literary Women*, London, 1978.

10 *Louis Billington*

Revivalism and popular religion

The Evangelical Awakening of the eighteenth century created Methodism, promoted a powerful new party within the Church of England and revitalised old dissent. Although often in disagreement, these movements shared a core of beliefs at the centre of which was the concept of conversion or 'new birth', a personal experience of repentance, forgiveness and cleansing from sin. A convert demonstrated this rebirth by adopting a new life style within a supportive congregation of like-minded believers whose language and behaviour marked them off from the worldly and the fashionable.[1] By Victoria's reign, evangelicalism had become respectable and powerful, 'the strongest binding force' in England according to G. M. Young in his classic account of the Victorian Age. Many historians have also emphasised the importance of evangelical religion in promoting political order and a class based morality.[2] Mrs Alexander summed up one version of this carefully ordered, deferential world in her famous children's hymn, 'All Things Bright and Beautiful':

> The rich man in his castle,
> The poor man at his gate,
> God made them, high or lowly,
> And order'd their estate.[3]

While anxious to preserve order, evangelicals also saw themselves as the conscience of the nation in the van of the anti-slavery and other humanitarian movements, but their beliefs also led them to create perhaps the most notorious symbol of nineteenth-century religious life, the 'Victorian Sunday' which has since become such a byword for extreme boredom and languor that few modern advocates of the restoration of Victorian values have attempted to revive it.[4]

If early Victorian England saw the continued growth of evangelical agencies designed to regulate a deferential lower class, the same era also witnessed the final phase of a more popular version of evangelicalism which enabled thousands of working people to develop a religious culture more in keeping with their own needs and aspirations. This popular evangelicalism found its most radical expression among the numerous sects which broke away from an increasingly authoritarian and socially respectable Wesleyan Methodism in the early decades of the nineteenth century. Quaker and Independent Methodists, Magic and Primitive Methodists, Gospel Trumpeters and Bible Christians are only the better known of a plethora of sects which drew upon the evangelical tradition to fashion a noisy, experiential religion which fostered a sense of shared and equal participation among its converts.[5] It was a syncretic religion which absorbed many elements of older folk beliefs, and it posited a magical world, where cunning men and wise women still held sway. These popular sects provided a supportive community which helped to sustain an autonomous sense of identity and purpose among small farmers, rural labourers, artisans and factory workers, experiencing the social dislocations of a period of rapid economic change.[6]

Although a few sects abandoned Wesleyan forms of government in favour of congregational autonomy, most retained typical Methodist structures which linked each local congregation through a circuit with a national conference which was the governing body. Unlike the Wesleyans, however, most of these sects gave equal power and representation to lay people, and the ethos within the sects worked to prevent the development of a separate and superior clerical order. The bulk of the work of teaching, preaching and evangelism was always undertaken by an unpaid laity, and indeed, a few Methodist sects were so anti-clerical as to oppose a paid ministry. Even when it was retained, the paid itinerant or travelling preachers were drawn from rank and file members, and distinguished for their spiritual gifts rather than superior or separate educational or professional training. Their pay was little better than that of the majority of their membership and was often barely sufficient to maintain a family.[7]

Low pay and lack of professional training marked the Methodist itinerants off from the evangelical clergy of more respectable denominations, but an even more dramatic symbol of that social gulf was the sects' acceptance of women into the ranks of both unpaid and paid preachers. Among the Primitive Methodists, Bible Christians and smaller sects, women preachers played key roles in establishing and sustaining congregations. Heroic 'mothers in Israel' were in the van of evangelistic campaigns which carried the gospel into the 'dark' regions of the country.[8] The Wesleyan Methodists' ban on female preaching in 1803 marked a key stage in the growing divide between official Wesleyanism and popular evangelicalism. Wesleyans, like Anglicans and Nonconformists, relied heavily upon women for fund raising and philanthropic work, but preaching and the work of the ministry were not defined by them as part of women's, 'proper sphere'. From early in the century, the Methodist sects defended female preaching, and well into the 1840s advocated a religious equality for women which contrasts sharply with conventional stereotypes of Victorian women's religious roles. A few energetic and gifted women found even the ministerial regulations of the Methodist sects irksome, and followed their own paths, forming a circuit of churches in the slums of the West Riding and issuing their own hymn book which tried to render meaningful the experiences of the destitute poor.[9]

The Methodist sects were suspicious of system and order in worship which impeded the working of the Holy Spirit, and their popular evangelism was essentially an invocation of direct supernatural action. Salvation was within the grasp of all, and sensational means were often necessary to extend the Lord's Kingdom. Much popular revivalism took place in the open air with street preaching, processions and vigorous singing. Large scale camp meetings, day or longer gatherings for continuous prayer, singing and preaching, were introduced from the United States, and were often held in competition with village feasts or parish wakes.[10] The Primitive Methodists celebrated the Jubilee of the camp meeting tradition in 1857, when they felt that the nation was still in need of plain, simple and energetic preaching. When pressing sinners to repent and receive the Holy

Spirit, preachers used extempore and colloquial language to stir their audiences' emotions, and sinners were encouraged to find release for their feelings by shouting, weeping and violent physical movements. Popular revival meetings were very different from modern stereotypes of staid Victorian chapel worship.[11] Among the most enthusiastic sects, emotional worship led to form of 'gospel dance' very similar to that emerging among the New Light revivalist sects in the United States. In Cheshire, for example, one Independent Methodist preacher found a congregation which at mid-century still delighted in clearing the room of furniture, joining hands and singing 'Step into the chariot of love, of love, of love'. Then they began to jump together in the most violent manner until they fell exhausted to the floor. Other preachers reported similar congregations of humble and devoted people who celebrated the rich blessings of Christianity in this vigorous fashion.[12]

'Gospel dancers' were not alone in putting music and song at the centre of their worship. Since the late eighteenth century, New Light revivalists in the United States had developed a tradition of spiritual songs very different in their words and music from the classic hymnody of Isaac Watts or Charles Wesley. Sung to well known popular airs, the spiritual songs were published in a succession of cheap collections which quickly crossed the Atlantic and grew to meet the needs of the people. Often close to doggerel, they embodied the actual language, experiences and hopes of working people, and the words and tunes were so simple or familiar that the songs could be quickly grasped by the illiterate, or those too poor to buy hymn books. Some collections were so popular that printers found it worth their while to issue pirated editions for their own profit.[13] At best, the spiritual songs possess a simple, vivid language which conveys 'a sense of being overpowered and simultaneously empowered by the Divine Spirit', and this vitality kept them popular for decades.[14] Such songs shocked respectable Christians by their casual informality and intimacy with God, as well as their use of popular tunes. The Wesleyan Methodists quickly objected to the 'light indecorous style of music of these effusions brought over from America', and this condemnation, plus a ban on American style camp meetings, came within five years of the Wesleyans' opposition to women preachers.[15] Yet among the Wesleyans themselves, especially in the North and West, there remained a fervent grassroots attachment to the tradition of popular evangelicalism which found expression through the work of a succession of revival preachers. Such men were increasingly lay preachers, not ordained ministers, and like Charles Richardson, 'the Lincolnshire Thrasher', they continued the extempore style of dialect preaching.[16] The 'depraved taste' and 'distorted religion' of these unsophisticated Wesleyan itinerants embarrassed many socially ambitious Wesleyans, but as long as 'revivals' were cherished among the Ranters – the sectarian Methodists – it was difficult to prohibit them in the Parent Society.[17]

Although popular evangelicalism was essentially an oral movement, cheap magazines and tracts were quickly used to reinforce the spoken word. This literature contained vivid reports of highly charged conversions, camp meetings, processions and the journals and letters of the preachers, which underlined their heroic perseverance and successes. Biographies and obituaries also provided readers with examples of godly living and dying. The format, content and tone of this literature differed sharply from middle class evangelical publications or the tracts intended to improve the poor. This was a religious literature written by and for working people, and reflected their beliefs and aspirations.[18] At a time when the preachers were feared as 'wizards' because of their magical ability to bring about conversions, the popular evangelical magazines mirrored a world in which traditional beliefs and customs were still strong. Numerous reports of visions, trances, miraculous healings and the wonderful transfiguration of the body at death are scattered through the pages of this literature, and apparitions and cases of exorcism are cited as evidence of the powers of the Holy Spirit in combatting the forces of darkness.[19] 'Praying Johnny' Oxtoby, a Yorkshire preacher 'of slender abilities, but zealous and useful', according to his biographer, was famous for his personal encounters with the devil and more than once battled with evil spirits until deliverance was achieved. 'Praying Johnny' died in 1830, but well into Victoria's reign, the Methodist sects had to rebuke not only members but local preachers for going to 'cunning persons' in cases of witchcraft, instead of relying on the powers of the Cross. More respectable evangelicals were always nervous of traditional beliefs and magical happenings, and were often as ready as the sceptics to investigate scientifically such occurrences in order to root out 'ancient superstition'.[20]

Much popular evangelism took place in the open air at camp meetings and village crossroads, but converts were usually gathered in cottages or barns, which also provided shelter for the itinerant preachers on their travels. Although by 1837, the Methodist sects had begun to open a growing number of chapels, these were often small, simple buildings architecturally, little different from the cottages where so many early congregations met. Popular evangelicals were harassed by fellow villagers, parsons and employers, and often found it difficult to obtain a chapel site, and when a site was found financial pressures limited the scale of construction.[21] The first volume of Kendall's classic history of the Primitive Methodists contains more illustrations of cottages than chapels and a very recent study comes close to idealising 'cottage religion' as refuge for humble people in a society which was destroying their economic independence and distinct culture. The cottage or cottage-like chapel provided the central focus in the lives of converts. Not only on Sunday but throughout the week, religious and social meetings encouraged all to play an active role in the spiritual life of the community. Praying in class meetings led on to exhorting and uncertain attempts at extempore preaching. The unconverted found salvation at these meetings and the converted could press on towards the second blessing of sanctification. Cottage meetings were also at the centre of a network of mutual support and aid in times of sickness, injury or death. This popular evangelical movement was very conscious of having created a vigorous and independent fellowship in the face of physical and legal opposition. The world of the cottage meeting was resented by middle class evangelicals, especially members of the Established Church, who found little there which matched their vision of a pious and deferential peasantry.[22]

Although Wesleyan Methodist leaders had long frowned on folk revivalism, for many years they had to tolerate 'thorough-paced ranters' in their own ranks because of local attachment to fervent awakenings. By 1837, however, the Wesleyans had opened their first theological college, and were intent on gaining social and intellectual parity with middle class Nonconformists.[23] Most Nonconformists themselves took a hostile or patronising view of popular revivalism with its emotional meetings and uneducated preachers, and this hostility was reinforced in the 1840s when 'vulgar' religion was seen as leading on to Mormonism, Millerite Adventism and worse.[24] By the forties, the Primitive Methodists, the largest and most stable of the revivalist sects had gradually begun to change. Even in the early days, Primitive Methodist leaders had been conscious of the disruptive tendencies of those claiming visionary gifts. Hugh Bourne, a fervent revivalist with a strong sense of the miraculous, nevertheless tried to regulate those who went into visions, and as early as the 1830s a somewhat better educated and respectable group of preachers began to emerge, who found support especially in some northern cities, where the Primitive Methodists began to attract a growing number of moderately prosperous members.[25] Local schisms prompted by calls for a 'free gospel' or by the ambitions of preachers who claimed special gifts of healing or prophecy drew off some of the more traditional minded membership who felt out of place in a religious fellowship, whose members and leaders now looked for social recognition from middle class Nonconformists.[26]

In 1844 the Primitive Methodists moved their publishing house to London from the moors of north Staffordshire, where the movement had begun, and their major magazine was given a new format. Reports of miraculous apparitions and visions disappeared and were replaced by formal sermonizing and popular educational pieces. In format and content, the *Primitive Methodist Magazine* came much closer to its Wesleyan counterpart.[27] A few years later, John Flesher, the preacher who had recognised the publishing house and the magazine, issued a much revised edition of the Primitive Methodist hymn book from which he deleted many of the old spiritual songs in favour of a more formal hymnody including some of his own creation. The new hymn book was greeted with howls of protest. There was some objection to Flesher's conceit in introducing his own hymns and mutilating those of Wesley and Watts, but the great majority took exception to the exclusions of the familiar spiritual songs. These had come to embody much of the Christian experience of grassroots members and for years, many circuits refused to use the new hymn book.[28] The shift towards denominational respectability was also marked by the disappearance of women preachers, especially from the itinerant ministry, and the rise of a more professional clergy. From the 1860s women preachers fade from the scene, and they receive less and less notice in the *Primitive Methodist Magazine.* Primitive Methodism was becoming a religion of the chapel not the cottage, and women were told that the home, not the public arena, was their appropriate sphere. At the same time, male preachers began to style themselves 'reverend', a title unknown to the pioneer generation, and acquired their own 'Quarterly Review and Journal of Theological Literature', quite separate from a growing number of publications aimed at the laity.[29] The Bible Christians, a smaller sect in the van of popular revivalism also grew increasingly self conscious about their noisy evangelism, and somewhat later reflected the same drift towards decorum, with a recasting of their hymn book and a succession of chapels in the gothic style. A few women continued as preachers, but they were transformed into 'female special agents' and excluded from the ministry, which began to receive a collegiate education.[30] Even the Independent Methodists, who clung to their objections to a paid ministry, reflected the same changes in styles of worship, chapel architecture and roles of women in their congregations.[31]

In 1837 the teetotal movement was barely five years old and contrary to popular stereotype did not enjoy the support of the evangelical churches. Methodist trustees were encouraged 'to provide wine for the use of the preachers, either before preaching to give them a little spirit for their work, or after preaching to revive their exhausted energies'.[32] Some of the most fervent popular revivalists viewed teetotalism with suspicion as an unscriptural movement too dependent on human means. Militant teetotalers among the Methodist sects created local schisms by insisting on the teetotal pledge as a condition of church membership and by abusing leaders who refused to endorse this new standard of purity. Even at mid-century, some Primitive Methodist leaders remained hostile to the new temperance movement, although Hugh Bourne, their co-founder, had given teetotalism his vigorous support. In spite of this hesitancy, however, it was the Methodist sects which provided much of the driving force in the teetotal movement, which drew upon popular revivalism for personnel, contacts, meeting places and techniques of propaganda and organisation. Although the larger and more respectable Wesleyans remained implacably opposed to teetotalism much longer, it was their own grassroots popular revivalists who pioneered radical temperance within the Wesleyan ranks.

The future of popular revivalism and temperance among the Wesleyans were two key questions in the great disruption of 1849. Thousands left the Wesleyans and joined a reform movement which became the United Methodist Free Church, a vigorous temperance body. This broad shift which led to the identification of popular Methodism with temperance reflected a general move away from the magical world of early nineteenth-century revivalism towards a more ordered, moralistic evangelicalism, such as was being reflected in the new style Methodist magazines as history and popular science replaced ghosts and miracles. The newer values were conveyed not only through the magazines but through the Sunday Schools and a religious literature designed specifically for children. By 1868, the Primitive Methodists had opened their first Theological Institute and a new generation of Wesleyans had started a popular *Methodist Temperance Magazine.*[33] The world views of the Wesleyans and the Methodist sects showed fewer and fewer differences. A folk religion had succumbed to more dominant values. Elements of popular revivalism were soon assimilated into a more commercialised style of professional evangelism, which had been growing since the 1830s.

Revivalism had long had informal American links through the camp meeting, spiritual songs and exchange visits of preachers, but from the 1830s a new style of professionalised American evangelism began to have a public impact of England. The move to introduce a new style American evangelism came less from the Methodist sects than from some English Nonconformists, anxious about their denominations' limited impact on the working class. Efforts at home missionary work had produced few results, and what was sought was a less emotional version of the popular revivalism which had created the Methodist sects but endowed them with a style of religion which middle class, well educated Nonconformists found 'vulgar', irrational and difficult to reconcile with their own Calvinist traditions. Such a revivalism was available in the United States where college educated ministers seemed able to blend effective evangelism with order, respectability and elements of a moderate Calvinism.[34] These men were a new breed of specialists in evangelism, and English Nonconformists welcomed a succession of them to Britain. The best known was Charles G. Finney, whose *Lectures on Revivals of Religion* marked a new stage in the development of revivalism. Finney introduced a more rational, scientific note. Revivals were not mysterious workings of divine grace but the use of right means: successful revivals could be promoted and Finney spelt out the techniques to be used. Both his theology and methods were too radical for many English Nonconformists who had welcomed Finney's less daring American predecessors to Britain, and his first visit in 1849–50 produced few of the 'great awakenings' which he had achieved in the United States.[35] But his *Lectures* were quickly taken up by sectarian Methodist leaders always on the look out for means of revitalising their own movements. It was the Methodists who also gave the most fervent support to another American, James Caughey, who first introduced large scale commercialised evangelism to Britain.[36]

A dramatic figure, who was accused of employing highly questionable methods, such as decoy converts to bring sinners to Christ, Caughey was popular among the Methodist sects and the Wesleyan reformers during the 1840s and 1850s. His theology and basic techniques were familiar, but his campaigns were long and carefully planned. Costs were justified in terms of detailed statistics of souls saved. He also combined evangelism with a passionate commitment to the temperance cause, a common feature of revival campaigns from mid-century onwards. Caughey came to England when Methodist folk religion was waning, and a more ordered denominational life was starting to develop.[37] He received support among those who clung to some updated version of the Methodist revival tradition, but by the 1860s, support for that tradition was declining in all branches of Methodism. For example, key leaders of the United Methodist Free Church, who had supported Caughey in the 1840s began to grasp that revival campaigns had little impact on long term patterns of denominational growth or decline, and that their super-charged emotionalism worked against a more cultivated and stable church life.[38] Fervent admirers of Caughey or his English disciple, William Booth, felt increasingly excluded from the centres of denominational life and were forced to publish their own magazines to establish a network of contacts which cut across Methodist denominational boundaries. Many revival enthusiasts were drawn off into Booth's Christian Mission (which became the Salvation Army), or into later Holiness sects.[39]

A similar evangelical sub-culture developed among some Nonconformists, Anglicans and Plymouth Brethren who produced a massive magazine and pamphlet literature in favour of revivals. Stimulated by awakenings in the United States and Ireland, these groups promoted innumerable revival campaigns in the middle decades of the century, and made grandiose claims for the success of their efforts. These campaigns were carefully planned and publicised, and aimed at all social classes. Working class evangelists like Richard Weaver, the converted coal heaver, retained something of the fire of the earlier Methodist preachers, but fervour was less appropriate for a gentleman evangelist such as Reginald Radcliffe or a specialist in drawing room meetings like Lord Radstock.[40] Propriety was also very much the hall mark of a new style of crinoline-clad lady evangelist, who differed sharply from the female preachers of an earlier generation. Both the male and female revivalists of mid-century were drawn increasingly from the laity, and this tendency is mirrored by a move away from churches towards public halls as the venue for evangelistic meetings. Professional revivalism continued to look towards the United States, and it was an American, Dwight L. Moody who headed the great revival campaigns of the 1870s which marked the high point of Victorian mass evangelism.[41] Moody was able to draw upon well funded publicity agencies and established networks of contacts, and his campaigns in the major cities made him a household name. An unemotional preacher, who presented his huge audiences with a simple message in colloquial language, extravagant claims were made for Moody's successes. His converts, however, came overwhelmingly from the Sunday schools and from those already in the habit of church-going, even if they had not experienced conversion. He strengthened a particular type of evangelical

Christianity, but like Caughey, he had little impact on long term patterns of church attendance.[42]

Victorian revivalism became increasingly identified with a distinct type of fundamentalism which flew in the face of dominant patterns of scientific and humanistic thought. It was these dominant patterns which influenced late Victorian Methodism and Nonconformity, where there was only limited support for biblical literalism and anti-evolutionary thinking. Moody-style evangelism had support among some evangelical Anglicans and in other quarters, but fundamentalism never enjoyed the popularity in late Victorian Britain that it did in the United States, where middle class conservative Christianity of the Moody type was complemented by a continuing rural folk religion which retained less and less vitality on this side of the Atlantic. Late Victorian revivalism became identified with a religious sub-culture whose values and preoccupations were only of marginal interest to the great majority of church and chapel goers.[43]

Perhaps late Victorian revivalism made its most lasting impact not on the churches but on popular culture. Professional gospel singers, of whom the great star was Moody's partner, Ira K. Sankey, performed commercial religious ballads which found wide acceptance far beyond the churches. Many of these ballads were more concerned with morality and sentiment than a distinct Christian message, with home as much as heaven being the focus of their lyrics. Indeed, in this sentimental genre, heaven seemed more and more like an idealisation of the Victorian parlour in which the ballads were so often sung. Sankey's *Sacred Songs and Solos* became one of the best loved books of late Victorian England, and its popularity carried over well into this century, but the man and his message underline the great changes that had occurred in popular religion since the beginning of the Queen's reign.[44]

Notes

1 J. Walsh, 'Origins of the evangelical revival', in G. V. Bennet and J. D. Walsh, (eds.), *Essays in Modern Church History,* London, 1966, pp. 132–62; W. R. Ward, *Religion and Society in England,* London, 1972, pp. 1–134; I. Bradley, *The Call to Seriousness: The Evangelical Impact on the Victorians,* London, 1976, pp. 19–56.

2 G. M. Young, *Victorian England: Portrait of An Age,* New York, 1954, p. 17; B. Semmel, *The Methodist Revolution,* London, 1973, pp.

110–98; D. Hempton, *Methodism and Politics in British Society 1750–1850*, London, 1984, pp. 55–110.

3 *Hymns Ancient and Modern*, London, 1924, p. 496.

4 F. K. Brown, *Fathers of the Victorians: The Age of Wilberforce*, Cambridge, 1961; J. Wigley, *The Rise and Fall of the Victorian Sunday*, Manchester, 1980.

5 R. Currie, *Methodism Divided: A Study in the Sociology of Ecumenicalism*, London, 1968, pp. 44–82; J. T. Wilkinson, 'The rise of other methodist traditions', in R. Davies, A. R. George, G. Rupp, (eds.), *A History of the Methodist Church in Great Britain*, London, 1978, 2, pp. 276–329; D. M. Valenze, *Prophetic Sons and Daughters: Female Preaching and Popular Religion in Industrial England*, Princeton, N.J., 1985, pp. 74–98.

6 J. Rule, 'Methodism, popular beliefs and village culture in Cornwall, 1800–1850', in R. D. Storch, (ed.), *Popular Culture and Custom in Nineteenth-Century England*, London, 1982, pp. 48–70; J. Obelkevich, *Religion and Rural Society: South Lindsey, 1825–1875*, Oxford, 1976.

7 In addition to sources cited for note 5, see J. S. Werner, *The Primitive Methodist Connexion*, Madison, Wis., 1984; T. Shaw, *The Bible Christians, 1815–1907*, London, 1965; J. Vickers, *History of Independent Methodism*, Bolton, 1920.

8 Valenze, *Prophetic Sons and Daughters*; J. Lightfoot, *The Life and Labours of Mrs Mary Porteous . . . 'A Mother in Israel'*, London, 1863.

9 W. F. Swift, 'The women itinerant preachers of early methodism', *Proceedings of the Wesley Historical Society*, 28–9, 1952–3, pp. 89–94, 76–83; F. K. Prochaska, *Women and Philanthropy in Nineteenth-Century England*, London, 1980; Valenze, *Prophetic Sons and Daughters*, pp. 187–204; D. C. Dews, 'Ann Carr and the female revivalists of Leeds', *Wesley Historical Society, Yorkshire Branch, Occasional Paper*, 4, 1982, pp. 15–31.

10 J. Kent, *Holding the Fort: Studies in Victorian Revivalism*, London, 1978, pp. 38–70; Werner, *The Primitive Methodist Connexion*, pp. 84–165.

11 W. Garner, *Jubilee of the English Camp Meeting*, London, 1857; Valenze, *Prophetic Sons and Daughters*, pp. 83–98.

12 W. Brimelow, *Life and Labours of William Sanderson*, Wigan, 1899, p. 72. Lightfoot, *Life of Mary Porteous*, p. 128, provides a similar report. For the American New Lights see S. A. Marini, *Radical Sects of Revolutionary New England*, Cambridge, Mass., 1982, pp. 89, 156, 166.

13 Marini, *Radical Sects*, pp. 156–71; G. P. Pullen, *Spiritual Folk Songs of Early America*, New York, 1937; H. B. Kendall, *The Origin and History of the Primitive Methodist Church*, London, n.d., 2, pp. 2–35.

14 Kent, *Holding the Fort*, p. 69.

15 J. T. Lightfoot, *Hymn Tunes and Their Story*, London, 1905, pp. 245–6.

16 J. E. Coulson, *The Peasant Preacher: Memorials of Mr Charles Richardson,* London, 1866. L. Billington, 'Popular religion and social reform: a study of teetotalism and revivalism, 1830–50', *Journal of Religious History,* 10, 1978–79, p. 283 cites numerous other biographies in the same tradition.

17 James Kendall, *Rambles of an Evangelist,* London, 1853, provides a good picture of a Wesleyan minister who hated 'wildness, extravagance, rant and loud noises'.

18 L. Billington, 'The religious periodical and newspaper press, 1770–1870', in M. Harris and A. Lee (eds.), *The Press in English Society from the Seventeenth to the Nineteenth Centuries,* London, 1986, pp. 116–17.

19 J. Thorne, *James Thorne of Shebbear: A Memoir,* London, 1873, pp. 51–2; *Primitive Methodist Magazine,* 10, Bemersley, 1829, pp. 128–235; J. Pallister, *A Brief Memoir of Mrs Jane Pallister,* London, 1834.

20 G. Shaw, *Life of John Oxtoby,* Hull, 1894; H. Woodcock, *Piety Among the Peasantry being Sketches of Primitive Methodism on the Yorkshire Wolds,* London, 1889, pp. 37–41; A. H. Patterson, *From Hayloft to Temple: The Story of Primitive Methodism in Yarmouth,* London, 1903, pp. 156–9. For middle-class evangelicals' objections to 'superstitions' see – L. Davidoff and C. Hall, *Family Fortunes: Men and Women of the English Middle Class, 1780–1850,* London, 1987, pp. 25–7, 92, 286–7, 402.

21 Woodcock, *Piety Among the Peasantry,* and W. C. Tonks, *Victory in the Villages: The History of The Brinkworth Circuit,* Aberdare, 1907, are typical regional histories which illustrate the struggle to open chapels.

22 Kendall, *History of the Primitive Methodist Church,* 1; Valenze, *Prophetic Sons and Daughters,* especially pp. 47–9.

23 A. Waddy, *Life of the Rev. Samuel D. Waddy, P.P.,* London, 1878, p. 58, for a young ambitious Wesleyan minister's view of his 'eccentric ranter' colleague. See also W. B. Brash, *The Story of Our Colleagues, 1835–1935,* London, 1935, and Ward, *Religion and Society,* p. 165.

24 Davidoff and Hall, *Family Fortunes,* p. 137; *Christian Witness,* London, March, 1844.

25 *Primitive Methodist Magazine,* 10, Bemersley, 1829, p. 22; Kendall, *History of the Primitive Methodist Church,* 2, pp. 360–1; Obelkevich, *Religion and Rural Society,* pp. 248–58.

26 Billington, 'Popular religion and social reform', p. 277; Valenze, *Prophetic Sons and Daughters,* pp. 274–5.

27 Billington, 'The religious periodical and newspaper press', pp. 127–8, 238.

28 J. Atkinson, *Life of Rev. Colin C. McKechnie,* London, 1898, pp. 114–9; W. J. Robson, (ed.), *Silsden Primitive Methodism,* Silsden, 1910, pp. 25–31.

29 Valenze, *Prophetic Sons and Daughters,* pp. 277–8. *The*

Christian Ambassador: A Quarterly Review and Journal of Theological Literature, first appeared in 1854.

30 Shaw, *The Bible Christians,* pp. 56–69, 82–5.

31 These changes can best be traced through the *Free Gospel Magazine* from the 1870s and in the histories of local chapels. See, for example, Stephen Rothwell, *Memorials of the Independent Methodist Chapel, Folds Rd, Bolton,* Bolton, 1887 and 1897.

32 Kendall, *History of the Primitive Methodist Church,* 1, p. 470.

33 Billington, 'Popular religion and social reform', pp. 275–86.

34 R. Carwardine, *Trans-Atlantic Revivalism: Popular Evangelicalism in Britain and America,* Westport, Conn., 1978, pp. 3–84; Kent, *Holding the Fort,* pp. 9–37. Moderate Calvinism represented a liberalisation of a faith which had emphasised both the exclusiveness of the elect and man's helplessness and inability to act in securing his own conversion.

35 W. G. McLoughlin, *Modern Revivalism: Charles Grandison Finney to Billy Graham,* New York, 1959, pp. 3–165; Carwardine, *Trans-Atlantic Revivalism,* pp. 134–55.

36 Carwardine, *Trans-Atlantic Revivalism,* pp. 107–33.

37 Carwardine, *Trans-Atlantic Revivalism,* pp. 107–33, 183 ff; D. A. Gowland, *Methodist Secessions: The Origins of Free Methodism in Three Lancashire Towns,* Manchester, 1979, pp. 109–10.

38 Kent, *Holding the Fort,* pp. 295–355.

40 J. E. Orr, *The Second Evangelical Awakening in Britain,* London, 1949; J. Paterson, *Richard Weaver, Life Story,* London, n.d.; J. Radcliffe, *Recollections of Reginald Radcliffe,* London, n.d.; Kent, *Holding the Fort,* p. 126.

41 O. Anderson, 'Women preachers in mid-Victorian Britain: Some reflections on feminism, popular religion and social change', *Historical Journal,* 11, 1969, pp. 467–84; Mrs (sic) Grattan Guinness, *Recollections of the Late Mrs Henry Dening,* Bristol, 1872.

42 Much of the huge literature on Moody is indicated in J. F. Findlay, *Dwight L. Moody,* Chicago, 1969, and Kent, *Holding the Fort,* pp. 132–214.

43 G. M. Marsden, *Fundamentalism and American Culture: The Shaping of Twentieth-Century Evangelicalism, 1870–1925,* New York, 1980; Kent, *Holding the Fort,* p. 67; W. B. Glover, *Evangelical Nonconformists and Higher Criticism in The Nineteenth Century,* London, 1954.

44 Kent, *Holding the Fort,* pp. 215–35; S. S. Tamke, *Make a Joyful Noise Unto The Lord: Hymns as a Reflection of Victorian Social Attitudes,* Athens, Ohio, 1978, 35 and 111.

11 *John Saville*

Imperialism and the Victorians

Britain was an old imperialist country in the nineteenth century, and as a body of ideas as well as of practice imperialism was pervasive throughout the decades of Victoria's reign. Ireland was especially important. It was England's oldest colonial possession. After centuries of savage fighting, the wars of the first Elizabeth more or less completed the conquest of Ireland by England and the imposition of English law over most of the country. In the next century the cruelties of years of fighting were ended with the Cromwellian Settlement, to be followed by a further period of killing at the end of the century. The now dominant Protestant Ascendency began to consolidate their power with the introduction of the Penal Laws against Catholics and the Catholic religion. The Laws were introduced in the 1790s, and assumed their worst features during the next thirty years. It was a barbarous period of English history. There was large scale emigration, particularly from among the upper classes, and those who remained, overwhelmingly peasants, lived in degrading poverty the like of which was nowhere to be found in Britain. Although Ireland in the second half of the eighteenth century gradually became more prosperous, with a marked growth in trade and a rise in agricultural rents, Ireland remained within the mercantilist system and the economic and financial benefits of growth accrued largely to the landowners, most of whom were English and many of whom were absentees from the Irish soil. There was a serious drain of capital from Ireland, one of the main features of classic imperialism, made up of rents to absentee landlords, the revenues of the Anglican Church – who practised a religion entirely alien from the mass of the Irish people – and a very large number of sinecures monopolised by the English, together with a growing Pension List. The Union with England in 1800 brought no relief, and the living standards of the Irish peasants, their numbers swelled by a rapidly growing population, remained far below the average of the poor in the rest of Britain. The growing crisis of the Irish economy culminated in the Great Famine of the middle and late 1840s when nearly a million died: the greatest single catastrophe in Europe during the nineteenth century. Emigration had been steadily increasing through the early decades of the century but with the famine the outflow became a flood, and the emigrant ships brought hundreds of thousands to the Americas and to Britain. The Irish population by the end of the century was about half its total before the famine.

The relations between Ireland and England exhibited the classic features of a colonial-imperialist connection: Irish poverty bred violence, corruption and a bitter hatred of the English, and on the English side there was an arrogance towards the 'natives' and the usual colonial beliefs in the intellectual and moral inferiority of the subject nation. As the Irish poured into Britain during the 1840s so the racism of the English, already pronounced against the Irish, became more and more evident; much assisted by the political agitation which Daniel O'Connell had developed in the twenty years before his death in 1847. After the failure of the widespread unrest of the later forties, the permanent presence of Irish communities in Britain, together with the revival of the violent agitation of the Fenians in the 1860s, encouraged the already marked prejudices of the English against the Irish. By this time popular cartoonists normally depicted Irish characters with clearly defined simian features: long upper lip, projecting mouth, a jutting lower jaw and a sloping forehead. Tenniel, in *Punch*, was probably the most influential cartoonist of his day – he began to draw the leading cartoon in *Punch* from 1862 – but the ape-like Paddy was common to all the comic weeklies and established the stereotype that the Irish were not only feckless and incapable of managing their own affairs, but would turn to violence and massacre on the slightest pretext.

Ireland was a special problem in Britain's Empire. Not only was it the oldest colony, but the economic and political connection with large sections of the English ruling classes was especially close. In the middle of the eighteenth century about one-eighth of all peers in the House of Lords owned Irish land or held Irish mortgages; by 1830 almost one peer in four possessed a property interest in Ireland, and the political consequences were obvious. There was no other colonial country where the economic and political relationships were so close. In 1848, for example, a year of considerable unrest and potential insurrection in Ireland, two out of the three leading Whigs in the British government were substantial property owners in Ireland. No where else was there this fusion of economic interest and executive and legislative power. Other colonial countries always had their special interest groups – the West Indian lobby is a well-known example – but only Ireland was actually part of the society which exploited it, and which theoretically and to a limited extent, actually shared in the developing democratic processes.

In addition to Ireland there was an old colonial Empire in 1815 which went back to the discoveries of the sixteenth century; and first in the New World against Spain in the seventeenth century, and then on a world scale against France in the eighteenth century, Britain gradually acquired a colonial Empire. What became the United States of America achieved their independence in the last quarter of the eighteenth century, but by then Britain was well entrenched in the Caribbean and in India, as well as the white settlements of Canada and Australasia. By the accession of Victoria in 1837, therefore, Empire and imperial sentiments were not new to the English and they were to be strengthened and extended by the economic developments of the rest of the century. British merchants swarmed over the whole of the economic world; and Britain alone, of all the advanced countries, developed a rate of capital accumulation in excess of the domestic demand. Capital export began after 1815 and stepped up to a higher level of outflow from about the mid-1850s. By the early 1870s the total invested abroad amounted to £1,200 million, not all by any means in countries of the Empire. The relationship between export of capital and the expansion of the imperialism of the advanced industrial nations is not a matter of simple correlation, and the question is discussed below.

In the early nineteenth century the expansion of the British Empire was certainly not a single-minded pursuit by British government. There were many cross-currents of opinion and it was the general growth of manufacturing and the export trade that were the main concerns of the industrial and commercial bourgeoisie. The exceptions were in those areas of the world where there was already a political control or a partial control; and the main country, or sub-continent, in this context was British India where the East India Company was slowly but inexorably extending its domination. After the Mutiny of 1857 the British Crown took responsibility for the administration of British India and in 1875 Victoria became Empress of India. Missionary work by various Christian denominations was often the dynamic force behind the penetration of the peasant and tribal societies of the world. It was in part, in the early decades, closely connected with the movement against slavery, the abolition of which was agreed at the Congress of Vienna at Britain's request. Missionary work went hand in hand with the encouragement of what were regarded as the civilised values of European societies. It was not sufficient to teach native peoples to read and understand the Scriptures; they had also to be taught to earn a living. 'Civilising' trade should take the place of the slave trade in Africa, and as David Livingstone was often heard to say 'Christianity, Commerce and Civilisation' must go hand in hand. Social reformers such as T. F. Buxton were always emphasising that the Bible and the plough must go together; and there is no doubt that the work of the missions in the early and middle Victorian decades led to the acquisition of colonies, although that was certainly not their intention. It was, however, inevitable. If the flag followed trade it was often the case that trade had followed the Cross.

What also requires emphasis is the acceptance of the superior values of Europe over the rest of the world and this was a strongly marked attitude both in Britain and in France, the latter beginning to acquire its second colonial Empire after 1815. The superior values were built around the values of Christianity, and they provided much of the intellectual and spiritual dynamic behind the great spread of missionary activity in Victoria's reign. There were broader considerations: the need to introduce order and security and to eliminate barbaric customs, such as the practice of *suttee* in India. The general belief that civilising the 'natives' was God's will imparted a sense of righteousness and moral certitude which was a central thread in all the discussions of the expansion of Empire. In the early decades of Victoria's reign it was largely the middle classes as well as sections of the aristocratic groups who were particularly concerned with the christianising aspects of the expanding British presence overseas. The Evangelicals in particular were especially concerned with the saving of heathen souls, and the various Missionary Societies received widespread support. To what extent, down to about 1870, these were sentiments widely diffused among working people, is difficult to say with any precision. Statements about attitudes are often liable to be selective. Before 1850 the radical movement associated with the National Union of Working Classes and the *Poor Man's Guardian* in the first half of the 1830s, and the Chartist movement from the late 1830s and throughout the 1840s, were firmly internationalist in general approach; and not only in relation to Europe. When George Julian Harney started publishing his *Red Republican* in June 1850 he carried at the masthead of his leading article a quotation from Robespierre: 'Men of all countries are brothers, and the people of each ought to yield one another mutual aid, according to their ability, like citizens of the same state'. The Chartists always supported the struggles of the Irish for independence, and in the last years of Chartism Ernest Jones exhibited the principled internationalism that had infused the radical groups when he vigorously upheld the right of the Indian people to rebel against their British overlords. The hysteria in Britain against the Hindus reached extraordinary levels of bitterness and hatred, and Jones did not deny the range and scale of atrocities that had been committed:

> We have been so much shocked with the dramatic descriptions of Nana Sahib's actions at Cawnpore, and the atrocities performed at other places, that, did we not believe they were the result of a long continued system of practices on the part of the British equally barbarous and repulsive, we should have no hesitation in joining even the *The Times* in its wild, wanton, and wicked demand for native blood.
>
> It is natural enough that men should forget the deeds of their own ancestors, and, in their own vaingloriousness, miscalculate the effects that inevitably follow. But, not forgetting is the great lesson taught the

Hindus by that race of tricksters, robbers and miscreants, who stamped the impress of cruelty and torture on the native mind, and who sowed the seeds of that sanguinary harvest which is but now being reaped in British India.

That the Sepoys have been treacherous and cruel, we might grant, but who taught them the lesson? We will see, by recurring briefly to the history of our Indian rule, and by recording some specimens of our 'mild and merciful sway', so much boasted of by those who believe in the justice of 'British Sepoyism', whilst they shudder to think of that of the natives themselves. (*People's Paper*, 31 October 1857.)

By the time Ernest Jones was writing these words the independent movement of working people was fast disintegrating and the radical groups became the left wing of the Liberal Party. Socialism died away quickly after 1850 and it was not until the 1880s that socialist ideas and a socialist movement, came back into British politics. During the years between, anti-imperialism was mostly a middle-class cause of radicals such as John Bright and Richard Cobden who spoke for those who objected to the use of force to acquire territory and who profoundly distrusted the State in costly overseas adventures. There was a distinction, however, between the white colonies, those that ultimately became Dominions, for which the radicals wished to encourage independence from Britain as soon as possible, and the colonies in the sub-tropics where the radicals accepted measures of paternalism, but where there was really no thought of these societies breaking away from Britain. The radicals like John Bright would attack abuses and financial and political corruption where they discovered it – India was an especial concern of John Bright – but a genuine independence was not regarded as being within the realm of the possible. It was a liberal tradition which always remained a minority trend within the Liberal Party but which carried over into the last thirty years or so of Victoria's reign when the attitude towards Empire underwent some important changes.

In the 1870s a more pervasive imperialist approach begins to be noticeable; and it had a number of different causes which came together in this decade. The first new development was the actual growth in the size of Empire. From 1870 until the beginning of the First World War around five million square miles were added to the existing British Empire, and the whole nation became much more conscious of imperialist matters and concerns. India was already under the Crown; Canada had become a federal grouping in 1867 but six out of her ten provinces were added from 1870 on. Australia was federated in 1900; New Zealand developed into a properous society by the end of the century; and South Africa became a Union in 1910. But it was the acquisition of vast new territories in the African continent that is the most striking feature of these closing decades of Victoria's reign. Nearly the whole of Britain's possessions in tropical and sub-tropical Africa were acquired in these years, and outside of Africa, Upper Burma was conquered and Malaya developed economically as a tin and rubber producer. The reasons for this vast expansion of imperial territory were complex, and by no means all were immediately connected with economic pressures. Obviously the growth of British manufacturing and trade was a necessary part of the historical process as was the growing and considerable export of capital; but political and strategic factors were often directly involved. The lifeline to India was always considered a central part of British world strategy, and the growing international competition with France and Germany – in Africa above all – contributed greatly to the sharpening of imperialist attitudes and policies in all these major countries of Western Europe. Some of the major British politicians of this period – above all Joseph Chamberlain – became fervent advocates of Empire and the relationships between Britain and her colonial territories, in both the temperate and the tropical areas of the world. The physical expansion of Empire was inevitably accompanied with the development of a body of ideas which justified and indeed exalted the role and place of Empire in the British scheme of things. In 1868 Charles Dilke published his *Greater Britain* which had a considerable success. It coincided within a few years of the opening of the Suez Canal, and the Franco–Prussian war; and the growth of nationalism which followed the latter, including the recognition by Britain of the changing character of power between the major countries of Europe, all contributed to the development of the new awareness of Empire. Much more influential than Dilke's book, however, was J. R. Seeley's *The Expansion of England* which first appeared in 1883, and three years later there was Froude's *Oceana, or England and her*

Colonies. All these volumes became classics of the ideology of Empire. They were concerned, it should be emphasised, only with the white-settled colonies and not with the dependent territories in the tropics and sub-tropics. The exception was India, always at the centre of Imperial concerns.

There were differences in approach. Dilke stressed the common bonds of culture and race between the various parts of the Empire and he emphasised the superiority of the 'British race', in which, it should be added, he included the Americans. The term 'Greater Britain' for Dilke meant the common bond between all the countries where people of British stock were to be found, with the 'Mother Country' as the centre of a beneficent Empire. For Seeley, whose book became one of the best-sellers of the country, – it sold 80,000 copies in the first two years – the emphasis was upon the significance of the ways in which the Empire had been established in the past, and it was he who turned the famous phrases that Britain had 'conquered and peopled half the world in a fit of absence of mind'. Unlike Dilke, Seeley did not encourage or recommend the further expansion of Empire; but both, as well as James Froude and other writers on the theme of Empire, all stressed the sense of belonging together, and related the pride of nationalism with the pride of Empire. Imperial themes were now, in the 1880s and after, discussed widely. A strong literary influence in this context was W. E. Henley's editorship of the *National Observer* (1888–92) but the most popular exponent of the Imperial idea – one can also write 'imperialist' – was undoubtedly Rudyard Kipling, the son of an Indian civil servant who began his own career as a journalist in India. His early writing was entirely connected with Indian themes, including accounts of the Indian army, and his influence became enormous. With Kipling, imperialism was a missionary activity for the British people. They were the Chosen People, superior to the 'lesser breed without the law' and it was Kipling who coined the phrase 'the White Man's Burden'.

One of the intellectual strands of the last thirty years of the nineteenth century which contributed to the intellectual and moral acceptance of imperialist ideas was social Darwinism. Charles Darwin's *Origin of the Species* had been first published in 1859. Its influence was wide-ranging and many sided, and when mixed with the evolutionary social theory of Herbert Spencer, there was produced social Darwinism. While there were varying interpretations of the general doctrine, in the context of the present discussion, social Darwinism provided the rationale for the survival of the fittest nation or race in the struggle between different nationalisms, or in the domination of the progressive white races over the backward coloured peoples. There were, as has been suggested, many variations upon the general theme of the survival of the fittest in social life; but the general ideas fitted well the apologetics of the imperialists in explaining their control and domination over large masses of the human race. The racial element had always been present in the writings of the imperialists from Dilke onwards, and the superiority of the Anglo-Saxon race was clearly and obviously illustrated by the extent of the Empire of the British.

Intellectual rationalisations normally have their more popular expression, and the voice of the people was heard with increasing power in the second half of the century, and especially in its closing years. It was a voice that included a number of different notes. Militarism was one. In some respects the military had always had a basis in popular opinion, but before 1850, while the military were not as despised as the police, their role in curbing and containing social agitation and political movements made them disliked and unsympathetic. The Crimean War saw the beginnings of a new attitude towards the military on the part of working people. In part it was a result of the complicated political processes which involved the decline of an independent working class radicalism with the demise of Chartism; in part it was a war against the hated Tsarist autocracy; and in part it was the first major conflict since Waterloo with sensational events such as the Charge of the Light Brigade: historical moments which captured popular imagination out of all proportion to their significance. And the Crimean War was followed by the bloody massacres of the Indian Mutiny, as well as by the recurrence of a war scare against the French. Among the mass movement of Volunteers in 1859–60 working men were to be found in considerable numbers. The changing attitude towards war, and the army, was reflected in changing attitudes within the Churches in Britain; well illustrated by an examination of hymns, tracts and sermons. The Church Militant had always been present in some periods of Christian history – vigorously so on many occasions – and it was quite remarkably pervasive during the third quarter of the century and through to the years of the First World War. When William Booth began his missionary work in the east end of London that led to the founding of the Salvation Army, it was wholly in keeping with his appeal to the under-privileged that he should introduce military rankings and military phraseology. The increased prestige of the military – not at all justified when the treatment of the ordinary soldier is considered – found national expression in support of the increasing number of small wars fought by the Army in far-off places of Empire, and reached its apotheosis in the sensationalised episode of General Gordon at Khartoum. By this time jingoism and bellicose nationalism had been given a vigorous outing during the diplomatic crisis in the Near East in 1878, and during the next decade jingoism began to be embedded as an integral part of the culture of army working class communities. The music hall was an important vehicle for jingoistic sentiment and during the 1880s there were at least 500 music halls in London alone. Concurrently with the expansion of the music hall as the entertainment centre for working people outside the home, alongside the public house, went the depoliticisation of the traditional working mens' clubs, a process which was in the main completed by the 1890s. Militarism and the Empire, the basis of jingoism, found its most complete social expression in the increasing acceptance by the public schools of curricula which emphasised all the qualities deemed to be necessary for future leaders and administrators. The games field encouraged team effort, acceptance of orders and submergence of the individual in the group. Cadet corps were to be found in most schools by the 1880s; and the Christian regimes which made a fetish of spartan self-deprivation, produced boys of eighteen with self-assurance, self-sacrifice and group loyalty. They also produced individuals who were conformist, conventional and mostly lacking in imagination: all qualities admirably suited to service in the armed forces or administration in an Empire that was geographically far-flung, or a Whitehall that was its directing centre. The paternalism that was a central part of this training encouraged a superior aloofness from the native peoples over whom they ruled that was the upper class parallel of the racism endemic among the military rank and file or the majority of working class communities in Britain: all encouraged by the portrayal of 'native' types – Indian and Chinese in particular – as obsequious, cunning, superstitious and so on in musical comedies or musical hall ballads.

Intertwined with this increasing glorification of war, and of the Imperial connection, went a popular reversal of attitudes towards the monarchy. Indeed it was an essential part of these changing ideas within civil society. The monarchy was not a favoured institution, either with the aristocratic classes or with the masses, in the first half of the nineteenth century. Victoria was certainly a considerable improvement on her predecessors and her family life with the Prince Consort had a rectitude which appealed to the growing social conservatism of the middle classes. But after the death of Albert, Victoria went into deep mourning and virtually retired from public life; and the monarchy no longer played a central part in public ceremonial. Throughout the nineteenth century until the mid-1870s there had always been an undercurrent of republicanism, but it was indifference among the working people rather than straight hostility. The first years of the 1870s actually saw a national republican movement, with between sixty to seventy republican clubs across the country. It was never a mass movement of significance, and as an organised movement it fell away remarkably quickly from 1873–4 on; and never returned. There were still some remnants of opposition to the Queen's Jubilee in 1887 – some trades councils for example refused to make a presentation – but by the time of the celebrations of 1897 there was no overt opposition. On the contrary. By this time the monarchy was seen as representing the nation, regardless of class division, and both 1887 and 1897 brought leading representatives of the white and coloured races within the Empire to the celebrations in London. From this time all monarchs have accepted their Imperial role, and monarchy and Empire have moved hand in hand.

These developing ideas on Empire inevitably found organised expression in a proliferation of societies concerned with the propagation of the themes of Britain and her Empire. The most important popular body, with a considerable working class membership was the Primrose League, established in 1884 in honour of Disraeli. It was a Tory organisation although in its later years it claimed to be non-party, but it was by far the most important mass society for the dissemination of ideas about Empire. It celebrated all the main episodes with lectures, exhibitions, magic lantern shows, leaflets and pamphlets, and events such as the death of Gordon at Khartoum were inevitably among the best known and the most commonly used in its work of propaganda. In the same year as the Primrose League was founded, there was also established the Imperial Federation League, an organisation directed not towards the masses but to the politicians and the élites of Britain and the white Dominions and Colonies. The League lasted only ten years, not least because of its acceptance of Imperial preference, a matter which inevitably caused a good deal of internal dissention, but on its demise in 1893 its various functions were taken over by a number of different bodies which came to be established during the 1890s. There was indeed a proliferation of imperial-oriented organisations in the two decades or so before the outbreak of World War One, and they testified to the response which ideas of Empire were evoking among the British people.

It was the Boer War which provided the climax to three decades of intensive Imperial propaganda. The leading members of the government, for the most part, were not especially belligerent, but considerable sections of the British were, and the Boers in Pretoria were to some extent influenced by the clamour which they heard coming from England. London was particularly bellicose; and the dramatic events of the war, such as the siege of Ladysmith, were capable of inciting great gusts of jingoism in its most unpleasant forms. The argument, developed by Richard Price, that jingoism touched working people rather less than has often been suggested, has in turn been modified by later research; and there is no doubt that large sections of manual workers, trade unionists as well as the majority of non-unionists, were infected in varying degree with the virus of imperialist opinions, some to the point of hysteria.

The question which remains is what happened to the radical opposition to Empire in the second half of the nineteenth century. As already briefly noted, the middle class radicals opposed the continued financial support of the white colonies, and campaigned against the corruption and unfair treatment of the peoples of the dependent territories, India especially. But there was no fundamental opposition to the concept of Empire, and much hedging of principle in times of crisis, as with John Bright at the time of the Indian Mutiny. There remained a small radical minority which continued to support the agitation and the struggles of the Irish – even the Fenians – and it was the coercive measures of the Gladstone government of 1880 in Ireland that helped to bring together radicals in the Democratic Federation, the immediate forerunner of the first socialist body in British politics for some thirty years. But in the 1880s the young socialist movement did not pay much attention to colonial or imperial questions, nor were they well equipped intellectually to do so; and it was their contact with European socialists at the Congresses of the Second International – the first of which was in 1889 – that slowly broadened the parochial vision of British socialists, whether of the marxist or the more liberal Independent Labour Party persuasion. There remained, however, considerable confusion of ideas and policies over colonial questions and the general issue of internationalism. H. M. Hyndman, the founder of the Social-Democratic Federation, illustrated the mixture of ideas within the socialist movement. He was generally in favour of imperial reform for colonial countries such as India but at no time was he in support of complete independence; and he was in favour of Britain defending her Empire against all comers. On the Boer War his attitude was mixed. He signed the manifesto against Britain which was drafted by the International Socialist Bureau, but he soon began to complain of 'the strong Continental prejudice against England' which the war generated. At heart Hyndman was an English chauvinist as his support of Britain in the First World War clearly indicated. It was especially based upon his ferocious anti-Germanism. There were others in the young socialist movement who took a broadly similar line. Robert Blatchford had founded the very successful *Clarion* weekly paper in 1891; and as a fervent 'Imperial – Socialist' he argued for the unity of the British people as well as of the Empire, in contrast with the doctrines of the international class struggle of the Second International. In the Boer War, as an old soldier, Blatchford supported the British but not just for nostalgic reasons. He believed in the Empire, and like Hyndman he developed a remarkable phobia against the German 'menace'. Germany, he argued, was striving for world domination, and the defence of the Empire, with Britain as its directing centre, was alone capable of ensuring the future of the British people.

The Fabian Society, first established in 1884, was never intended to be a mass political organisation. They were largely London based and were content with their few hundred members. As an intellectual power-house for the merging socialist and labour movements, they were, of course, very important; and their influence was both considerable and long-lasting. In their political essence, the Fabians were liberal-collectivists of an advanced kind; and on matters of foreign policy and on questions of Empire they had no distinctive socialist views. In the case of the Boer War the 'old guard', that is the Webbs and Bernard Shaw above all, were not in favour of a campaign against the British government. They persuaded the Fabian Society – it was done through a postal vote – to issue no public statement of policy on the issue of the Boer War on the grounds that it was a subject 'outside the special province of the Society', and that the war, having already begun, could not now be altered or solved by a Fabian Society declaration. The Society voted 259 against 217 for the old guard view; and fifteen of its members resigned, among them Ramsay Macdonald. Shaw produced an apologia for the Fabian attitude in a famous pamphlet, *Fabianism and the Empire* in which the division of the world among the large imperialist powers was approved and justified. Small nations like the Boers, Shaw argued, were anachronistic in the new world of the twentieth century. There was another element in the Fabians' argument. They accepted the need for the maintenance and the strengthening of Empire, but this could only be achieved by the acceptance of the need for a much greater 'national efficiency' which in turn demanded improved housing, health, and educational reforms as well as the reorganisation of government departments such as the War Office. In the years between the Boer War and the beginning of the First World War the connection between Empire and the urgent need for increased efficiency in all departments of social life was commonly made, against the backcloth of the increasing competition from industrial and commercial rivals such as Germany; a rivalry which was also more and more seen in military terms.

The first serious analysis of imperialism came in the year after the death of Victoria. This was J. A. Hobson's *Imperialism. A Study.* Hobson had been writing in a number of journals during the 1890s developing some of the ideas in his later book, but it was the Boer War which encouraged him in its publication. He had visited South Africa in 1899 and his 1902 book was an indictment as well as a treatise on his subject. It was to have both an immediate impact upon public opinion as well as a long term effect; and it remains today essential reading for any analysis of the imperial phenomenon. In Britain it was the beginning of a liberal-radical critique of imperialism of a kind which had been absent in the closing decades of Victoria's reign from any intellectual or political group; and it provided the first volume in a series of critical appraisals of the role of the western industrial nations in their relations with the economically more backward societies of Asia and Africa. In 1907 there appeared the remarkable study of Egypt by Wilfred Scawen Blunt, one of the most interesting men of his generation: a Sussex squire, ex-diplomat, poet, and champion of all oppressed peoples. Blunt became a friend of the marxist Theodore Rothstein who himself published *Egypt's Ruin: a financial and administrative record* in 1920 and which, together with E. D. Morel's exposé of the atrocities of the Belgians in the Congo territory, helped to provide the beginnings of an anti-imperialist literature which greatly influenced the young radicals of these years. It was H. N. Brailsford's *The War of Steel and Gold,* published in 1914, which brought together much of the anti-imperialist writing of these years and which in turn was to have a very considerable influence upon the generations which followed. All these writings, however, came after the Victorian era proper; and what is notable about the decades before 1900 is the absence of a sustained critique of the methods and objectives of imperialist expansion. There were isolated protests. John Stuart Mill and the Governor Eyre episode of the 1860s is an obvious example of what became a large-scale challenge to established authority; and there were a number of prominent people, John Bright among them, who kept a close watch on Indian affairs. But there was no sustained critique, and it was only an advanced liberal such as Hobson who was able to develop a theory of imperialism from within the liberal tradition.

The absence of a principled opposition to the ideas and the practices of imperialism, and the failure of the merging socialist movement to develop a coherent critical analysis, meant that imperialist ideas and concepts became part of the 'common-sense' of the greater part of the British people. In its popular forms, this commonsense expressed itself in the jingoism of the Boer War years and of the early years of the war which began in August 1914. For the historian the interest in the aftermath of World War One lies not only in the considerable weakening of the militarist tradition and the growth of pacifism, but also in the continuation of the imperialist traditions of the years before 1914. Certainly in the schools the Empire still figured powerfully in the teaching of history and contemporary affairs, and the new medium of the film was a very effective way of presenting the romantic version of Empire, in which the white imperialists usually have the better of whatever crisis is being portrayed. Ideas and traditions have considerable staying power, and even after the Second World War, when the decolonisation process was more or less completed by the mid 1960s, the memories of Empire, filtered through the various forms of media and almost all historically inaccurate and often wholly misleading, continued to exercise a quite powerful influence. Another role was still eluding the British people.

Select Bibliography (published in London unless otherwise stated)

There are general surveys in B. Porter, *Critics of Empire. British Radical Attitudes to Colonialism in Africa 1895–1914*, 1968, and idem, *The Lion's Share. A Short history of British Imperialism 1850–1983*, 2nd edn., 1984; H. Gollwitzer, *Europe in the Age of Imperialism 1880–1914*, 1969; an excellent marxist introduction in V. Kiernan, *Marxism and Imperialism*, 1974; G. Jones, *Social Darwinism and English Thought. The Interaction between Biological and Social Theory*, Brighton, 1980; and a succinct introduction to the economic theories of imperialism in W. Baumgart, *Imperialism, the Idea and Reality of British and French Colonial Expansion 1880–1914*, Oxford, 1982.

For the ideas of the earlier part of Queen Victoria's reign, and especially those of the middle-class reformers, see: B. Semmel, 'The philosophical radicals and colonialism', *Journal of Economic History,* 21, 1961, pp. 513–25, and E. Stokes, *The English Utilitarians and India,* Oxford, 1959. The most useful contemporary source for the ideas of the commercial and industrial bourgeoisie are the issues of the *Economist,* published weekly, and for the best summary of moderately advanced liberal opinion, see Thorald Rogers, *Cobden and Modern Political Opinion,* 1873. There is much useful material in John Morley's *Life of Richard Cobden* and in the speeches and biographies of John Bright, for which see especially, G. B. Smith, *Life and Speeches of Right Hon. John Bright,* popular edn., 1882.

There is now a considerable discussion of popular attitudes in Victorian Britain. On the general themes of this article see: H. Pelling, *Popular Politics and Society in late Victorian Britain,* 1968; H. Cunningham, 'Jingoism and the working classes, 1877–8', *Bulletin of the Society for the Study of Labour History,* no. 19, 1969, pp. 6–8; L. Perry Curtis, *Apes and Angels. The Irishman in Victorian Caricature,* 1971; R. Price, *An Imperial War and the British Working Class. Working Class Attitudes and Reactions to the Boer War 1899–1902,* 1972; S. Humphries, ' "Hurrah for England": schooling and the working class in Bristol 1870–1914', *Southern History,* 1, 1979, pp. 171–207; J. M. Mackenzie, *Propaganda and Empire. The Manipulation of British Public Opinion, 1880–1960,* Manchester, 1984.

For the labour movement and imperialism, see J. Saville, *Ernest Jones. Chartist,* 1952; A. R. Schoyen, *The Chartist Challenge. A Portrait of George Julian Harney,* 1958; C. Tsuzuki, *H. M. Hyndman and British Socialism,* Oxford, 1961; T. Rothstein, *From Chartism to Labourism,* 1929; new edn. with introduction by J. Saville, 1983; A. M. McBriar, *Fabian Socialism and English Politics, 1884–1918,* Cambridge, 1962.

12 *Eric M. Sigsworth*

W. S. Gilbert . . . the wisest fool

William Schwenk Gilbert was described as the wisest of Victorian fools by the eminent economic historian, Sir John Clapham,[1] quoting from *Utopia Ltd* on the advantages to the company promoter of the legal device of limited liability . . .

Some seven men form an Association
(If possible all Peers and Baronets),
They start off with a public declaration
To what extent they mean to pay their debts.
That's called their Capital . . .
If you come to grief and creditors are craving . . .
Do you suppose that signifies perdition?
If so you're but a monetary dunce –
You merely file a Winding-up petition,
And start another company at once . . .'[2]

Most aspects of Victorian society were to Gilbert the object of fun. Although they seemed so solemn in their public presentation of themselves, the Victorians flocked to the Gilbert & Sullivan Operas and enjoyed hugely the lampooning of their institutions and attitudes.

Gilbert was born in 1836 and died in 1911, truly a Victorian. His father had been a choleric naval surgeon. Of his mother little is known except that she provided him with three sisters, about whom history is equally reticent. When only two years old, on holiday, he was surrendered by his nursemaid to Italian kidnappers, but returned unharmed for the ransom of £25 – a sum sufficiently derisory to have impressed the memory on him for the rest of life. Educated at Ealing School, he learned classics, wrote plays, became head boy and went on to King's College,

London, whence he graduated, having been disappointed in his attempts to become an artillery officer by the (for him) premature ending of the Crimean War. More prudently but less glamorously he sat the recently instituted competitive examinations for the civil service, passed and became an assistant clerk in the Education Office of the Privy Council. For four years he endured (in his own words) 'the detestable thraldom of this baleful office' enlivening their tedium with brief bouts of service with the Militia in which he was commissioned for twenty years. Shortly after, a modest legacy enabled him to resign his clerkship and pay his way to become a barrister (another highly theatrical role). This career only lasted for four years. If less boring than being a clerk, lack of success in the law meant that his income was sharply reduced.

In the long intervals spent waiting for briefs, Gilbert passed the time trying to write and, indeed by the age of twenty-four had written fifteen farces and burlesques. His first success was in a publication optimistically called *Fun* whose staff he joined in 1861 and it was here that he published the *Bab Ballads* which are important in containing many of the ideas used in the plots of the operas and in showing the development of the use of paradox which he so often exploited as a humorous device – the idea that by inverting accepted social situations and attitudes . . . by turning them, as he would have said, 'topsy turvy', one could expose their intrinsic foolishness, stimulating audiences to laugh not only at the inversion, but at what was being inverted, often themselves.

These skeletal details of Gilbert's early career are important since they provided much of the material for his libretti.[3] His father's naval background gave him an interest in the navy reflected in the *Bab Ballads* in which the intention to marry the whole of Captain Reece's female relatives to his ship's company the better to ensure their happiness and contentment, clearly foreshadows the plot of *H.M.S. Pinafore* and provides a good example of Gilbert's device of turning things upside down . . . in this case – and it was a very meaningful one in the social context of Victorian Britain – the inversion of class relationships.

His being surrendered to Neopolitan brigands by his nursemaid similarly served as a key part of the plot of the *Pirates of*

Penzance, in which Ruth, a member of the pirate band, confesses on the eve of Frederic's completing his indentures to become an accredited pirate, that he had in infancy been the victim of her mistake as his nursemaid. As she confesses to the Pirate King

Making my instruction, which within my brain did gyrate
A sad mistake it was to make and doom him to a vile lot
I bound him to a pirate – YOU – instead of to a pilot.

Similarly, in *Pinafore,* Buttercup mixed up as babies Ralph Rackstraw an Able Bodied Seaman and Capt. Corcoran his commander (formerly Capt. Reece of the *Bab Ballads*).

The same theme recurs at the end of the *Gondoliers* when Inez, the Prince's foster mother clarifies a confused situation by declaring that in that capacity she had substituted her son for the Prince, allowing him to be kidnapped.

Gilbert's military propensities are recalled in the famous patter song in the *Pirates* sung by Major General Stanley as the very model of a modern Major General.

His brief and conspicuously unsuccessful legal career provided Gilbert with repeated opportunities to profit humorously from the law, ranging from the early short operetta *Trial by Jury,* through the character of the Lord Chancellor in *Iolanthe* to Sir Bailey Barre, QC, MP in *Utopia Limited* and finally in the last of the operas, the *Grand Duke,* in which there occurs The Notary.

There are several themes in Gilbert's operas and underlying attitudes to consider but first a brief outline of some of them and their chronology is appropriate.

For Gilbert the 1860s was a decade of increasing literary and dramatic success. He had become well known as an author. From this position of strength he was introduced to Arthur Sullivan in the autumn of 1870. Unlike Gilbert, Sullivan had been born into poverty, his father Thomas earning one guinea a week in the Surrey theatre orchestra. It was thus a musical family, if poor. By the early 1870s Sullivan had succeeded in elevating himself to a position of some eminence in the world of serious music. He had won a scholarship to the Royal Academy of Music, from being a chorister at the Chapel Royal. He then studied at the Leipzig Conservatoire, and was offered the post of

Professor of Pianoforte and Ballad Singing at the Crystal Palace School of Art. His first music to be publically performed, *The Tempest* in 1862, was instantly successful, seeming by its high tone of seriousness, to lay the foundation and at the same time point the way for his musical career. It also marked his entry into society where unlike the testy Gilbert his pleasing and ingratiating personality lent itself eagerly to being lionised. He had also written an opera, *Kenilworth,* now forgotten. The geniuine grief he felt on the death of his father inspired him to tap the rich vein of musical solemnity and melancholy which so appealed to Victorian concert audiences. In 1866 this orchestral work *In Memoriam* swept him on a tide of tears to the front rank of contemporary composers. Although in private life he rejoiced in wine, and women and doubtless song and certainly gambling, like many Victorians his private practices contrasted with his public *persona.* The public knew him as the composer of what was known as sacred music . . . *In Memoriam,* an oratorio called *The Prodigal Son* and a work of crushingly high flown sentiments, *The Lost Chord* inspired by the death of his brother. He was on friendly terms with European Royalty, Queen Victoria commanded a complete set of his works and the Duke of Edinburgh was one of his closest friends, while the Duke of Albany was, in his own words, a 'chum'. He appeared set to become the great British heavyweight composer of his day. And yet there bubbled in him the well springs of lighter music which were first revealed when the editor of *Punch* asked him to write the music for a burlesque play *Cox and Box.* Sullivan and his librettist Burnand, pleased with the little piece's success (it is still sometimes performed) tried their hands at a longer opera *The Contrabandistas* which failed, sending Sullivan back to his serious music. He then met Gilbert. Their first operatic venture *Thespis* also failed. To the relief of his admirers who regretted this frivolous side of his talents, Sullivan returned to write the awfully serious *The Light of the World* which was much more befitting the author of that militantly Christian hymn, *Onward Christian Soldiers.* Once again, however, he tried collaboration with Gilbert, creating their first successful operetta *Trial by Jury,* which opened in March 1875 in a triple bill, which included Offenbach's *La Perichole* and a farce entitled *Cryptoconchoid Syphonostomata.* It was an immediate success, not the least ingredient of which was Gilbert's mockery of a great British institution . . . the Law and all its pomposity.

Between 1875 and 1896, the year of their last collaborative effort *The Grand Duke,* Gilbert and Sullivan wrote thirteen operas, most of which are still regularly performed to full and enthusiastic audiences. Remarkably only four of the thirteen operas dropped out of the popular repertoire, *Ruddigore, Princess Ida, Utopia Limited* and *The Grand Duke.* They have, moreover, and until very recently, been performed with little change in the manner of their presentation, other than as a quick response to the critics when they were originally presented. They are as pure a set of Victoriana as one could meet, a truly remarkable enduring legacy when one reflects how little otherwise of the things seen by Victorian audiences survives apart from foreign Grand Opera.

The law received rather gentler treatment in *Iolanthe* than had been the case in *Trial by Jury* through the characterisation of the amiable Lord Chancellor which nevertheless leaves little doubt of Gilbert's attitude in his autobiographical ditty . . .

When I went to the Bar as a very young man
Said I to myself said I
I'll work on a new and original plan
Said I to myself said I,
I'll never assume that a rogue or a thief
Is a gentleman worthy implicit belief
Because his attorney has sent me brief
Said I to myself said I
Ere I go into court I will read my brief through
Said I to myself said I,
And I'll never take work I'm unable to do
Said I to myself said I,
My learned profession I'll never disgrace
By taking a fee with a grin on my face,
When I haven't been there to attend to the case
Said I to myself and I.

The institution which *is* lampooned of course is Parliament, particularly the House of Lords. The Peers of the realm are figures of fun, from the moment when they make their splendid entry, marching on to the stage in coronets and robes singing

Bow bow ye lower middle classes
Bow, bow ye tradesmen, bow ye masses
Blow the trumpets, bang the brasses . . .
We are peers of highest station
Paragons of legislation
Pillars of the British nation.

As one of the characters remarks later in the opera, 'For self contained dignity . . . combined with airy condescension give me a British representative Peer.' Lord Mountarrarat has explained why a House of Lords selected by competitive examination as opposed to heredity would be unthinkable. 'I don't want to say a word against brains – I've a great respect for brains – I often wish I had some myself – but with a House of Lords composed exclusively of people of intellect, what's to become of the House of Commons? . . . If there is an institution in Great Britain which is not susceptible of any improvement at all it is the House of Lords.'

British triumphs of arms however had been achieved without much help from them . . .

When Wellington thrashed Bonaparte
As every child can tell
The House of Lords throughout the War
did nothing in particular
And did it very well.

The song ends with sentiments which were highly relevant to the contemporary controversy about the constitutional role of the Lords in Parliament . . .

And while the House of Peers withholds
Its legislative hand
And noble statesmen do not itch
To interfere with matters which
They do not understand . . .

Then all will be well with the country. Not content with ridiculing the Peers, Gilbert did not let the Commons escape. The opening of Act II finds Sergeant Willis on sentry go outside the House, pondering first the strangeness of the two party system whereby Nature

always does contrive
That every boy and every girl
That's born into this world alive
Is either a little liberal
Or else a little conservative

and then reflecting on the equal oddity of voting behaviour in the House . . .

When in that House MPs divide
If they've a brain and cerebellum too
They've got to leave that brain outside
And vote just as their leaders tell em to
But then the prospect of a lot
Of dull MPs is close proximity
All thinking for themselves is what
No man can face with equanimity.

Neither the sound broadcasting of the proceedings of the Commons and certainly not the televising of the House of Lords has, in the intervening century, done anything to mitigate Gilbert's view of these great British institutions.

In *H.M.S. Pinafore* it was the office of first Lord of the Admiralty which came in for ridicule, an appointment held until 1957 by a politician with no necessary naval experience.

Sir Joseph Porter KCB, the First Lord of the Admiralty explains in song how he rose in the legal profession from office boy who polished up the handle of the big front door, through the post of junior clerk and articled clerk to a junior partnership . . . 'the only ship I ever had seen', then via a pocket borough into Parliament where as a reward for always voting at his party's call and never thinking for himself at all he became the Ruler of the Queen's Navee, giving rise to the golden rule

Stick close to your desks and never go to sea
And you all may be rulers of the Queen's Navee.

In the *Pirates of Penzance* Major General Stanley, another eminent booby, after a prolonged display of information, vegetable, animal and mineral, concedes that his actual knowledge of military matters is nil.

For my military knowledge tho I'm plucky and adventury
Has only been brought down to the beginning of the century
But still in matters vegetable, animal and mineral
I'm the very model of a modern Major General.

The performance of Major and other generals in the Boer and the Great War provided little alternative optimistic evidence.

A similarly critical note with radical overtones was struck in the same opera by the Pirate King.

> But many a king on a first class throne
> If he wants to call his crown his own
> Must manage somehow to get through
> More dirty work than *I* ever do
> Though I am a pirate King.

Eminently fair comment when you survey the assembled crowned heads of Europe, always excluding of course our own monarch who was anyway a queen and pretty well impotent within the constitution, though of her eldest son, and her nightmare grandson the Duke of Clarence, whose sexual catholicity embraced post office telegraph messengers, there was not much to be said in favour.

The penultimate opera *Utopia Ltd.* is one of the most interesting as a vehicle for Gilbert's much more direct satire upon British life than that presented in Japanese disguise in *The Mikado.* It is set in a south sea island with a despotic government tempered only by the ability of two watch dogs to have the king blown up by dynamite should he lapse from political or social propriety. King Paramount has sent his daughter Zara to be educated at Girton College whence she returns to remodel Utopia entirely along English lines bringing with her to achieve this 'six Representatives of the principal causes which have tended to make England the powerful, happy and blameless country which the consensus of European civilisation had declared it to be' – to wit, company promoter, a naval captain, a soldier, a county councillor, a Lord High Chamberlain and a QC, Sir Bailey Barre who can

> demonstrate beyond all possibility of doubt
> That whether you're an honest man or thief
> Depends on whose solicitors has given me my brief.

Mr Goldbury the company promoter proposes to turn the whole country into a limited company – 'there is not a christened baby in Utopia who has not already issued his little prospectus'.

The Anglicisation of Utopia however succeeds too well

These boons have brought Utopia to a standstill.
Our pride and boast – the Army and the Navy –
Have both been reconstructed and remodelled
Upon so irresistible a basis
That all the neighbouring nations have disarmed
And war's impossible. Your county councillor
Has passed such drastic sanitary laws
That all the doctors dwindle starve and die,
The laws remodelled by Sir Bailey Barre
Have quite extinguished crime and litigation
The lawyers starve and all the jails are let
As model lodgings to the working classes
In short –
Utopia swamped by dull prosperity
Demands that these detested flowers of progress
Be sent about their business and affairs
Restored to their original complexion.

What then can have gone wrong? The answer is that the missing ingredient has been the failure to adopt the British model of party government.

> Introduce the great glorious element . . . at once the bulwark and foundtion of England's greatness . . . and all will be well. No political measures will endure, because one party will assuredly undo all that the other party has done and while grouse is to be shot and foxes worried to death, the legislative action of the government will be at a standstill. Then there will be sickness in plenty, endless lawsuits, crowded jails, interminable confusion in the army and navy and in short general and unexampled prosperity.

The *finale,* sung by Princess Zara, looks forward to the emulation of the achievements of England, when this final measure is adopted, so that Utopia will become like that monarchy sublime

To which some add (but others do not) Ireland.
Such at least is the tale
Which is borne on the gale
Form the island which dwells in the sea
Let us hope for her sake
That she makes no mistake –
That she's all she professes to be.

The criticism of party government allied with the pointed scepticism of the last lines provoked a hostile reaction from the critics who were ever lying in wait, illustrating a problem which

Gilbert constantly faced and of which he was well aware. There must be no departure from the prevailing concept of good taste, no transgressions from the *public* display of high moral purpose. How *dare* Mr Gilbert criticise party government or cast doubt on the perfection of the British way of life? As far as morality was concerned, Sullivan's private life hardly matched his exalted public image or the ponderous religiosity of his serious music. It was indeed a matter for constant rebuke that he allowed his lighter side expression in the often witty music of the operas, which were felt to be beneath him. Gilbert, according to his biographer Hesketh Pearson was a fluent composer of unprintable limericks and a great and well known raconteur of bawdy tales in the clubs which he frequented.[4] There is also apparently a play, which according to Pearson was 'stealthily shown and furtively read in certain circles' which bears strong evidence of Gilbert's authorship.[5] He was well known to delight in the company of young women, preferably around seventeen, which was his favourite age. He and his wife adopted one, and another caused his death when he tried to rescue her from drowning. This propensity is of course not necessarily naughty, but it was surely far from what *public* morality would have sanctioned. Look at the odium which was attached to Mr Gladstone's highly principled attempts to reclaim prostitutes!

Whatever may have been their private inclinations neither contributor to the operas would allow anything in their productions which would infringe that general injunction on public morality . . . 'never to bring the blush to the cheek of modesty', or in Gilbert's own words to cause 'the sensitive modesty of a young girl (to) shrink from hearing'.[6] He therefore kept within the constraint, but it was nevertheless irksome, as is clear from the interview which he gave to the *Daily News* in 1885. 'English dramatists are driven within the limits of bourgeois thought imposed by the survival of Puritanical prejudice. The English dramatist dances his hornpipe in fetters.'[7]

In spite of his attempts to cater for his eminently Victorian audience he still fell foul of accusations of lapses from good taste. Lewis Carroll, on hearing Capt. Corcoran R.N. say the line 'Dammee it's too bad', dashed off an agonised letter to the *Times* protesting at the outrage on the moral senses . . . there might be *children* in the audience . . . could any responsible father take his wife and family to the theatre to hear such language . . . 'he said *Dammee'* . . . repeated Carroll to underline the enormity of the offence.[8] Even more splendidly, the title of the opera *Ruddygore* originally spelled with a *y* created a chorus of horror as being morally offensive and coarse, so loud that Gilbert changed the title to *Ruddigore* eleven days after the first night to assuage public opinion.[9] Only at the last minute was an even deeper abyss avoided . . . the title for Gilbert's Japanese fantasy was to have been called *The Town of Tittipoo* which is the location of the opera, but at the last minute it was changed to *The Mikado.* This emphasis on the Japanese setting of the opera, which had always been recognised as a satire on England, caused offence on other grounds. The Home Office banned its performance for six weeks in 1907 to avoid offence to the visiting Crown Prince of Japan . . . officials in the British Embassy in that country wished to have it banned for ever.[10] How difficult especially when, having tried so hard to avoid offence on moral grounds, Gilbert was criticised about the costumes of the girls' chorus, which while admitted to be graceful, evoked the comment from a reviewer that they failed to emphasise their femininity . . . 'they obliterate the natural distinction between the sexes, imparting to the prettiest girl's figure the shaping of a bolster wrapped up in a dressing gown'.[11]

Poor Gilbert, who made it a cast iron rule never to have men playing women's parts. His plots are, though aware of the distinction between the sexes, as sexless as could be wished – the most that is permitted being the occasional chaste kiss and the odd cry of 'Oh Joy', or 'Oh Rapture' – occasionally both together. Even the line which was inserted when Yum Yum protests to Koko to whom she is now engaged, 'You're not going to kiss me before all these people.' . . . 'Well I'm certainly not going to kiss you after them.' was expunged in 1914.[12]

In intention therefore, though with occasional lapses, Gilbert truly reflected the hypocrisy of Victorian society in which private vice of every kind flourished behind a public facade of moral probity. Not surprisingly, though curiously overlooked at the time, his plots reflected another outstanding feature of Victorian society . . . its class structure. For a writer whose main literary stock in trade lay in the exploitation of paradox as a satirical device it was inevitable that he should find the social relationships, as well as the institutions in which they were embodied in the British class system, a rich vein to be exploited.

If the Gods could change places with the strolling players in the early opera *Thespis,* for a time only and with resultant chaos, then what might happen if somehow social class relationships were turned upside down-again, if only for a time? It was a theme to which Gilbert repeatedly returned. It is at the core of the opera *The Sorcerer.* John Wellington Wells, a dealer in magic and spells, has created a love philtre which would cause those who took it to fall in love with the first person encountered . . . it is clear that persons of opposite sexes only are to be so affected, nor, as explicitly stated in the text, would it affect people already married. Having already stepped aside from that potential quagmire of moral turpitude, the way is open to administer the potion to an entire village. Prior to this Alexis, an officer in the Grenadier Guards and son of Sir Marmaduke Pointdextre is betrothed to Aline the daughter of Lady Sangazure. Their love is so high and noble that they wish everyone to share their great gift . . . hence the business of the potion. Alexis declares

> Oh that the world would break down the artificial barriers of rank, wealth, education, age, beauty, habits, taste and temper and recognise that in marriage alone is to be found the panacea for every ill . . . I have made some converts to the principle that men and women should be coupled without distinction of rank. I have lectured on the subject at Mechanics' Institutes and the mechanics were unanimous in favour of my views. I have preached in workhouses, beershops and lunatic asylums and I have been received with enthusiasm. I have addressed navvies on the advantages that would accrue to them if they married wealthy ladies of rank and not a navvy dissented . . . [however] it can't be denied the aristocracy hold aloof.

To which his fiancee replies 'Ah! The Working man is the true Intelligence after all!' 'He is' agrees Alexis, 'a noble creature when he is quite sober'.

The whole village takes the potion. Sir Marmaduke falls in love with Mrs Partlett, a pew opener, a humble person . . . who tells her less than enthusiastic son-in-law to be . . .

> I am aware that socially I am not heverythink that could be desired, nor am I blessed with an abundance of worldly goods, but I can at least confer upon your estimable father the great and priceless dowry of a true, tender and lovin' 'art.

To which Alexis replies (coldly) 'I do not question it. After all a faithful love is the true source of every earthly joy', and Aline points out 'Zorah is very good and very clean and quite sober in her habits and that is worth far more than beauty.' Lady Sangazure falls in love with John Wellington Wells; Aline meets and falls in love with Dr Daly the vicar, a very old fogey, which is too much for Alexis. His lofty aspirations thrown aside, how can things be reversed? The answer is by the self sacrifice of John Wellington Wells who, obligingly makes amends by exiting to the devil through trap door 'amid red fire' as the stage direction has it.

A similar theme is found in *H.M.S. Pinafore.* Josephine, daughter of Capt. Corcoran R.N. is loved by Ralph Rackstraw an able seaman, in love with 'a lass above his station . . . Oh pity pity me Our Captain's daughter she And I her lowly suitor.' As he reflects, 'it's a strange anomaly that the daughter of a man who hails from the quarter deck may not love another who lays out on the foreyard arm. For a man is but a man whether he hoists his flag at the main truck or his slacks on the main deck.' She in turn is sought in marriage by the First Lord of the Admiralty whom we have already met. Confessing to her father that she has already given her heart to a common sailor . . . her father counsels her

> Come my child let us talk this over . . . I attach but little value to rank or wealth but the line must be drawn somewhere. A man in that station may be brave and worthy but at every step he would commit solecisms that society would never pardon.

Josephine replies that she will never reveal her love. Enter Sir Joseph who imbues the ship's company including Ralph with the fine democratic sentiment that 'a British sailor is any man's equal, excepting mine'. Emboldened, Ralph declares his love to Josephine who returns it and they plan to elope. Capt. Corcoran tells Sir Joseph, who complains of Josephine's lack of affection, perhaps the reason is that she is aware of her social position being so far below his own. Why not, he suggests 'assure her officially that it is a standing rule at the Admiralty that love levels all ranks' which Sir Joseph does, being unaware of the real cause of his failure. He goes on to state his official opinion that 'love is a platform upon which all ranks meet' which convinces

Josephine of her correctness in wanting to marry Ralph. Sir Joseph and Capt. Corcoran mistake her delight as being due to the acceptance of Sir Joseph. However, the plot to elope is revealed. Ralph appeals to the democratic ideals with which he has been influenced claiming above all that he is an Englishman. Capt. Corcoran replies

In uttering a reprobation
To any British tar
I try to speak with moderation
But you have gone too far
I'm very sorry to disparage
A humble foremast lad
But to seek your captain's child in marriage
Why dammee it's too bad.

Sir Joseph, outraged at the Captain's language, sends him below and orders Ralph to be chained in a dungeon. The way out of this social dilemma is Buttercup's confession that she mixed up the Captain and Ralph as babies, so that really their ranks are reversed and Sir Joseph rectifies the situation observing to the former Captain Corcoran

'Well, I need not tell you that after this change in your condition, a marriage with your daughter will be out of the question.'
'Don't say that your honour,' pleads the ex. capt., –
'love levels all ranks.'
'It does to a considerable extent,' agrees Sir Joseph, 'but it does not level them as much as that.'

He becomes engaged to his cousin Hebe; ex. Capt. Corcoran now a seaman, to Buttercup; Ralph is united with Josephine and all the class relationships are ironed out if not very logically.

Gilbert has never been conspicuous in the gallery of radical thinkers who have sought to devise societies alternative to that of the capitalist structure in which he was so conspicuously successful, with abundant wealth, a magistracy and a knighthood. His plots hardly ever portray members of the working class except as figures of fun. He should reasonably be classed as a choleric elderly Tory. In the end perhaps his view of social change tending to greater equality may probably be that enunciated in the Gondoliers

When every blessed thing you hold
Is made of silver or of gold
You long for simple pewter
When you have nothing else to wear
But cloth of gold and satins rare
For cloth of gold you cease to care
Up goes the price of shoddy . . .
In short whomever you may be
To this conclusion you'll agree
When every one is somebodee
Then no one's anybody.

Though his operas were very popular with all classes, providing popular ditties and catch phrases, he was above all a court jester to that bourgeoisie whose moral corsets he found so chafing. His allusions often demand a high standard of literary and classical education for their full appreciation. His role as a social critic was rather as the ancestor of latter day socially satirical entertainments like *Beyond the Fringe* or *TW3* or *Not the Nine O'Clock News* and their regular mouthpiece *Private Eye.* Intended to be critical, iconoclastic even, they lead nowhere very much except to amused scepticism. Like Harold Macmillan, turning up at the theatre to be seen laughing at the parody of himself in *Beyond the Fringe,* audiences seem to have achieved a similar relationship to Gilbert. He acts as a safety valve against committing the British sin of being seen to take anything too seriously.

There can hardly be a weekday evening of the year in which his words are not being performed somewhere a century and more after he wrote them about and for Victorian society at its peak. He was indeed the wisest of Victorian fools and perhaps it is the enduring Victorian legacy within and about us which enables him still to strike a responsive chord.

Notes

1 Sir John Clapham, *An Economic History of Modern Britain,* Vol. 2, 1932, p. 137.

2 All of the extracts from the lyrics of the operas are taken from W. S. Gilbert, *The Savoy Operas,* London, 1959.

3 The biographical details in the study are drawn from the extensive literature on Gilbert and Sullivan, including the following – R. Allen, *The Life and Works of Sir Arthur Sullivan,* New York, 1975; L. Ayre, *The Gilbert and Sullivan Companion,* London, 1974; L. Bailey, *The Gilbert and Sullivan Book,* London, 1952; L. Bailey, *Gilbert and Sullivan and Their World,* London, 1973; H. Benford, *The Gilbert and Sullivan Lexicon,* New York, 1978; I. Bradley, *The Annotated Gilbert and Sullivan,* 2 vols., Penguin Books, 1982 and 1984; S. Dark and R. Grey, *W. S. Gilbert: His Life and Letters,* London, 1923; G. E. Dunn, *A Gilbert and Sullivan Dictionary,* New York, 1971; *Martyn Green's Treasury of Gilbert and Sullivan,* New York, 1961; H. Pearson, *Gilbert and Sullivan,* Penguin Books, 1950; J. W. Steadman (ed.), *Gilbert Before Sullivan,* Chicago, 1967; A. Williamson, *Gilbert and Sullivan Opera, A New Assessment,* London, 1953.

4 Pearson, *op. cit.,* p. 302.

5 *Ibid.*

6 Williamson, *op. cit.,* p. 70.

7 Bradley, *ibid.,* Vol. II, p. 313.

8 Carroll's letter to The Times is reprinted in Bradley, *op. cit.,* Vol. I, p. 70. As he points out, it is the only time that a swearword occurs in any of the operas.

9 *Ibid.,* p. 278.

10 Bradley, *ibid.,* Vol. I, p. 264.

11 *Ibid.,* Vol. I, p. 306.

12 *Ibid.,* p. 280.

Index